THE LIFE AND LOVES
of the
COUNTESS OF WARWICK

Daisy

THE LIFE AND LOVES
of the
COUNTESS OF WARWICK

SUSHILA ANAND

PIATKUS

PIATKUS

First published in Great Britain in 2008 by Piatkus
This paperback edition published in 2009 by Piatkus

A CIP catalogue record for this book
is available from the British Library

ISBN 978-0-7499-0977-2

Edited by Steve Gove
Text design by Paul Saunders
Typeset in Sabon by Phoenix Photosetting, Chatham, Kent
Printed and bound in the UK by
CPI Mackays, Chatham ME5 8TD

Papers used by Piatkus are natural, renewable and recyclable products sourced
from well-managed forests and certified in accordance with the rules of the
Forest Stewardship Council.

Mixed Sources
Product group from well-managed
forests and other controlled sources
www.fsc.org Cert no. SGS-COC-004081
© 1996 Forest Stewardship Council
FSC

Piatkus
An imprint of
Little, Brown Book Group
100 Victoria Embankment
London EC4Y 0DY

An Hachette UK Company
www.hachette.co.uk

www.piatkus.co.uk

For Ann, Jane and Jenny

Contents

~

Acknowledgements

~

There are a great many people who helped in the writing of this biography. I could not have done it without them, and it is a pleasure to record my thanks. In the early days of my research, I contacted Brian Creasey of the Easton Lodge Gardens project. Brian lives in a small wing, the only surviving part of Lady Warwick's Lodge. He and his wife received me there, and I was able to look through his large collection of memorabilia before he gallantly photocopied a lot of it for me.

Emma Temple allowed me to use the huge number of letters written by Lady Warwick to her grandfather, Joe Laycock. Apart from her generosity in allowing me to keep the whole collection in London, Emma never tried to influence the way I interpreted the crucial relationship between Joe and Daisy.

Maynard Greville's granddaughter, Caroline Spurrier, also made her family archive available to me, and generously gave me the opportunity to work on the material in London at my own pace. It was Jane Clargo, one of Lady Warwick's great-granddaughters, who put me in touch with her cousin Caroline. Jane also accompanied me to Essex and helped me research, a very welcome extra pair of hands! She has been supportive in a wider sense.

The late Keith Kyle read some of my early chapters and gave me the benefit of his expert knowledge. I am only sorry that he slipped away just before I managed to finish the book, but his early encouragement was so valuable. His wife, Sue, also drove me to Essex on one occasion, which helped me to make progress.

There are two other people to whom I owe so much on a personal level. Though separated geographically, my cousin Ann Jasper has been supportive from the time I was diagnosed with breast cancer while in the early stages of this project. She has been understanding and encouraging about the many challenges over these last few years. Then, very near the end of writing, I was poleaxed suddenly by a severe illness which lasted several weeks. During that time, Jenny Watt truly was my Good Samaritan, and it is entirely due to her that I got through. The kindness and dedication she gave cannot be expressed in words.

Laura Morris always believed that the story of Lady Warwick's life was worth telling, despite many rejections! Happily, Alan Brooke, my editor at Piatkus, agreed with her. Thanks to both.

∽ 1 ∾

The Heiress

ON A CRISP WINTER day in the 1890s, hansoms clattered down Piccadilly, coachmen cracking their whips and steam rising from the horses. A certain father and son sat together on a knifeboard bus that morning as their driver negotiated his way down the thoroughfare thronged with vehicles. The boy was Philip Tilden, who would one day become a fashionable architect. Suddenly a figure came into view whom his father recognised: a strikingly beautiful woman with deep blue eyes whom he knew to have a personality of great charm, and who possessed great wealth. This celebrated lady was the Countess of Warwick, who at that time held an unassailable position in society. Darling of the Prince of Wales for ten years, she dominated the Marlborough House circle, and the style in which she entertained at her country house became part of her legend.

However, her life was far from transparent. Although a certain amount was known about her, there was much that was hidden, as it had to be. She appeared to be a perfectly dignified wife and mother, but while that was undoubtedly true, there was another reality. Impetuous and strong willed, Daisy Warwick's passionate nature dictated the course of her life.

This remarkable woman was born in conventional and comfortable circumstances on 10 December 1861 at 27 Berkeley Square, one of London's best addresses. Her father, Colonel the Hon. Charles Maynard, was nearly fifty; his wife Blanche, née Fitzroy, only eighteen. Their newborn daughter and first child was named Frances Evelyn, but informally would always be known as Daisy.

Her family had a long history: one ancestor of her father was said to have accompanied the Black Prince to France. The Maynards had become prominent in the sixteenth century as landed gentry who owed their fortune to the court of Elizabeth I. Blanche's side of the family was historically more interesting, both her parents being descended from Charles II. Her mother, Jane Beauclerk, stemmed from Nell Gwynne's son James, the first Duke of St Albans. Her father, Daisy's maternal grandfather, the Rev. Henry Fitzroy, was collateral to the Dukes of Grafton, whose lineage started with Charles Fitzroy, a son born to the Merry Monarch by the Duchess of Cleveland.

Those sexual shenanigans at the Restoration court seem light years away from the parish of Hartwell, Northamptonshire, where the Rev. Fitzroy held the living. Although well connected, the family in the rectory was not possessed of great wealth, but they would have enjoyed the dignity and respect given to gentry. Blanche may well have met her eligible husband when Charles Maynard visited Passenham, one of his family estates in the county. If the clergyman's daughter wanted to marry money, she could not have done better than attract him. Heir to Viscount Maynard, Charles would one day inherit the fabulous wealth that went with his father's title. Everything could be overlooked, even by a clergyman, when a daughter was being offered such a promising future. Virginal young Blanche would probably have known next to nothing about Charles' past. She was to be his second wife; his first marriage is something of a mystery, but it produced no children. Silence would be maintained about any possible mistress during the intervening years, an association which would have ended with his engagement.

Colonel Maynard of the Blues was physically impressive, with a reputation as a brilliant equestrian and a *beau sabreur*. He had a well-known fondness for wine, and during his military career had shown a tendency for madcap exploits. When the marriage between Charles and Blanche was celebrated at Hartwell in October 1860, it was the cause of much rejoicing within her family. There must have been even more happiness the following year when the couple had their first child, a daughter. She was given the names Frances Evelyn, and christened at St George's, Hanover Square on 21 January 1862.

Thereafter, when her parents wanted a change from town, they could either go to the three thousand acres of Passenham or to Shern Hall, the seventeenth-century family property in Walthamstow. Land on the eastern fringe of London's city had not as yet been spoilt by mass speculative building, and in the early 1860s Walthamstow remained more village than town. There were several attractive houses, dating mainly from the seventeenth and eighteenth centuries, some long-established shops, a pub or two and a church. This modest environment was where Daisy spent some time during her earliest years, a marked contrast to the sophistication of Berkeley Square and the rolling acres of Passenham.

Charles and Blanche were in a marriage which may have lacked the excitement of great romantic love, but if Blanche felt any lack of passion, her future as Viscountess Maynard looked promising. To begin with, there was Easton, the family estate. Easton Lodge, completed in 1596, had been built by Sir Henry Maynard, whose career at the Elizabethan court had flourished with his appointment as secretary to Lord Burleigh. The fortune he accumulated was sufficient to buy around fifteen hundred acres of land in north-west Essex, which lay within the ancient manor of Estaines. The mansion he commissioned, built in Jacobean style, was set perfectly in a deer park, and was in every way a suitably imposing residence for a retired courtier. His son, another Henry, also took up a career in service of the Crown, and was granted a peerage in 1628.

The family history thus far seems very worthy, but not exciting. However, in the eighteenth century a much more interesting character came to the fore, a figure who could have materialised from one of Henry Fielding's novels. She was Nancy Parsons, born a Bond Street tailor's daughter. She came under the protection of a West India slave trader named Horton, whom she accompanied to Jamaica, either as his wife or quite possibly as his mistress. Perhaps Nancy did not take to life on the other side of the world, or perhaps she fell out with her protector, but she left him in the West Indies and fled back to London, where she flourished as an actress and courtesan. She sat for both Gainsborough and Reynolds, whose portraits show Nancy Parsons, 'Mrs Horton', as a vibrant beauty. However, by the 1760s, Horace Walpole was describing her in a letter to Lord Hertford as 'one of the commonest creatures in London, once much liked but out of date . . . everybody's Mrs Haughton' [sic], and naming the Dukes of Grafton and Dorset, who apparently shared her. Lord Maynard was a third interested party, and he eventually married her in 1776.

Having become chatelaine of Easton Lodge, with social cachet as the wife of a wealthy peer, Nancy seems to have become restless, to the extent that she eventually eloped to France with a young man, said to be one of her husband's servants. On leaving Easton, however, she remembered to take with her some of the fabulous Maynard jewels. One version of Nancy's story ends with her being murdered by the young lover near Fontainebleau, where her body was subsequently found in a ditch, but neither the jewels nor the young man were ever seen again.

∽

Charles Maynard had been born in 1814, the possible date of Nancy's death. By the time Blanche gave birth to his own daughter,

half a century later, a transformation had taken place. The exotic
Regency world seemed long past, and even more remote was the
bold eighteenth century in which Nancy Parsons had cut such a
dash. Publicly at least the atmosphere was much more restrained,
with industrial enterprise and moral seriousness the keynotes of
Queen Victoria's third decade on the throne. True, there was the
demi-monde, with supper clubs for men, which provided every
pleasure, and ballet girls at the Alhambra who were not shy.
However, now that he had a wife and daughter, Charles would no
longer be a man about town. For some reason, possibly linked to
some of his wild exploits, or perhaps his fondness for wine, the
heir had become estranged from his father. However, all seemed to
be going well with his marriage. A second daughter was born on
St Valentine's Day 1864 and named after her mother, but she
would always be known as 'Blanchie' to avoid confusion.

Any possible disappointment that the new baby was not a son
would have been offset by knowing it likely that there would be
future additions to the family. Life must have seemed promising,
but eleven months later fate struck dramatically. On 2 January
1865, Charles died of a sudden seizure at the family's Berkeley
Square house. With Daisy only three and Blanchie still a baby,
their young mother would have to rely on Grandpapa's sympathy.
Things looked not entirely unpromising when, soon after Charles'
funeral – he was buried in the Maynard vault of Little Easton
church – Viscount Maynard invited his daughter-in-law to bring
the two small grandchildren to Easton. Although fire had
destroyed the original house, Easton had been rebuilt in fashionable neo-Gothic style during the 1840s, and remained impressive.
This visit was enormously important in determining the young
widow's future, because Viscount Maynard decided just in time to
take a great interest in his three-year-old granddaughter.
Naturally, to a small child the house seemed vast, and Daisy's most
vivid memory was of Grandpapa being wheeled from one stately
room to another by a liveried footman.

When Viscount Maynard died, three months afterwards, it became clear just how much had depended on that family meeting. Grandpapa had changed his will, bequeathing his entire estate to Daisy, making her overnight one of the greatest heiresses in the land. Her annual income, estimated at £40,000, would be held in trust for her till she reached the age of twenty-one; until then she would be a ward of court. The heiress was already a very distinctive child, with signs of future beauty, and with such a fortune at her disposal she would have unique power. Had she been old enough to understand what had happened, the implications would have been overwhelming, but she would realise the meaning of her position only gradually.

Viscount Maynard had four daughters, and it had been a reasonable assumption that his fortune would go in part to them, with perhaps a generous bequest to his grandson, Charlotte's child. Charlotte, the Hon. Mrs Capel, probably expected nothing less. We know that other members of the family who had hoped to benefit were furious when they heard that Daisy had been named as sole heir, and having gathered to hear the will read, they hurled pats of butter at Canevari's portrait of Lord Maynard. Blanche on the other hand must have been elated. Her new circumstances made her a highly eligible young widow, as well as the mother of a very important daughter. No matter what the future held, she would be mistress of a great estate until Daisy came of age.

How deeply Blanche had been in love with her husband is impossible to say. There is a tradition within the family that she had married him reluctantly, so she may not have felt the deepest grief. Whatever the truth, naturally she would keep a year's conventional mourning.

Within a short time, Blanche and her daughters left Shern Hall permanently for Easton. Travelling on the railway it was no great distance, about thirty miles, but the journey was fairly slow and tedious for small children. Daisy recalled sixty years later 'The long drive from the station on a wet night, the plop plop of the horses' hooves, and the swaying motion of the heavily closed brougham . . . making me physically sick'.[1]

Once arrived at the mansion which was now home, the two children settled into their nursery wing with Nanny and nursemaids. Their mother continued to experience hostility from other family members who had not shared her good luck. In fact, so nervous was she about their intentions – even fearing that Daisy might be abducted – that a footman always accompanied the children when out with their nurse.

Blanche the young widow was a good looking and ambitious woman, and she became acquainted with one of the most eligible bachelors in Society. Francis St Clair Erskine, fourth Earl of Rosslyn, was a great catch. Although he could sometimes be autocratic, he was also an intelligent and charming man, who was said to have the best cook in London. His family had been established in the Scottish lowlands for centuries at Dysart, an estate that overlooked the Firth of Forth. Rosslyn's circle included the erudite Lord Beaconsfield (the former Benjamin Disraeli), who was one of his closest friends, and he was also a favourite with the old Queen, who appreciated his wit and charm. Blanche did not miss the opportunity with which fate had presented her. Just under two years after Charles Maynard's death, she became the Countess of Rosslyn at St George's, Hanover Square in December 1866. Both Daisy and her sister seemed to feel affection for their stepfather. They called him 'Papsy', and he was equally affectionate towards his stepdaughters. Lord Rosslyn became principal trustee for Daisy while she remained a ward of court, and took it upon himself to act as her agent at Easton. He had already gained a reputation as a breeder of horses, and was well known in the racing world. On coming to Essex, he built new stables for his establishment at Brook End on the Easton estate, and during the 1870s also undertook some remodelling of the house at considerable expense.

The first child born to the Rosslyns, in 1867, was a daughter named Millicent. In 1869 came James, known as 'Harry', and in

1870 another son, named Alexander Fitzroy, known as Fitzroy or 'Fitzy'.

~

From an early age Daisy realised vaguely that she was an important child, subtly different from Blanchie with whom she shared nursery education. Miss Phillips, their first governess, was recalled as 'a dear good lady of Victorian sensibilities, who favoured lavender water and cheap scent, and who would faint at the sight of a mouse'.[2] She gave the children their first piano lessons, and quite soon Daisy was attempting 'The Bluebells of Scotland'. The children's playground was the deer park, and they learnt to ride, with an attendant groom walking beside the ponies. Daisy had inherited a great affinity with horses from her father and became an outstanding rider, exhilarated by galloping fast across country.

Eventually, Miss Phillips was succeeded by Miss Blake. Known as 'Blakey', she believed herself to be the secret love child of an aristocrat, possibly with a royal connection. Whether this was true or merely the figment of her imagination, she certainly had an aristocratic manner. Even if it was a little biased towards kings and queens, her teaching of history inspired Daisy. She also enjoyed nature study, for which her own estate offered ample opportunities, with its ancient trees and wild flowers, and from an early age she derived pleasure from watching the changing seasons. A boisterous child, belying her delicate appearance, Daisy described herself as 'climbing, running, jumping and challenging all rules'.[3]

As the years passed, she began to understand why people showed deference towards her. For instance, after Sunday service in Little Easton church, everyone stood and waited for her to leave first, estate workers curtseying or nodding heads as she passed. The little girl must have seen the vast difference separating her level of existence from that of such people, a strong influence in early childhood. Her tenants and workers were comparatively fortunate in the help extended to them in hard times.

The Rosslyns were good landlords, generous and sympathetic, and Blanche would often take her two older daughters to visit cottages on the estate, bearing appropriate gifts: baby clothes, blankets, broth and coal perhaps. Daisy's mother had a strong religious faith, and her daughter would have absorbed this ancient tradition of largesse dispensed from the manor house. It taught her a lesson, as it was meant to: that from those who have much, much will be expected.

When Daisy was ten, her second half-sister Sybil was born, and when she was nearly grown up at fifteen, Angela was born in 1876, the last of five Rosslyn children. The family was typical of that time, the older children nearly adult and the younger ones still occupying the nursery.

At the age of twelve, Daisy sat for a pencil portrait by Frank Miles, which entailed several visits to his Chelsea studio. Miles, who was much admired among theatrical and literary people, had been her stepfather's selection. On her final visit, Daisy and Lord Rosslyn arrived to find Lillie Langtry in the studio. Lillie had not been long in London, but her appearance was unforgettable, as Daisy described many years later:

> I found the loveliest woman I have ever seen . . . She had dewy violet eyes, a complexion like a peach, and a mass of lovely hair drawn back in a knot at the nape of her classic head. But how can words convey the vitality, the glow, the amazing charm, which made this fascinating woman the centre of any group she entered . . .[4]

Lord Rosslyn promptly invited Lillie to dine at the family's Grafton Street house the following evening, when Daisy and Blanchie watched her arrive from high up on the staircase above the hall. Naturally, she was accompanied by her husband Edward, although his part in Lillie's life was increasingly on the margin. Mrs Langtry in her signature black dress was radiant and as yet unspoilt. She was also invited to Easton, where Daisy and Blanchie took her riding.

Lillie's appearances in Hyde Park were eagerly awaited. At this impressionable age Daisy would have been absorbing ideas about the adult world and its values, including the fact that sexual power could be exerted by beautiful women. There were many influential people within her parents' circle – her parents entertained lavishly, and among the many guests in London and at Easton Lodge were prominent Tory politicians. She would enter the adult world easily when the time came, but during her childhood, Daisy would not have been part of her parents' sophisticated world. Innocence and simplicity were the keynotes in her upbringing.

Aged seventeen, Daisy was accompanied by Lord Beaconsfield to see Henry Irving and Ellen Terry in *Hamlet* during their inaugural season at the Lyceum Theatre in 1878, when she remembered being dressed demurely in white muslin. The occasion was a sort of audition, because Beaconsfield was subsequently to report to the Queen about this promising young girl.

About a year later, the Rosslyns moved to a new London house, 51 Grosvenor Street, conveniently near Hyde Park for Daisy to be seen there during the season, another sign that childhood was nearly over. It was *de rigueur* to appear daily if one was to claim membership of the elite circle of people who rode between the statue of Achilles and Knightsbridge. Ladies in skin-tight habits were to be seen, mounted on beautifully groomed horses. When carriages arrived on a summer afternoon, friends and acquaintances enjoyed a kind of garden party beneath the shady trees, with cakes and ices supplied by Gunters in Berkeley Square. However, *The World* complained that the rules of decorum in Rotten Row were being flouted by characters like 'the galloping snob' cannoning against quiet riders. There were even some young women 'in habits of hideous misfit', whose grooms loitered near the railings and then charged off 'as if in a steeplechase'.[5] It is unlikely that either Daisy or Blanchie would have worn anything but perfectly fitting habits or allowed their grooms to indulge in such louche behaviour.

Although barely an adult, Daisy already had the kind of aura that attracted men. Among the friends regularly entertained by the Rosslyns was Prince Leopold, youngest son of Queen Victoria. He was accompanied by one of his equerries, Francis Greville, Lord Brooke, heir to the Earl of Warwick. Soon after leaving Oxford without a degree, 'Brookie' had moved smoothly into an appointment as aide-de-camp to Lord Lytton, Viceroy of India. To one of 'the heaven born', as elite officials were called, the subcontinent offered plenty of pleasurable distractions. Aside from formal duties, Brookie and his compatriots had bagged several tigers and stuck a few pigs. Further travel in the East beyond Hindustan had been an enjoyable preparation for his intended political career, and he had been appointed equerry not long after his return.

It was during a visit by Prince Leopold to Dysart that Brookie first met Daisy Maynard, and he showed an immediate interest in her. Daisy's interest in him was equally instant. Being on the verge of election to the House of Commons and eight years her senior, Brookie must have seemed sophisticated, and he possessed innate charm. He was not tall enough to be an imposing figure, but he was of sound character, had an ease of manner and a droll sense of humour. Though primarily a sportsman, he took his sketch book on country visits.

Daisy's parents noticed the attraction which had been sparked between the two young people, and did not entirely welcome it. Such a young girl, they felt, was not ready even to think of a serious commitment. It was much too early. Brookie's family were of ancient lineage, with an historic title and an impressive family seat at Warwick Castle, but they were not among the richest of the aristocracy. There was plenty of time for other eligible men to come forward – maybe a prince, who could tell? Daisy and Brookie were constantly thinking about each other, but had to keep their feelings secret.

Lady Rosslyn told Brookie at one point that his Lordship was annoyed about his talking to Daisy so much. Meanwhile, the Queen had been consulting Lord Beaconsfield about a bride for Prince Leopold, and had heard Beaconsfield's favourable impression of his evening at the theatre with Miss Maynard. Her photograph looked very promising. A beautiful heiress whose stepfather was known at court might do nicely, Her Majesty thought.

A visit to Windsor followed, which was enough to make even the most poised young girl nervous, but the occasion went well. Daisy was self-possessed, and the Queen was charmed. She hoped that Leopold would take his mama's advice. He had found it most difficult to form an enduring attachment, and it would be a comfort to see him settled. The Queen, a shrewd judge of character, felt that Daisy Maynard could be the girl to inspire him. Although Leopold was not physically robust, and was handicapped by haemophilia, he had a degree of sensitivity which was attractive. Unlike his brothers he took an interest in the arts, particularly music. It is difficult to judge whether he had developed significant feelings for Daisy before her meeting with his mama, though it seems likely. Even a prince might feel that a beautiful and eligible girl deserved more than a passing glance.

It was in December 1879 that *Vanity Fair* heralded an important event: Miss Maynard, the great heiress, would soon be 'coming out into the world',[6] and a splendid ball was being planned for her at Easton Lodge. It was rumoured that half London would 'flash down' to attend. The social column was right. On the night of Daisy's debut, hundreds of guests arrived from far and near to celebrate the occasion, which also marked her eighteenth birthday. Masses of Mediterranean flowers decorated the house, and the event was reckoned to be the last word in style, as *The World* duly reported:

How am I to describe better the magnificence of the Earl and Countess of Rosslyn's ball last month than by calling attention to the fact that Mr Carlo, the eminent Knightsbridge coiffeur arrived early in the day to crimp and powder the lacqueys?

My informant adds however that the curled darlings were rather the worse for the festivities towards night. Was it not enough to turn their heads in every sense of the word?[7]

In early February 1880 the Prince gave a house party at Claremont, his country residence, at which both Daisy and Brookie were present. It seems that Leopold made a tentative approach to Daisy. It was a delicate situation, but she seems to have been able to deal with it confidently, despite her lack of worldly experience. Daisy knew that she was not in love with the Prince; she was madly attracted to Brookie, but to what extent Leopold was aware of his equerry as a rival is uncertain. After his talk with Daisy he could be in no doubt.

The most significant event of that visit took place swiftly afterwards. The previous year Daisy had cried over Brookie's first bouquet, because seeing him had given her 'the greatest pain as well as the greatest pleasure'.[8] Now Brookie and Daisy went for a walk in pelting rain in order to be alone, and having just turned down a royal prince, Daisy joyfully accepted Brookie's proposal of marriage. Drenched but elated, the couple returned to the house, secretly engaged.

~

Early in March Daisy made her first appearance at the Queen's Drawing Room, dressed in silver tissue. *The World* described the occasion:

Miss Maynard and Miss Violet Hankey, two charming debutantes of opposite types, were considered to bear away the palm for beauty. Two Chinese in native costume, wearing shoes with thick white soles, such as one sees on handscreens were moving about watching the proceedings with great curiosity. Lord

Beaconsfield moved alone and noiselessly through the brilliant throng . . .⁹

Such was the secrecy of Daisy's engagement that, three months later, the Queen believed that the question of Leopold's own engagement to Daisy was still alive. She was anxious for news, and awaited the messages sent by Lord Rowton, Beaconsfield's secretary, which were communicated through Horatia Stopford, her maid of honour. The Queen was growing impatient, and Rowton received a note from Horatia:

> The Queen has seen your letter to me and dictated these words . . . That her Majesty's wishes are *these* viz If they feel *disinclined* it would be better to say so *before the Prince goes to Canada*, and not allow the matter to be hanging on, and for him to be refused in the end, for this, the Queen could *not allow* and wishes you therefore to put it to them strongly.¹⁰

Lady Rosslyn was ambitious for a royal marriage, and an indication of the consideration she gave to the Prince's proposal is the delay, during which she seems to have been trying to persuade her daughter to accept. There may even have been just a glimmer of doubt in Daisy's mind as well. What would life be like as Princess Leopold? However, it was no more than a glimmer. Daisy was essentially resolute in character. She was promised to Brookie, and her formal decision in respect of Prince Leopold was given on 11 May 1880. Rowton broke the news to Beaconsfield:

> The young lady writes today – through Horatia – finally declining. I have been to the Palace: but could give no useful advice. I am to return this evening, to hear whether He and the Great Lady (who is furious or said to be!) – have taken any steps.

I expect to be sent on an Embassy of rebuke only, for the final letter leaves no opening for further pleading.[11]

That evening Daisy had an audience with the Queen, who hoped that the issue was not dead. Afterwards Prince Leopold also engaged Daisy in conversation. Rowton believed that external influences had borne a part in the decision 'with much consulting of friends who, jealous or prejudiced',[12] had settled the question. So by dinner, the whole affair had become 'a dissipated dream', and the Queen did not hide her annoyance. Above all she was anxious that no word of what she regarded as a humiliating refusal should leak out. Rowton tried to pacify her, as he told his boss: 'I succeeded in averting any irritating messages by showing that they would provoke revelations not desirable, or else misrepresentations, and that "nothing has occurred which may not be explained so as to clear the young gentleman, a visit, a gracious invitation in return" . . . etc. The Fairy readily took this view . . .'[13]

However, the Queen's remarks, such as 'How angry Lord B will be!', show that it took some time before she was completely reconciled. It was all so provoking, and a disappointed Prince Leopold left for Canada.

Daisy's strong will had been made clearly manifest. An early letter conveys all her eagerness:

How can I tell you what *great* pleasure your letter this morning gave me. It was such joy to see your handwriting again! Yesterday I met Miss Charteris riding in the Park, and she said that your people were not coming to town for some time, but that you were to be in London on Thursday.

In the afternoon Mrs Farquahar came to see me, and told me you had written to her, and I settled to go to tea with her about five tomorrow to meet you! What a good idea it was of yours to think of her, for I don't think you had better come to see us till the mother returns on Friday. Servants are such a bore, and the children too . . . Oh Brookie how delightful it will be to meet you after so long! I have been in a state of excitement and tearing spirits since I saw Mrs Farquahar . . .[14]

There was no doubt that she was completely in love with her very dear Brookie.

~ 2 ~

Marriage

DAISY'S ATTRACTION TO LORD BROOKE was not deterred by her parents' opposition. Their daughter had strength of character. Brookie was a man about town, attending the House of Commons, to which he had been elected as MP for East Somerset that year. He made his maiden speech during the winter at the behest of Harry 'the Squire' Chaplin, Conservative MP for Mid-Lincolnshire, and daily letters full of inconsequential gossip were written to Daisy from the Carlton or White's. They were sometimes amusingly illustrated with little drawings. Though not over-enthusiastic about his parliamentary duties, Brookie liked to be there on the big occasions, as for instance when Charles Stewart Parnell was to speak.

Romantically, Brookie's path had not been completely smooth, as he implied in a letter written soon after their secret engagement:

My own dearest Daisy

How good of you to think of writing to me so soon . . . one looks for the hand one knows so well but has not seen half enough. It is so hard as you say to talk to anyone in a letter . . .

·and I am so stupid at writing. Do you really think that I think
of you *sometimes* just a bit – dearest you don't know how I do,
and how wretched I felt the day we parted after house hunting.[1]

Since their first meeting at Dysart there had been times of unhappiness. He mentions a letter given to his youngest brother Sidney
Greville to deliver by hand to Lady Rosslyn, which she had refused
to receive. However, all difficulties could now be accepted philo-
sophically: 'What does it matter now that I know you love me –
you don't know how I have always believed in real true love, don't
laugh at me for saying so, but I am sure that it so seldom exists
and now that I believe I have found it I do hope that I may be able
to keep it . . .'[2]

Daisy responded: 'My whole heart is yours. I do love you so,
better and truer every day.'[3]

At the end of April 1880, while her parents were at Newmarket,
Daisy was settling into the house they had rented at 51 Grosvenor
Street, and records having been to a charming ball given by
Captain Fitzwilliam, where she had danced all night. During her
year as a debutante, Daisy was left in no doubt about her immense
popularity, 'feted, feasted, courted and adored in a continual
round of pleasure',[4] ineligible men having been screened out by
vigilant hostesses. During the London season she attended balls in
all the great houses, which seemed like fairytale palaces 'with
lovely beings in diaphanous tulle and chiffon'[5] gliding across the
rooms. Waltzing induced such feelings of ecstasy that it was almost
disturbing. The revels sometimes continued till sunrise, when carriages transported those lovely beings home through the morning
mist.

There were also moments even more exciting than the waltz,
when she contrived to be alone with Brookie. Sometimes they sat
on a certain blue sofa, which became the focus for some of his
secret thoughts and desires. Daisy remembered 'a mad mad afternoon'[6] when they had kissed passionately in the middle of a piano

duet. There was obviously a strong sexual attraction. Brookie imagined a good deal: 'I long to kiss you with my arms all round you,' he confessed, and had dreamt about it, but then 'how vile it was to wake up.'[7] When circumstances kept them apart, they eagerly waited for the post:

> I have been longing for a letter all the morning my darling Brookie . . . your dear loving words have given me such joy . . . I can never feel half good enough for you . . . you are so perfect and I am only a little goose that giggles! But I *do* love you . . . Somehow I can't settle down to things as I used to do, and I think how lonely the world is without you . . . We shall be happy! Shan't we? Tell me, do, that you are coming to give your little Daisy a *big* kiss on Friday![8]

Miss Maynard would much rather have been going to the theatre with Brookie than living her secluded life driving a phaeton round Easton with Papa. Early in the summer, after several weeks pursuing Daisy's stepfather, Brookie managed to see him. During the formal interview, always something of an ordeal for an eager suitor, Lord Rosslyn agreed to the formal engagement, and the bride-to-be wrote to her fiancé in May 1880, radiantly happy

> because you love me and because I belong to you now and always . . . Brookie, dear, our love is a thing far too sacred to be mixed up with any horrid mercenary considerations. If I am glad that I am rich it is only at the thought that it may be of use to you, and we will help one another to make good use of it.[9]

Daisy was anxious to put his mind at rest about potential opposition from her parents. Nothing she might be told could ever influence her – his love meant more to her 'than all else in the world'. She made a point about wishing their future together not to be like the lives of some couples known to them: 'it *cannot* be, for we love each other so and I will help you and be useful to you, and live for you . . .'[10]

The engagement was duly announced by Lady Rosslyn during a ball at Grosvenor House in June, and Lord Rosslyn gave his friend Beaconsfield a warm appraisal of Brookie:

> He is a steady and domestic young man, who is not tarred with the brush that so often disfigures the golden youth of this century but so far as we can see he gives promise of making a true and loving husband. He is fortunate in his choice, and in this I am sure you will agree with me. He must wait a year, but in his case the impatience of his love will be calmed by the serenity of his prospects.[11]

The couple received many congratulations, and particularly warm wishes from Lord Beaconsfield, who thought that the approaching event 'will possess every element of happiness . . . romance, youth, wealth, beauty and love, a lofty rank and an historic name to sustain and inspire . . .'[12] *The World* claimed to speak for Society when it pronounced that 'the marriage of Lord Brooke, eldest son of the Earl and Countess of Warwick, with Miss Maynard, very early removes from the scene one of the greatest heiresses of modern times . . . many manly hearts are broken . . .'[13]

When Daisy was enjoying life as a debutante, her best friend and confidante was Violet Lindsay, whose unusual beauty and intelligence were much admired. Her father, Colonel the Hon. C.H. Lindsay, third son of the Earl of Crawford, was an equerry to the Queen, and with this pedigree, Violet naturally had an entrée to the best Society. As a young child, she had shown a great talent for drawing, and had later been Edward Burne-Jones' muse. Much of her time was now spent as a professional artist, producing exquisite silverpoint portraits, and she was to exhibit regularly at the Royal Academy and elsewhere for the whole of her life. She was a good friend to have when Daisy wanted an assignation with

Brookie, to whom she wrote typically: 'I am going to luncheon with Violet, and we will probably go on to the Grosvenor about three. Do come there!'[14]

After the rendezvous, a brief note said all that the meeting had meant: 'It was such happiness being near you again . . .'[15]

∾

Once her engagement had been announced, Daisy might reasonably have expected that the path to her wedding would be smooth, but in fact there was to be a great deal of friction in the months ahead. Soon after the announcement, Lord Rosslyn made an embarrassing remark about Daisy having refused Prince Leopold, which had spoilt his chance of a royal son-in-law. It was a surprising gaffe for a man who was used to court protocol. Brookie later told his fiancée that the Prince was 'much enraged with his Lordship for saying about town that you refused him'.[16]

The family went up to Scotland to spend the late summer at Dysart as usual. The windswept seashore, their private beach, was an ideal playground for the children. Daisy and Blanchie had time to spend by themselves, and enjoyed climbing over rocks, soaked by spray from breaking waves, running along with their dog Smidge who darted hither and thither pouncing on crabs. The mood was free, and with their Charteris cousins across the Firth of Forth at Gosford there was some mingling when they were so inclined.

When Brookie arrived to stay the atmosphere was lighthearted, but when he left to join a stalking and shooting party Daisy's mood became flat. If only it had been possible for her to accompany him, she thought, as she visualised herself striding energetically over the hills. Brookie's host at Glenfishie was Sir Charles Mordaunt, now comfortably distant from the scandal created by Harriet, his first wife, who had admitted to being 'very wicked' with the Prince of Wales and many others in his circle. After the divorce hearing, all the named men had emerged unscathed, Sir Charles had found a dull second wife, but Harriet had been committed to an asylum. However, there was usually capital sport with Sir Charles. In the evenings, whisky flowed like water, and his valet played the fiddle. Brookie was also shooting at Duchal and Kingussie that autumn. Amongst the bag one day at Duchal were thirty-two brace of grouse which had been brought down by his gun.

Neither visits to the Charteris cousins nor lawn tennis at Dysart were sufficiently engaging to stop Daisy thinking longingly of Brookie, to whom she wrote a very flattering letter: 'You are always perfect, the more I see you the stronger my love for you grows – There is nothing in the world that I would not do for you – for I could not live without your love . . .'[17]

However, the party at Dysart had its highlights, with some traditional Scottish dances. When the good weather eventually broke, there were dramatic thunderstorms, and huge waves pounded the harbour wall. Then disturbing news travelled north: there had been an outbreak of scarlet fever in Easton village, which had spread quickly in the neighbourhood. In spite of this danger, the Rosslyns decided to go south. They had scarcely settled back in mid-September when ten-year-old Fitzy collapsed. Two local doctors called in wrongly concluded that he had succumbed to scarlet fever or possibly diphtheria. Both were usually fatal. Brookie, who had recently been staying, was now in his constituency of East Somerset, and received an urgent letter:

12pm *Monday Night*

My darling Brookie

Before going to bed I must write you a hasty line to tell you how very troubled and anxious we are tonight. Dr Playfair came this evening and has completely upset Hawksley's theories as to Fitzroy's illness.

He says that the child has something (I forget the exact word) on the brain, produced by either sunstroke or a blow or a fall,

and nothing whatever to do with scarlet fever or dyptheria [sic].
Nor can he conceive it possible that the two doctors can have
deliberated even as to the possibility of it being either the one
or the other. Of course this relieves everyone from the fear of
any infection . . . but the fears are very great and the doctor . . .
can hardly give us any hope. The child is *quite* unconscious
tonight . . . it is a case of *weeks* even *months* in this condition.

Nothing can be done . . . for no medicine will affect the *brain*,
and the only thing to do is to keep up his strength with nour-
ishment . . . I am very tired my darling and unhappy, for the day
has been a very trying one . . . I can but tell you that the danger
is *very very* great . . .[18]

Playfair most feared what he called 'tubercules on the brain'. The
condition was probably a form of meningitis, but in an age before
antibiotics doctors were powerless in the face of such diseases,
many of which affected children. Even this senior physician could
not be certain about what had caused the little boy's unnatural
sleep. Apart from the comfort and general benefit of good nursing
there was no treatment. Quite broken down, the parents sat beside
his bed, and they probably put all their faith in prayers for him.

Brookie communicated, saying that he was thinking about
them all in their great trouble, and Daisy tried to manage the
household so as to leave her mother free. Days and nights passed
in the limbo of uncertainty. Then came a small improvement,
when Fitzy briefly became conscious. Dr Playfair returned to
London, and sent instead one of his junior colleagues from King's
College Hospital to stay for the duration. Nurse kept the patient
perfectly quiet in a darkened room, and he remained stable. Then,
gradually regaining consciousness for longer periods, Fitzy began
to recognise people and say a few words; it seemed that he had
passed the crisis and returned from the borderland. When he eventually sat up in bed to eat one of the peaches Brookie had sent, it
was a sight that looked not far short of a miracle.

Fear about the little boy was now dispelled, and by Michaelmas Day he was talking about playing cricket, wanted to get up, and had an enormous appetite. Daisy went off to secure a goose for the celebration dinner.

~

Normal life was resumed, and thought was given to the marriage settlement. It was to become the cause of much friction: the bride-to-be and her parents did not live harmoniously over the next few months. There were arguments and angry silences, all of which affected Daisy's well-being. Brookie naturally did not like his 'dear soul' being upset, but his position was awkward, since the Warwick wealth could not compare with that of the Maynard heiress. Daisy, for her part, was completely in love, and wanted her future husband to be respected and not sidelined, as she wrote eloquently: 'Please please never say you feel uncomfortable, because what is mine is yours . . . What is all I have worth against such love as yours . . .'[19]

She was disconcerted that agreements were being discussed secretly, and the couple were not being given information about what income they would have. Besides, there were signs that Mama and Papa were expecting a great deal too much for themselves. Their plans were inadvertently disclosed by Grandmama, who had heard from Blanche that the Rosslyns were expecting £5,000 a year to be given as the mother's jointure. Moreover, Daisy was to be entirely responsible for debts contracted at Easton, which included an estimated £50,000 for extensive building undertaken by Lord Rosslyn, without sanction either from the other trustees or the Chancery Court. He also insisted on his reappointment as sole agent for the estate. Daisy confided all this to Brookie: 'darling, isn't it hard that everyone is trying to rob one . . . and my own mother too!'[20] She thought her parents' demands outrageous, describing her stepfather as 'the greater evil'.[21]

It was only thanks to Grandmama that the truth had been revealed. The old lady had obviously felt that an injustice was

being done, and let the cat out of the bag. Armed with this knowledge, Daisy was able to play her own hand, and insisted that
Brookie be allowed an appointment with the family solicitor, Mr
Walford of Piccadilly. Independently, she decided to give her sister
Blanchie a generous allowance. Two thousand pounds a year
would be sufficient for all her expenses, including dresses and a
maid. However, the idea of providing for the St Clair Erskine children was not something to which the heiress took kindly.

It would be three years before Daisy would be able to enjoy
complete independence. Meanwhile, her parents were blithely
confident that they would achieve their aims, thinking that their
future son-in-law was malleable and mistaking his perfect courtesy for weakness. Brookie had always treated Lady Rosslyn
chivalrously, and she was under the impression that he would
agree to anything. Instead he commented acerbically that Lord
Rosslyn was 'inordinately fond of money',[22] and quietly but firmly
resisted. At one stage there was even some doubt as to whether the
wedding would take place.

The financial negotiations had revealed blatant greed, to the
extent that Lord Warwick was expected to settle £3,000 annually
on his son, but finally the haggling came to an end. Now that all
was agreed at last, plans could be made for a wedding in the spring,
but there was some lingering tension which caused the bride-to-be
nervy headaches. Daisy had been incensed by her parents' behaviour, and was certainly averse to sharing Easton with them, as they
proposed. She had been compelled to play the dutiful daughter to
some extent, but was nevertheless longing for her independence.

∼

In November a change of scene was offered by an invitation from
Lady Louisa Mills to join a shooting party at Wildernesse, an
eighteenth-century house in Kent set in ample parkland. The estate
had formerly been owned by the Marquis Camden, who had entertained George III there. Lady Louisa's untitled husband Charles

had made his fortune as an industrialist, and the couple were major social players. Other young ladies invited included Violet Lindsay and Violet Paget, the latter of whom was to achieve prominence as a novelist under the pseudonym Vernon Lee. Without a great deal to do while the men were shooting, the girls spent a lot of time sitting around gossiping. Both Violets had brought their drawing pads; having persuaded Daisy to model, they complained that she did not keep still enough, and so gave up. There were impromptu concerts, with guests encouraged to play the piano and sing. The weather was bitterly cold with a hard frost, but well wrapped up, the young ladies went for brisk walks, sometimes as far as the woods to watch the men shoot and to join them for lunch. After the intense cold, it was a relief to get back into the house and sit round a fire. Tea was served when the guns returned, a time for the girls to wear seductive silks and velvets. When everyone had dressed for dinner, they assembled again downstairs, and it only remained to see with whom one was going to walk in.

Brookie, absent from Wildernesse, received a teasing reminder: 'We are by way of dancing this evening. Shall I be good and dance only with my Papa?'[23] The name 'Oliver' was mentioned in letters once or twice, as if Daisy had another admirer, and Brookie teased her. The secret admirer was most likely Oliver Montague, a bachelor courtier. But Montague was devoted to the Princess of Wales, so Brookie had little cause for worry.

On the anniversary of their decisive day at Claremont he wrote a reflective letter:

Today I ought indeed to love you more than any other day and to think myself the happiest man in the world. Just one year ago, since then, *how much* delight to me, just a little mixed perhaps with anxieties but always full of the knowledge that there was someone who loved me and whom I loved better than anything in the world.

In years to come if I am still alive there will never be a day more precious except perhaps one which I do trust won't be long in coming.

Darling Daisy, if devoted affection from me can ever make up to you for the sacrifice you made in curtailing the excitements and pleasures which a young lady must always experience on first beginning life – you will get it to the fullest from me.[24]

Two months before her wedding, Daisy was sent to Brighton. She had been run down for some time, having suffered an attack of measles, and Dr Gull, Queen Victoria's physician, had said that she needed sea air, which tended to be the advice for a good many patients in those days. Besides, her parents seem to have had a hidden agenda. Unfortunately, the weeks spent exiled in Brighton succeeded merely in testing her endurance rather than raising morale. Away from friends, accompanied only by Alice her personal maid, Blakey her former governess, and a footman, time dragged. With nothing much for a spirited girl to do on the south coast in winter, the experience was no help in releasing any tension which had been brought on by her troubles with the family. She longed for Brookie's visits, but he was discouraged by the Rosslyns at every turn.

He in turn longed to be with Daisy, and she dominated his thoughts, but it was only with permission from her parents that he could appear at the Palmeira Square house in Brighton, and that was not very often. In fact he himself was run down, describing himself as 'headachy' and 'cobwebby'. On that account he was taking time off and missing divisions in the House. His state was probably a good deal to do with sexual frustration. However, failing to turn up for parliamentary business and giving feeble excuses displeased his father.

The Rosslyns did not improve his mood, making it quite clear that his separation from their daughter was desirable. They were unaccountably strict, and considering that their daughter was officially engaged, unreasonably so. In the days when Daisy had been laid low with measles, he had been told to stand outside her bedroom and could only talk to her from behind the door. Despite her mother's antipathy – she did her best to curtail his visits – he had continued to call every morning, always courteous but determined. When the Rosslyns gave Brookie permission to visit Brighton, they instructed him to stay in an hotel, an order that was quite superfluous. Brookie would never have taken liberties with etiquette.

During those gloomy days, Daisy swam once or twice in the freezing sea. Brookie joked about bringing her a bucket and spade. Even late in February, he wrote to her, there was a lot of snow lying about the lawn at Warwick Castle, and at the end of a hard winter thin ice on the lake. Brookie wondered if the sea had really been good for his darling, and if so thought that 'the nasty parents' were sure to say that it was because he was being kept away: 'How dear of you to miss me so . . . do tell me often that you love me it makes me so happy,'[25] he concluded.

The home news at Warwick was small beer, which some of the elected Conservative aldermen had been accused by 'the Rads' of offering as a bribe. A protest petition had been drawn up, and Brookie thought that the accusation was probably true. But the Radicals were going to lose anyway, and a good thing too.

When Brookie was at last able to visit Daisy, naturally the couple were overjoyed, but the time went too quickly. He confessed to feeling low when he found himself alone again, and expressed some of his frustration about the enforced separation: 'My dearest I do love you so . . . why are we so much apart? We should be so happy always together, and you are so dear when you say that you never will be bored with me . . . Everyone who has been at Brighton complains of headache, so you and I are not exceptions . . .'[26]

Word had come from Claremont that Prince Leopold was also

in bad health, and lying in bed with sad thoughts, complaining that all his friends were getting married and that he was the only one from whom nuptial bliss seemed to be withheld. The hard winter seemed to have got everybody down, but Brookie's Himalayan orchid had flowered at last, and he sent Daisy some sprays, hoping that they could look forward to lovely days ahead, sitting under the cedars at Warwick.[27]

~

By the middle of March, Daisy's sojourn in Brighton had thankfully come to an end. She returned to London, where her parents had rented 7 Carlton Gardens from Lord Warwick. The couple became immersed in pre-wedding activity, with Brookie taking the main responsibility for getting together all they needed for their ménage. This included everything from carriage and pair to silver candlesticks, and he went plodding round to salerooms and horsedealers. Only the best would satisfy him, but he always wanted to find a bargain. Presents continued to arrive, some of which were very desirable: gold and silver plate, *objets de vertu*, beautiful tea services and some dazzling jewellery, including a sapphire and diamond bracelet from the Prince and Princess of Wales. Lord Beaconsfield did not live to see the marriage celebrated, but he had chosen a brooch for Daisy, which was sent on by Lord Rowton.

The Chancery Court had given formal permission for her marriage, and granted her £2,000 for her trousseau. Brookie took a great interest in her dresses, some of which were from Paris. At last the long period of waiting was nearly over. Much of the engagement had been difficult, but the way now seemed clear. And family relationships had improved, although Daisy made a pointed reference about paying for the wedding herself, adding 'Not much shall we be indebted to his Lordship for!!'[28]

However, in one sense she was very fortunate in her parents. They had shown a degree of wisdom in giving her freedom of choice. Their daughter was marrying for love, which was far from usual. Very young girls were often pushed into marriages arranged entirely on the basis of wealth and status, ignoring the subtle matter of sexual compatibility. Having approached their wedding in a haze of romantic ideas, they might then find themselves locked into a distasteful relationship.

The novelist Elinor Glyn belonged to the Society about which she wrote, and portrayed it with witty understanding. Her novel *The Reflections of Ambrosine* gives an account of the heroine's marriage to a man whom she finds repulsive, and makes the comment: 'No one can imagine the unpleasantness of a honeymoon until they have tried it. No wonder one is told nothing about it.'[29] When the book was published in 1904, nearly twenty-five years after the Maynard–Warwick wedding, its theme was still valid. Yet Daisy looked forward to marriage with serene happiness, and Brookie gave material proof of his devotion with the gift of a diamond necklace.

On 30 April 1881 the cream of Society assembled at Westminster Abbey, led by the Prince and Princess of Wales, to see 'one of the richest hands in England joined to one of its oldest titles'. Prince Leopold had honoured his promise to be best man, and there were hundreds of guests, including tenants from both Easton and Warwick. At precisely 3.30 the large congregation stood 'in hearty welcome to the lovely bride', who entered with her stepfather. She looked dazzling in a classic dress of white satin 'deluged with old lace', her veil held in place by a single spray of orange blossom. Twelve bridesmaids accompanied her up the long nave, with Beethoven's chorus 'Twine ye Garlands' resounding.

If the bride glanced round, among the congregation she might have seen Princess Louise in a large hat with crimson feathers, and her mother rather subdued in an outfit of smoky velvet, whereas Lady Charles Beresford was resplendent in pink under black Spanish lace. Splashes of white, gold and turquoise were to be seen among the congregation. One of the Prince of Wales' earliest lovers, Patsy Cornwallis-West, had chosen a flame-coloured outfit. According to *The World*'s report, 'notwithstanding this brilliant entourage, the service was quietly and impressively celebrated by a large and imposing staff of clergy . . .'[30]

The marriage was duly solemnised by the Bishop of St Albans, and the service included a favourite Victorian wedding hymn, 'O Perfect Love'. The Prince of Wales signed the register with Lord Rosslyn, and then old Dean Stanley pronounced the blessing. Mendelssohn's triumphal music resounded as Lord and Lady Brooke emerged to a welcoming crowd, buzzing with interest. The re-gilded Warwick state coach was waiting in the abbey forecourt, and with some help from attendant footmen Daisy's long train was carefully arranged and the couple seated. The coach moved off, catching the last rays of spring sun, which had shone all afternoon. Innumerable broughams converged on Carlton Gardens, bringing guests to drink the couple's health, for which an excellent Steinberger had been provided. There was even a sonnet in honour of the occasion, written by 'H.W.':

Thronged are the Courts of Britain's ancient Fame
With eager feet, while mellowed beams disclose
Ancient heraldries, where honour finds repose,
And monarchs, heroes, genius, all obtain
The resting-place ambition craves to gain!
Today, lo! Youth and beauty's gathered host,
With Royal and noble, England's boast,
Around the fairest flower of our Queen's Reign!

Sweet Daisy – bloom! A wealth of love and joy,
In thy bright Springtime ta'en a line to grace
Whose lore historic ancient pages prove!
Long years and happy may thy future trace!
Thrice Heaven's favour be, without alloy, –
As Royalty today smiles on thy love![31]

❧ 3 ❧

Grand Passion

DAISY'S WEDDING TO BROOKIE had undoubtedly been one of the most memorable ever celebrated in London. Daisy had shed a few tears before leaving Carlton Gardens, a natural reaction to the emotional demands of such a grand ceremony.

Instead of being lured by the Mediterranean or a European city for their honeymoon, the couple had accepted Ditton Park, beside the Thames, from the Duke of Buccleuch. It was perfect weather in May for lazy boating trips, and the seclusion offered on a private estate must have been very welcome. Daisy's family sent a stream of affectionate letters, and even visited the newly-weds for a day. Lady Rosslyn's concern was for her daughter to rest, although the bride had written to say how happy she was. Daisy was plainly giving her parents a reassuring message, and they must have been relieved. Lord Rosslyn wrote to Brookie: 'Daisy's letters are too charming, full of natural feeling and a happiness that brings tears to my eyes. May God bless you and continue it through happy years of ever increasing love. Your kindness and love will be repaid a hundredfold . . .'[1] One can read the subtext as 'thank you for being a sensitive husband'. Writing of married love, he adopted a quasi-clerical tone, describing it as 'the one thing that grows deeper and holier as death draws near'.[2]

Brookie seemed entirely at peace with himself and the world when he wrote to his mother-in-law two days after the wedding, calling her 'dearest Lady Rosslyn'. He was sending 'a little line of gratitude for giving one the dearest little wife that any man ever had. I am *so* happy, and I think dear Daisy is too . . . We couldn't have a nicer place to stay . . . The woods are one mass of primroses.' Daisy was sitting opposite him in a speckled tweed dress, and might need a day or two to get over 'all the excitement and worry'.[3] During their idyllic honeymoon, Brookie was all chivalry.

There was only a single engagement that the couple had to keep before their stay at Ditton was over. Although not something they would have chosen, it could not be declined. The Queen had commanded that Lord and Lady Brooke should dine and sleep a night at Windsor. In her romantic way, Her Majesty had asked the bride to appear in her wedding dress. Daisy wrote to her mother about the occasion:

> We had a very nice time on the whole last night. A very small party, the Harry Bowkes, Lord Hartington, Lady Churchill . . . Princess Louise and Beatrice and Leopold and ourselves . . . The stewarding after dinner was dreadful. For the Queen stayed such a long time. H.M. was so kind and nice, and she asked after you and said she had read with great pleasure Papa's sonnets to Lord Beaconsfield, and she talked much about Lord B. She thought my dress lovely and she put her nose into the orange blossom and fingered my lace and looked at all my jewels and admired Papa's catseye bracelet. They were all charming, and I really enjoyed it.[4]

Those lines come from an ingénue, fresh and unspoilt. Over the next few years Daisy would develop the bold behaviour more conspicuous among people in the Prince of Wales' circle. There would be a later visit to Windsor, on which occasion Daisy ignored protocol and left the castle very early in the morning, wearing her riding habit, en route to the Essex Hunt races. Watching her untimely departure, the Queen was heard to mutter: 'How fast, how very fast.'

There was a brief pause in London before the couple continued their honeymoon in Scotland, spending the time at Dysart. By June they were busy getting their establishment together at 7 Carlton Gardens. Daisy was now there in her own right, and was also the chatelaine at Easton. It must have felt very good to be in command of her own destiny, and she now took her place in sophisticated society. Lord and Lady Brooke were members of a distinguished circle, sometimes joining the elite that surrounded Lord Salisbury, Conservative opposition leader, in his Arlington Street home. Royalty was often present, and at a dinner in July other guests included the Prince and Princess of Wales, with the Crown Prince and Princess of Germany.

Lady Brooke's parents had moved to Leicestershire and were settling into a new home in Stamford. It was of modest size, but later enlarged by the acquisition of adjacent houses. Being in the middle of a bustling town was a novelty, as Daisy's stepsister Angela remembered: 'a house in a street was in itself an excitement.'[5] She spent half her days hanging out of the window, watching all the passersby. To her Stamford seemed brimful of possible adventures, and besides watching people, there were ancient churches and old curiosity shops to see. Her father, described as 'a heaven born horse dealer', now had his bloodstock establishment at Burleigh Paddocks. Astute in buying and getting his mares at good prices, Rosslyn became one of the most successful men in the business. He had the distinction of breeding Tristan, winner of the Queen's Vase and Ascot Gold Cup in 1893, a triumph which he sadly did not live to see.

Daisy's younger sisters were now reaching an interesting stage: Blanchie was seventeen, Millie a great beauty at fourteen who had already met her future husband, Cromartie, heir to the Duke of Sutherland, at the family seat of Dunrobin Castle on the beautiful and remote coast of Sutherland. They were to be married on her seventeenth birthday, 17 October 1884, at St Paul's, Knightsbridge.

~

Daisy's Easton estate was always to be her favourite home, and she relished taking possession of it in her own right. Easton Lodge was undistinguished architecturally, and indeed the refurbishment carried out in the 1870s had not made it any more aesthetically pleasing. However, with at least fifty indoor servants and double that number of estate workers, Daisy created a house with a unique atmosphere and every luxury. The forty acres of gardens at Easton were among the finest in Victorian England. Everyone looked forward to the Saturday to Monday house parties. Love affairs flourished, and as long as they were conducted according to Society's rules, a good deal of freedom was allowed. This depended on maintaining conventional appearances at all costs; it was no matter who was in bed with whom as long as these unofficial couples avoided scandal. *Fait ce que vous voulez* was the accepted philosophy, but Society exacted a heavy price from those who failed in their duty of discretion. As Elinor Glyn observed:

> It might be a lovely lady's own lover who was sitting beside her, but he would never lean over her or touch her arm to accentuate his speech, for all touching in public was taboo . . . By the end of the first evening, you usually knew which member of the party intended to make it his business to amuse you, in a discreet way, during the visit, in the hope of who knows what reward?[6]

Put in plain English, she meant that men sounded out which of the married women might be available. There is a story, maybe apocryphal, about the importance of secrecy. An innocent young girl once told a company of guests lazing in the garden that she believed the house to be haunted. Last night this debutante had seen a figure in white walking down a corridor and then suddenly vanishing. She got no reaction, and a long silence followed. The experienced guests knew that the mystery figure was very much of this world, and had vanished into a bedroom not his own. Many a guest would walk down the corridors at Easton after midnight, and a certain amount of danger made the game more piquant.

When a couple wanted to be alone by day, their hostess would suggest a walk in the direction of Stone Hall, tactfully diverting any third person who seemed likely to attach themselves. This Elizabethan cottage was a halcyon retreat, and the old English garden in which it stood was Daisy's creation. There were areas with plants put in by her friends, their names engraved on heart-shaped plaques, and a Shakespeare border with many of the old English herbs and flowers. There was also a gingko tree, and a boxwood topiary sundial. Perhaps Elinor Glyn was thinking of such an environment when she wrote:

> Love affairs at this time were sentimental and refined . . . they always contained an element of romance . . . were never under-taken either for money or out of sheer lust. The whole matter, surrounded by glamour, perhaps rendered temptation all the more irresistible . . . Nothing was allowed to appear crude and blatant, and what were essentially ugly facts were made to seem beautiful or even admirable . . . [7]

In other words, when the location was one of beauty and luxury, extra-marital sex had a degree of refinement which it might have lacked in less salubrious places.

~

It was not until September 1882 that Daisy produced a son and heir, who was given the name Leopold Guy, but was always known as Guy or 'Guido'. Lady Rosslyn had been present during the painful labour, and once the ordeal was over, church bells rang out in Warwick and Dunmow, while a bevy of nurses attended to the baby.

His twenty-year-old mother was soon hunting again. Hunting was a sport about which she was as passionate as Brookie was about shooting. Daisy grew increasingly bored with shooting parties, although she held many at Easton. Other great houses were often cold, lacked creature comforts and served indifferent food. Ladies were expected to spend much time alone while the guns were out, or stand around freezing, and Lady Brooke began declining invitations to shooting weekends, leaving Brookie to go alone. By contrast, the Saturday to Monday parties Daisy gave gained a reputation for good food and stimulating conversation. Her guests were drawn from the cream of Society, and might include a sprinkling of Tory politicians and distinguished ambassadors. Invitations for a Saturday to Monday house party were coveted, especially when it was known that the Prince of Wales would be present.

His Marlborough House circle naturally reflected his own tastes, namely shooting, racing and sex. In his New Year message to Daisy of 1883 Lord Rosslyn gave an unflattering picture of the beau monde, warning that 'The society of women whose only thought is dress and gossip who paint their faces . . . and of men who are stupid if not vicious and vicious when not stupid palls after a time – but it is so difficult to get rid of.'[8]

If that style of life was adopted in youth, it led to a sort of dance of death, 'knowing how wrong things are – how untrue – yet without the courage to free yourself from the thraldom . . . You grow like them, you imitate their manner and their habits – and you die, if you survive the princelings and the paint, a toothless old hag without love and without respect.'[9]

Pleasure loving and indulgent as the Brookes' circle was, it could hardly be described as vicious. Perhaps Rosslyn saw the particular temptations to which a young, beautiful and rich woman might be subject. If he sounded a little on the heavy side, reminiscent of an evangelical preacher, his view came from a deep religious faith. He described the life he wished for his beloved stepdaughter as one 'surrounded by all the clever, the pure and noble-minded'. She should preside 'over a society that is witty without profanity and religious without intolerance ... Welcoming mighty travellers, learning the wonders of foreign lands, even seeing some far away places, and always listening to the thoughts of noble-minded patriots and statesmen . . .'[10]

It was an idealised picture of aspirations held by the more intelligent women in Society. Was Lord Rosslyn aware of the uninhibited lifestyle in Daisy's circle?

She herself would soon have her name linked with several men, including Lord Randolph Churchill, his brother Blandford, and Sir William Gordon-Cumming. When the Brookes attended Prince Alfred's ball that year, the Prince of Wales was noticeably paying court to Lady Randolph, a sensuous raven-haired beauty whose forthright American manner appealed to him. In the 1880s the Churchills were often guests at Easton.

Among others who frequently signed the visitors' book were Lord and Lady Charles Beresford. Lord Charles was a volatile, charismatic Irishman who had served the Prince of Wales as equerry in the 1870s, and notwithstanding the deference due to royalty, they had enjoyed a close friendship. One of his brothers, Lord Marcus, was the Prince's stud and racing manager. William, a younger brother, was to serve as Lord Dufferin's aide-de-camp in India, and in the South African war would win a Victoria Cross. Curraghmore, the family estate in Waterford, reflected the family's importance. Beresford's wife, Mina, was at a disadvantage in being a few years older than her husband, and in a world where appearance was everything, her lack of beauty mattered.

Daisy Brooke and Charlie Beresford started what was to be a fiery love affair perhaps as early as 1883, or at the latest by the beginning of the following year. Forty years later she stated that he was the father of Lady Marjorie, her elder daughter, born in October 1884.[11] Very quickly after Marjorie, Daisy's second son arrived in November 1885, and was named Charles Algernon Cromarty. This frail little boy, who died aged sixteen months, might just possibly also have been Beresford's child.

At any rate, if her statement concerning Marjorie is true, Daisy drifted away from her marriage with unusual speed. Normally there would be several children in the nursery before such a departure in pursuit of pleasure. What reason can be found for her straying so early, after so many heartfelt pledges of love for Brookie? Possibly, as they became adjusted to marriage, Brookie's sexuality proved unequal to his wife's. It seems as if Daisy craved greater sensual fulfilment, became restless and looked elsewhere. She did not have to look far. Charlie Beresford had the kind of masculinity that a lot of women found irresistible. What is certain is that the pair had a relationship which both remembered for the rest of their lives, and at the time they were obsessed by it. Their liaison was interrupted when Charlie was put in command of the naval brigade on the expedition sent to rescue General Gordon from Khartoum in September 1884. Having shown exceptional courage under fire, he returned a hero, and was to be decorated by the Queen. The Liberal government resigned, having been widely criticised for botching the Sudan campaign and leaving gallant General Gordon to the mercy of the Mahdists.

The lovers' enforced separation predictably meant that they enjoyed a passionate reunion. Charlie had brought Daisy a reminder of the great Sudan expedition, a tent embroidered with Arabic script. Sir Donald Mackenzie Wallace, a noted Arabist, when asked to translate refused to do so, saying the words were too indelicate to be spoken in front of ladies.

In the election of autumn 1885 Beresford became MP for East Marylebone. No sooner had Lord Salisbury taken office than his government suffered a defeat on an amendment to the address brought forward by Jesse Collings, and in January 1886 he resigned. The Liberals under Gladstone were not in office much longer, being defeated in July of that year on the Home Rule Bill. In August Beresford was appointed Junior Lord at the Admiralty, and retained his parliamentary seat at the 1886 election, when the Conservatives under Lord Salisbury were returned again, much to the Queen's relief. The opposition now included 118 Radicals and Home Rulers.

In 1886 the turbulent political atmosphere was matched by equal turbulence in private, when the Beresfords were guests at Easton. Daisy's affair with Lord Charles had been an open secret in Society for some time, but one evening she impetuously walked into Lady Beresford's bedroom and announced that she intended to elope with him. Brookie, she said, had already been asked for a divorce.

Lady Beresford had known about her husband's affair with Lady Brooke for a long time, and had accepted adultery, knowing it to be unexceptional within her circle, but she thought Lady Brooke's announcement was simply outrageous. Furious at what she regarded as Daisy's insolence and high-handedness, Mina Beresford refused to countenance the break-up of her marriage, and left Easton immediately with Charlie in tow. His career was not to be sacrificed to 'such an insane project'.[12]

The idea of divorce did not find favour with Daisy's husband, but it was later said that the marriage had come very close to ending over Beresford. Daisy seems to have accepted the impossibility of escaping, although impetuously she had wanted to do so. After 1886 the Beresfords' names do not appear again in the visitors' book at Easton. The affair might have continued spasmodically until the following year, but gradually Charlie's passion died down and he ended the relationship. Daisy had unfortunately broken the rules governing romantic adventures by becoming emotionally involved with her lover.

Somehow the Brookes managed to come through this crisis for the time being. But more rules would later be broken, causing bitterness and a semi-public scandal. An enormous amount of self-control was needed to maintain the required dignity during an affair, and it is not surprising that sometimes people failed to maintain the façade.

~

By December 1888, Daisy was in the throes of a political campaign. A by-election was to take place in Colchester, Essex, owing to the death of its MP in a hunting accident. Brookie was asked to stand as the Conservative candidate against the popular local Liberal, a sportsman named Sir William Brampton Gurdon. The fact that Lord Brooke was also a local man probably accounted for his nomination, because his attendance in the Commons when representing East Somerset had been less than impressive. Both parties were facing challenging circumstances. Lord Salisbury's Conservative government had suffered a number of defeats in recent by-elections, and the Liberals had lost a number of supporters because of Gladstone's Home Rule Bill. Lady Brooke went on the offensive in support of her husband in Colchester, canvassing with her customary energy. It was largely due to her ubiquitous presence in the town that the Tory campaign gathered momentum, with leaflets urging electors to vote against Brampton Gurdon, 'beaten in Norfolk and beaten in Rotherhithe'. Daisy brought a dash of glamour to the campaign, driving her four-in-hand round the constituency, and on polling day, 18 December, provided transport for reluctant voters. Whether her persuasion was decisive or not, it can't have done her husband any harm, and he not only won but increased the Conservative majority. After this resounding success, Daisy and Brookie went to the Riviera, to spend Christmas in their villa at Beaulieu.

Early in the new year of 1889 something prompted Daisy to write a letter to Charlie, making a dramatic appeal for him to return to her. There is no indication as to why she decided on her action at that particular time; perhaps anger at being rejected had been simmering for some time, or maybe some emotional crisis prompted her. When the letter arrived, Charlie was on the Continent, collecting statistics on foreign navies, enabling him to urge Parliament to spend an additional £20 million on the British fleet. He had apparently instructed his wife to open any mail during his absence. Therefore it was Mina Beresford who read Daisy's letter. The salient points made were that Charlie was to leave his wife and join Daisy in the South of France, and that he had fathered one of her children. Moreover, jealousy prompted Daisy to assert that Lady Beresford's own pregnancy was a betrayal; she had no right to have a child. This was a statement to which Mina took great exception. She later pronounced Daisy's letter to have been 'of a most extravagant and shocking description'.[13]

Lord and Lady Brooke were still at Beaulieu when the Beresfords arrived at Monte Carlo, having gone to the Riviera for Mina's health. An avalanche of forthright notes arrived for Charlie from Daisy. Worse, Lady Brooke's wounded vanity resulted in what Mina Beresford was to call 'disgraceful and disagreeable' stories.[14] As the result of wishful thinking, Daisy even claimed that Lord Charles was persecuting her with his unwanted attentions. Lady Beresford acted to put an end to the harassment from Lady Brooke. Unless some restraint was imposed, she felt Daisy might indeed persuade Charlie to resume their relationship.

The person to whom Lady Beresford turned to impose that restraint was George Lewis, doyen of solicitors and a key figure in Victorian Society. Lewis had made his reputation by dealing with prominent people who had got into personal entanglements that might remove them from fashionable Society, should their affairs become public. Thanks to him many secrets were kept, and disagreeable law suits avoided. Lewis was instructed to inform Lady Brooke that her letter had been opened and read by Lady Beresford.

Receipt of the solicitor's letter was naturally a great shock, and Daisy became distraught. When she recovered some equilibrium, there was no doubt in her mind about what she should do. One evening, appearing at Marlborough House in all her fragile beauty, she tearfully revealed to the Prince of Wales everything that had caused her such dreadful unhappiness. Her confidence was not misplaced. Daisy found the Prince to be the soul of sympathy, a man who longed to protect this beautiful young woman, and he looked at her 'in a way which all women recognise'.[15]

It was a meeting that would change her life: with her combination of beauty and vulnerability, before long she was to replace Lillie Langtry in the Prince's affections. Their liaison would last for almost nine years.

The same night His Royal Highness took an unmarked cab to George Lewis' house, where he arrived at 2 am. Roused from bed, Lewis had no choice but to ask his visitor in. The Prince demanded to see the incriminating letter, and having been allowed to do so, declared it to be the most shocking he had ever read. Some days later the Prince descended from a cab at 100 Eaton Square, the Beresfords' house, where he asked Lady Beresford to hand over her copy of Daisy's letter. Refusing to do so, she warned the Prince that he had no business to be meddling in such an affair, but was given the royal command that she was to communicate her terms through Mr Lewis.

When Lady Beresford responded, she stipulated that if Lady Brooke wanted her letter returned, she was to withdraw from London and Society for a year. If she were to agree, a veil of silence could be drawn over the episode, but nothing less than those terms were acceptable. Charles Beresford was to say later that he considered it 'a most dishonourable and blackguard action' on the part of His Royal Highness even to ask to see the letter, much less to read it. He castigated Mr Lewis for his 'sycophantic servility',[16] which had made him forget his honour and duty as a member of the legal profession, and must surely have been unprecedented.

Daisy could never have agreed to Lady Beresford's proposals, and she had no need to do so. Knowing that the Prince was protecting her, she had nothing to fear. Society's inner circle knew of the close relationship that had developed between them, and wherever the Prince was invited he let it be known that he wished Lady Brooke to be there. The Prince arrived at the Beresfords' house for a second time, and his attitude was sterner. He wanted that letter, and despite his profession of friendship for Lord Charles, Lady Beresford understood all too clearly that their position in Society would be damaged unless he got it. She felt aggrieved, aware at this point that both the Prince and her husband were favouring Lady Brooke. The husband felt himself to be in a position of maddening perplexity, but he was intent on saving the person who had written the offending letter. Mina agreed eventually that it should be sent to her brother-in-law John, Marquess of Waterford, for safe keeping. Lord Charles then believed and hoped that the incident had been closed; Lady Beresford, however, maintained that she was being deliberately excluded from Society, and considered that the Prince's behaviour amounted to a defamation of her character.

Charlie Beresford felt that the Prince of Wales was taking Lady Brooke's side for reasons that were not entirely altruistic, and went to confront him at Marlborough House in January 1890. Deep feelings were involved, maybe even a touch of jealousy, and the atmosphere became heated. When challenged about his affair with Lady Brooke – which was now openly acknowledged among his circle – the Prince called Beresford a blackguard, but Charlie responded 'with some warmth and considerable clearness that there was only one blackguard in the case at all',[17] and that was His Royal Highness. So saying, he aimed a blow at the Prince. The Prince stood accused of interfering in a private quarrel. Beresford warned that he had no intention of allowing his wife to suffer from the aftermath of a liaison which he had repudiated. Serious notice would be taken if his wife suffered more in any way as a result of the Prince's influence.

The following month Charlie Beresford took command of his ship *Undaunted*, and was expected to be at sea for several months. In his absence a sensational pamphlet appeared, with the title

'Lady Rivers', which was thought to be the work of Lady Beresford and her sister, Mrs Gerald Paget. It not only included some text from Daisy's notorious letter, but also revealed her position as the Prince's *maîtresse en titre*. Several copies were in circulation, and any hostess who managed to obtain one found that she had a full drawing room for the most popular after-dinner entertainment in town. Some of the old guard took a dim view of Society's rules being flouted, but 'Lady Rivers' was talked about everywhere. The Prince was an old hand at dealing with unwelcome publicity, but it is not recorded what he himself thought.

~

When Daisy's stepfather Lord Rosslyn died in September 1890, after a brave struggle with cancer, sixteen year old Angela, his youngest daughter, was the most affected. She had been exceptionally close to him, and had accompanied her father on the journeys undertaken for his health, and finally to Paris, where he had undergone treatment by the renowned neurologist Jean-Martin Charcot. That month, the Brookes were to have been with the Prince of Wales at Tranby Croft, the Yorkshire house of shipowner Sir Arthur Wilson. And considering what took place, Daisy probably regretted not having been there.

Sir William Gordon-Cumming of the Scots Guards, a well-known man about town, was strongly suspected of cheating during a game of baccarat. Five other guests claimed to have seen him raise his stake once he had surreptitiously seen the cards. Having conferred about what to do, the assembled company decided to ask Sir William to sign a statement that he would never play again. He reluctantly agreed, and his fellow guests promised to keep silent about the affair.

Unable to be present at Tranby, the Brookes travelled to Scotland for Lord Rosslyn's funeral, and saw him laid to rest in the family chapel. While on their journey north they stopped at York to meet the Prince of Wales, who was on his way back to London.

It seems that he forgot the pledge of silence about Gordon-Cumming. Within a few weeks the secret was out, and everyone believed that Daisy had been a 'babbling brook'. She emphatically denied spreading the news, but suddenly everyone knew about it. No doubt feeling that a solemn undertaking had been broken, Sir William brought a libel action.

At the ensuing trial in June 1891 the Prince was called to give evidence, and his appearance did nothing to dampen down the high profile publicity. Sir Edward Clarke, the Solicitor General, made some caustic remarks about the kind of entertainment enjoyed by people well known to His Royal Highness. Gordon-Cumming lost his case, but it cast a murky shadow on the royal circle in which he had moved.

Partly to shield her husband in the Beresford affair, the Princess of Wales swiftly invited Lady Brooke to a dinner at Marlborough House. Privately, the Princess felt antipathy towards her husband's mistress, but by extending her invitation an appearance of normality could be created. It was really an attempt at damage limitation. Mina Beresford was in no doubt about the motivation: it had happened 'by means of the strongest pressure on the part of the Prince of Wales and probably with a view to shielding *him*!'[18] It was the moment when a fresh scandal would be distinctly undesirable. The Princess had received this unabashed adventuress at dinner at Marlborough House, and the effect of this had been apparently to render the Prince of Wales' conduct reckless towards herself: 'He has cast all sense of decorum to the winds . . . he has now proceeded to boycott me in the most open manner . . . To such an extent has this been carried that amazed spectators have brought the matter before Lord Charles' notice . . .'[19]

Under the strain caused by this unfair treatment, the Beresfords' marriage had reached breaking point. According to Lady Beresford, matters had continued to be in a very uncomfortable state for some time, 'people not knowing what to think of such remarkably perverse conduct on the part of the Prince of Wales . . .'[20]

On board *Undaunted*, Charlie received news of Daisy Brooke's triumphant appearances in Society, and was grieved to hear from various friends that his wife was being ignored and suffering 'a species of Society boycotting'.[21] The Prince's antipathy to her was apparently well known, and people had actually apologised for not inviting her to certain parties. In response Lord Charles had told his wife to absent herself from any entertainments where she was likely to meet their Royal Highnesses and might be subject to open insults from the Prince of Wales. In a letter drafted but not sent, Beresford accused the Prince of treating Lady Charles in such a way as amounted to 'a distinct insult . . . perfectly uncalled for . . . monstrously humiliating and unjust'.[22] He could not see 'a shadow of an excuse for the ungentlemanly manner'[23] in which His Royal Highness had acted through this painful business. As head of what was called Society, it might have been thought that he would not have interfered in a quarrel, and certainly not in order to throw his influence on the side which was palpably in the wrong.

For years he had endeavoured to shield the person who may have been led astray by him, 'often at the sacrifice of every true thought, comfort and happiness at home'.[24] He accused the Prince of doing everything possible to make the scandal public. Matters had now reached a stage where Beresford was compelled to decide whether to go on shielding a former friend and see his wife taking the consequences, or to expose the lady and the Prince who was acting on her behalf. He wanted an unequivocal apology. If that was not forthcoming, he planned at the first opportunity to give his opinion of His Royal Highness publicly, and to state that the Prince had behaved to him 'like a blackguard and a coward'.[25] He had not taken this step without most careful thought, and was quite aware of the momentous issues involved. If compelled to take the grave course of making the whole matter public, Beresford stated, he would be filled with little regret at the annihilation of a friendship which had lasted twenty years.

It was now the end of the London season, the capital was all but abandoned, and nothing had been resolved. Rumours circulated that Lord Brooke might be seeking a divorce: an American edition of *The World* claimed to have information that were he to do so, fourteen co-respondents would be cited, and when he decided not to go ahead with a petition, the only losers were certain sections of the press. For about three months the whole Beresford affair remained dormant, but in the autumn it took on a new life. There was much coming and going between Lord Salisbury's Hatfield estate and Marlborough House. Intense discussions took place between the private secretaries, S.K. McDonnell for Salisbury and Francis Knollys for the Prince, about how they would deal with all eventualities. There was considerable apprehension, and McDonnell's notes made after the meetings convey it all. Everyone in authority realised that there was substance in Beresford's threat, and that a catastrophe had to be averted somehow. Equally, the Prince's dignity had to be maintained and his private life protected. Moves were afoot to consult senior government lawyers.

The Queen, tucked away at Windsor, knew as much as most of the people involved, and was said to be 'much distressed'[26] after Princess Louise had discussed it with her. The Queen had asked her private secretary if the Prince of Wales was concerned about the affair or did not think it serious, and was upset on being told that he was very much troubled. The people who surrounded her heir were far too dedicated to pleasure for her liking, and her characteristic comment was: 'If ever you become King, you will find these friends most inconvenient.'

Privately, members of the Beresford family were also suffering anguish. The 'Lady Rivers' pamphlet had come to the attention of Lord Marcus; indeed it was difficult to avoid. Attempting to uphold the importance of traditional aristocratic values, he had written to Charlie about it, but had not received a reassuring reply. Even more disturbed by the whole affair as time passed, in November he had written again:

Your answer to my letter disappointed me very much, and your letter to our mother disgusted me . . . I wrote and told you that Lucy Paget and your wife were circulating pamphlets in Society and elsewhere which contained a copy of a certain letter, which you ought never to have allowed to remain in existence . . . Your answer to me was not the answer of Charlie Beresford the brave sailor, who has hitherto been looked up to as the soul of honour. You expressed no horror about this letter being published . . .[27]

Not only did Charlie appear brazenly unrepentant, he was full of threats against the Prince of Wales, who had been his greatest friend. It was vital to maintain the family's honour, little else mattered: 'You have a name which has hitherto been untarnished, and to the glory of which you have been no small contributor. That name at this moment is in the greatest danger of being dishonoured in the blackest possible way . . . Why?' Lord Marcus had heard that the pamphlet, 'stamped with dishonour from its infancy', was being circulated with Charlie's sanction: 'Can anything be more terrible or damning to you, to your family, to your children. If you are reckless about yourself, for God's sake remember them . . .'[28]

Their mother, the dowager Lady Waterford, had, he said, been utterly ignorant of the whole business until receiving a letter from her son. Now, at any moment, she might be struck with paralysis from the sudden shock. Lord Marcus denied that Lady Beresford had been boycotted by the Prince of Wales up to the time when she started circulating the pamphlets, 'and people who tell you to the contrary are only doing so to work you up and to provide an excuse for ruining you'. Marcus recalled that there had been a scene at Newmarket, when Charlie had renounced his wife in the presence of witnesses. It was hardly convincing now when he talked about sticking to his wife 'against the whole world'. The very existence of the pamphlet was tangible proof that honour and chivalry were 'no longer synonymous with the name of Beresford'.[29]

Early in December, Lady Beresford telegraphed her husband, asking him to come home, and they were both in fighting mood. On 17 December, McDonnell made a morning call on Beresford at Eaton Square, and after waiting some time, finally saw him at the door of his dressing room. Beresford first spoke about his election address, and then said that he was 'about to write to the Prince of Wales demanding an apology from him . . . he should use temperate language, as he felt the delicacy of his position with regard to Lady Brooke'.[30] As Lord Salisbury had said to him: 'If you have stood in a certain relation to the anonymous lady . . . it must not be your face or hand that brings her into any disgrace because she yielded to you.'[31]

At the subsequent midday meeting held at Marlborough House with Knollys and Colonel Oliver Montague, all agreed that the only way out of the impasse was some concession. Mention was made 'that nobody could approach Lady Brooke because the Prince of Wales would not allow it'.[32] The following day Charlie wrote a letter to the Prince 'on a very serious matter', accusing him of 'openly slighting and ignoring' Lady Beresford. His wife had announced that she would live abroad rather than be humiliated in this way. He mentioned some malicious rumours recently circulating:

> I perceive in all this however such a direct intention to damage my wife that I am determined that this sort of thing shall no longer continue: and I as her husband agree with all her friends and relations that such a state of things is brought about entirely by the line of conduct your Royal Highness has thought fit to adopt. I now demand an apology from your Royal Highness on behalf of Lady Charles Beresford, failing which I shall not only apply for an extension of leave, but I shall no longer intervene to prevent these matters becoming public.[33]

As the festive season approached, there was intense activity among the secretaries and civil servants. On 19 December, a meeting was convened at Marlborough House with Charlie's letter in hand. Accompanied by McDonnell and Oliver Montague, Knollys read it to the Prince, who immediately denied all the accusations. He failed to see anything for which he needed to apologise. Far from ignoring Lady Beresford in public, he had always shaken hands with her, or made a bow of acknowledgement. As he replied:

> I am at a loss to understand how Lady C can imagine that I have in any way slighted or aggrieved her during your absence abroad, as you state is the case. As a proof of which I may mention that Lady C was invited to the Garden Party at Marlborough House this last summer, to which she came.[34]

Lord Charles was not satisfied, and responded that he could not accept the Prince's letter as an answer. He wanted an expression of regret, tantamount to acknowledgement that there was cause for an apology. The crisis was deepening. The private secretaries feared that if no way could be found out of this impasse, they would have to clear the way for legal action. The opinion of Sir Edward Clarke and the former Attorney General, Lord Russell, should be sought. Lord Salisbury repeated his advice that some concession was really the only possible way out, and Beresford wrote him a confessional letter:

> The great respect I hold for you and the respectful affection I have for Her Majesty as well as my sense of duty to her, compels me to do what lays [sic] in me without sacrificing my own honour, to enable the Prince of Wales to write me what I consider my due . . . I have asked no advice. On myself and on myself alone is the burden of this dreadful matter. I may be crushed if the Prince refuses my demand, but I would be crushed like a man and not like a worm. I have not asked one

of my thousands of friends to come to me, in order that I may be chivalrous *not* to the Prince of Wales but to the Queen's son . . . Through stories put about I am believed to be hiding, and my honour is in question. That will come as bright as the sun again, without my attempting to defend it . . .[35]

It was the Prime Minister who had the task of drafting another letter for the Prince. This again was less than a wholehearted apology:

I regret to find from your letter of 23rd instant that circumstances have occurred which have led Lady Charles Beresford to believe that it was my intention publicly to wound her feelings. I have never had such intention, and I regret that she should have been led to conceive an erroneous impression upon this point . . .[36]

Though surely disappointed by its tone, there was no real choice for Beresford but to accept this letter, which in formal terms ended the matter, without recourse to law.

The Beresfords held their marriage together and did not emigrate, but they suffered exile from Marlborough House for many years. Lady Brooke could not have been impervious to all that happened during the crisis. However, when it was over not only did she flourish more than ever. She was becoming a legend.

In March 1892, while travelling in Egypt, the Marquess of Waterford wrote kindly to her and returned the provocative letter, hoping that the matter was now entirely at an end; mentioning that Lady Charles had given permission for the letter to be given back '*entirely of her own free will*',[37] he hoped this would be remembered. A few weeks later, the Prince and Princess of Wales were at the Cap Martin Hotel in Menton. While there they received the news from Waterford, to which the Prince responded:

I have no desire to revert to what occurred at the end of last year; but I shall never forget and can never forgive the conduct of your brother and his wife towards me. His base ingratitude after our intimate friendship of about twenty years hurt me more than words can say. You who have so chivalrous a nature and are such a thorough gentleman in every sense of the word will be able to form some idea what my feelings on the subject are![38]

4

Queen of Society

DURING THE 1890S DAISY was at the height of her influence over the Prince of Wales. He adored her, and many a gilt invitation went out for a Saturday to Monday at Easton, making it clear that he was the star attraction. Entertaining the Prince was the summit of social success. Daisy spent prodigiously, apparently never giving a thought to the cost. Because she had always taken for granted her fortune and the style of life it enabled her to enjoy, it never occurred to her to question the expense. The Prince was said to contribute £2,000 a year towards shooting over the estate.

Elinor Glyn and her husband, Clayton, had settled at Sheerings, a manor house not far away, and the couple were often among the guests at Easton. Glyn later recalled the experience: 'Easton in the nineties was the centre of all that was most intelligent and amusing in the society of the day. Its hostess, Lady Warwick, was literally a Queen, the loveliest woman in England, of high rank, ample riches, and great intelligence. Her immense prestige made every invitation a great honour . . .'[1]

There was a certain ritual about the Saturday to Monday visit. In winter guests arrived at about five o'clock and were greeted by Hall, a distinguished character in his own right. Seemingly omniscient, Hall knew everyone, and was totally in command. Nothing seemed to be beyond his ability, 'Whether it was a telegram sent to Timbuctoo or your train or boat connections worked out to Hades or the moon . . .'[2]

Footmen carried each guest's luggage to the appropriate room, maids unpacked, and during their stay the guests' every possible wish seemed to be anticipated. Tea was a very important occasion, when ladies wore 'the most exquisite gowns of sable trimmed velvet, satin brocade . . . silk gauzes and lace'.[3] Laid out on a big round table was a feast of muffins, crumpets, sandwiches, scones, jam with Devonshire cream and cake. It was a time for enjoying the latest gossip, and perhaps the men would cast an eye around the room and have thoughts about future action. There could be as many as twenty guests, and some men accepted invitations unaccompanied, as did the Prince of Wales. No introductions were made, on the assumption that everyone would automatically know everyone else. The house was beautifully warmed and lit, unusual comforts in those days.

While ladies were dressing for dinner, young Guy would arrive with a spray of gardenias, stephanotis, or perhaps orchids. Again Elinor Glyn sets the scene:

> When the men joined the ladies, whichever of them had been admired would be singled out for the attentions of the most dashing and adroit of men, but good manners were such that no lady was ever left alone, and all of them would find that some man had sat down beside her. Men did all the chasing and contriving to see the ladies of their choice.[4]

Men concentrated on pleasing women, did their utmost to be agreeable, and began conversations on topics which they believed would interest their companions.

In Glyn's novel *The Reflections of Ambrosine*, Easton would become 'Harley', while the character of Margaret Tilchester, whom the young girl Ambrosine sees as 'the most fascinating personality with something of the sun's rays about her',[5] was based on Daisy. When Margaret spoke in her mellifluous voice, people listened. 'How fine a thing life seemed when one spent half an hour with Lady Tilchester in the glorious garden at Harley. A gruff sounding man handed Ambrosine a cup of tea, while engaging at the same time with a bob-tailed sheepdog. Suddenly she realised that *he* was her host!'[6]

Among the guests in the house party 'everyone's life seemed full of interest – interest in something great', but there was occasional talk of scandal, rather exciting for an ingénue: 'Only Lady Tilchester seems noble and above all these earthly things. Her beautiful nature would stand any test.'[7] It is a flattering portrait, but an injection of realism comes when the girl discovers that the perfect lady has borne a child to her lover. It is not, however, seen as a character flaw, neither does it cause surprise. It is simply what happens in that circle.

Sir Anthony Thornhurst, the lover, is very recognisably based on another frequent visitor, Seymour Wynne Finch, a colonel in the Royal Horse Guards who was dubbed the handsomest man in England. Elinor herself was whirled into a passionate affair by Finch, and their affair lasted three or four years. But eventually the puritan streak in her character made her feel too much guilt, and regretfully she parted from him.

～

Although Daisy maintained her high profile in Society, the 1890s was also a decade in which she took initiatives of a far from frivolous kind. Two friendships became important to her at this time. At a dinner party given in 1892 by Moreton Frewen, dissolute uncle of Winston Churchill and the instigator of numerous failed business projects, she met W.T. Stead, who was then editor of the *Review of Reviews*. He had brought conviction to Fleet Street, and had initiated journalism of a more daring kind. Possessing dynamic energy, Stead was one of those characters in late Victorian England who seem to be larger than life. The son of a Congregational minister in the north, he had grown up hearing great preachers, and he carried their moral fervour and idealism into his adult life. As editor of the *Pall Mall Gazette* he had been in the vanguard of the new investigative style of reportage.

His exposé of the child sex trade, 'The Maiden Tribute of Modern Babylon', published in the *Gazette* of July 1885, had generated a furore. Stead had paid the price, finding himself in the dock at the Old Bailey accused of the very crime he had attempted to expose, though the prosecution relied on a technical breach of the law. Found guilty and sentenced to three months in prison, he had been firmly supported by such people as Josephine Butler and Cardinal Manning. In fact he had been guilty of nothing more than shining a light into one of the darkest areas of Victorian society.

As well as crusading against society's evils, Stead had a flair for gaining access to leading figures in every sphere, from historian Thomas Carlyle to Slatin Pasha, the Austrian adventurer who fought alongside General Gordon in North Africa. Gordon himself had granted Stead an exclusive interview before leaving for the Sudan. Stead was also a fervent Spiritualist, finding time in his frenetic professional life to produce *Borderland*, a psychic quarterly. At a time when membership of the Society for Psychical Research included some distinguished academics and there was widespread interest in the paranormal, Stead's belief was not unusual. Even the Queen had sittings with her own psychic medium.

Although an embodiment of the Nonconformist conscience, Stead seemed drawn to Lady Brooke. He saw that part of her nature was unfulfilled, became her mentor and encouraged her interest in social questions. Though unconvinced by Stead's communication with 'spooks', Daisy had a high regard for him. In an early letter from Dunrobin she wrote: 'I can never be thankful enough for a friendship that helps me more than you imagine, to lead the life I wish to lead in future . . . a few lines from yourself will always give intense pleasure.' She praised him for his splendid work, inspiring people 'to higher and better things', and expressed how much his encouragement meant: 'Do not forget us all, toiling to find our ideals, or forsake us for the world of "Spirits" who have had their day on this earth, and who need your sympathy and friendship less than *we* do!'[8]

Whether Stead was her inspiration for greater commitment to charity work or not, Lady Brooke certainly seems to have undertaken more from the time when she came under his influence. But then philanthropy had never been more fashionable. *The World* reported: 'Almost every great lady has freely bestowed time and attention upon some scheme calculated to give employment or happiness or comfort to the less fortunate of her sisters.'[9]

One of Daisy's flagship projects was a school of needlework for Essex girls, which gave them a choice of career other than domestic service. Young village girls who had left school at thirteen, if strong enough, might find work in a household for the princely wage of a shilling a week. For delicate or handicapped girls, however, their health made life as domestics impossible. Such girls remained unemployed, and consequently a burden on their families. Daisy discovered that some of them had an aptitude for intricate needlework and could achieve high standards. Why not harness their talent? It seemed such an obvious and positive solution. The Easton Needlework School was set up in a room at the Lodge, and it was not difficult to find recruits. Girls trudged miles from the neighbouring villages. During their three years' training, they would be paid two shillings and sixpence a week, rising to ten shillings when they became fully proficient. No wonder there was a big demand for places, among the frail and healthy alike.

One of their specialities was embroidered lingerie, for which there was a ready outlet among Daisy's Society friends. When the volume of business became too great for personal distribution, Daisy boldly rented a shop in Bond Street, on which her name

featured. The shop was in fact more of a showroom where customers could be measured and choose from samples on show.
Hidden away from the customers a workroom flourished, with
girls producing elaborate tea gowns and other items. Not only
were they paid handsomely at between twelve and sixteen shillings
a week, but accommodation was provided for them, and there was
a whole new world to explore in the heart of Mayfair.

The school from which they had graduated moved to a building in the grounds of Easton Lodge, catering for about thirty girls.
The enterprise did not always run smoothly, and made no profit,
but it was imaginative and worthwhile. The shop was a talking
point in London Society, but in its piece on philanthropy *The
World* had made a covert attack on Lady Brooke, implying that
she was inefficient and her plan a failure. Daisy had a statement
inserted the following week, defending the scheme: 'financially it
was not a success, but after all that is Lady Brooke's own affair'.[10]

No greater contrast could have existed between Stead and
Daisy's other great friend, the patrician Lord Rosebery. She felt a
strong affinity with the shy statesman, and early in 1892, after he
had declined an invitation to meet the Prince of Wales, she wrote
of her admiration for Rosebery's 'brilliant career, and an intense
wish to know more of a great man'. However, she was sympathetic
about his reluctance to do much socialising: 'I so thoroughly
understand the preference for solitude and a book to any of the
distractions offered by tiresome people . . .' A great sorrow placed
one on a lonely height, looking down on all humanity playing life's
great game, 'absorbed in thoughts known only to an aching
heart'.[11]

The great sorrow referred to was the death of Rosebery's wife,
Hannah, following which he had become somewhat reclusive.
Society gossiped that Lady Warwick was pursuing him, but she did
so no more than she pursued others whose company she enjoyed.
It was inevitable that they should sometimes meet at the same
gatherings. They were also in Paris together on one or two

occasions, when they dined and went to the opera. If they had a love affair, it was conducted with the utmost discretion.

~

In 1893 Brookie succeeded his father, becoming the fifth Earl of Warwick, which was the signal for Daisy to install electric lighting and other comforts in the ancestral castle. She also arranged for some extensive interior decoration, including a Chinese suite and rooms for the Prince of Wales near her own. It was a vast and in parts sombre dwelling, but there were reception rooms of great beauty and the new Countess made the most of them.

The following year Daisy stood for election as trustee of the Warwick workhouse, hoping to bring about an improvement in the conditions there. She also became a Poor Law Guardian. Speaking at the time, she mentioned 'the great principle which is gradually gaining recognition of the joint and mutual responsibility of man and woman',[12] something which applied as much in community affairs as in domestic. Once elected as a guardian and trustee, Daisy escorted the Prince of Wales round the workhouse to introduce him to some of his future subjects. He was not unaware of social conditions at their worst, having visited the slums of Holborn and St Pancras incognito and subsequently spoken in a debate on housing in the Lords. He had admitted that conditions prevailing in some areas of London owned by the Duchy of Cornwall were just as bad. At the time of the Royal Commission for the Housing of the Poor, he had urged the appointment of Octavia Hill as a commissioner, and, according to his private secretary, Knollys, had been anxious for the inquiry to be a success. The Prince was more progressive than Gladstone, who had thought it would set an inconvenient precedent if a lady were to be placed on a Royal Commission, and had asked His Royal Highness not to press the matter.

Writing to Stead from Chatsworth that winter of 1894, Daisy told him about her recent visit to Colchester where she had sorted, packed and sent ten thousand garments to poor districts. She had also spent two days in East London near the Victoria Docks doing charity work. Almost in passing she mentioned having established a nurses' home at Leyton. Even her critics could not deny that Daisy Warwick was a woman of action, and to participate more fully she had rented a house near Westminster. She hoped that by being on the spot she could focus better on some of the political issues in which she was beginning to become interested. Of these, education was high on her list.

~

Celebration of her husband's succession had waited for two years, but when it happened it was spectacular: Lady Warwick's *bal poudre*, on 1 February 1895, became a legend. Five hundred guests had received invitations in white and gold. They were to dress in costumes from the periods of Louis XV and XVI. The ball took place in near-Arctic weather, with several feet of snow lying over the grounds, and one can imagine the reaction of guests as they entered the castle, which had assumed the brilliancy of the eighteenth-century French court. Radiating from a central chandelier, electric light illuminated the hall, but with all the mellowness of candlelight, and five thousand wax candles were also burning. Hung over the hall's stone walls were Beauvais tapestries and yellow-silver embroidered cloth. 'Belle', *The World*'s reporter, was impressed: 'Each room seemed lovelier than the last one. The gold drawing room was absolutely brilliant . . .'[13]

Dancing took place in the Cedar Drawing Room, hung with Van Dyck family portraits. Daisy chose to be Marie Antoinette, in a dress of rose-tinted brocade, with woven pink and blue flowers and roses embroidered in gold thread, all studded with exquisite diamond stars. A sapphire-blue train fell in folds from her shoulders, secured by a *rivière* of diamonds. Twelve-year-old Lady Marjorie and another young girl were dressed as shepherdesses in white, the Queen's maids of honour.

As Worms' famous Austrian band played appropriate music for the dancing, several guests could be identified in 'cunning combinations of colour and coquetries of costume'.[14] Brookie wore a ruby velvet coat, profusely trimmed with gold lace, and a wig *à la mousquetaire*. Millie Sutherland was Louis XV's consort, Marie Letzinka, wearing white and silver brocaded satin, with a ruby velvet train and masses of diamonds. There were guests who came variously as ladies of Louis XVI's court: Madame de Pompadour, the Duchesse de Polignac and the Duchesse d'Orléans. Dom Luis de Soveral, the Portuguese minister, was one of several '*mousquetaires*' present, including le Viscomte de Bragalonne (Prince Henry of Pless), and le Comte d'Artagnac (Lord Lovat). They were Dumas come to life. Harry Rosslyn was the Duc de Nemours, and the millionaire bachelor Joe Laycock – who was soon to play a much larger part in Daisy's life – an officer of the Pondicherry Regiment in eighteenth-century India. There was the 'Abbé Bevet', slightly sinister in black velvet with skull cap. Mrs Alice Keppel, future mistress of the Prince of Wales, was wearing Rose du Barri antique brocade with silver thread, had powdered hair with three Rose du Barri feathers, and pink satin shoes with diamond buckles.

At midnight three trumpet-blowing heralds summoned the guests to supper where forty tables had been laid in the hall, and the menu included *chauds* and *froids*. Dancing continued till dawn, and 'it was fairly morning before the echo of the last carriage wheels died away'.[15]

Pleased with the resounding success of her ball, confirmed by all the Society journals, the Countess was unprepared when she found some unfavourable reportage in certain radical papers. She sent cuttings to Stead, her accompanying letter full of the unfairness, as she perceived it, of the way the ball had been described in those periodicals. Obviously stung by the criticism, she said that it had been no more expensive than an ordinary ball, of which hundreds were given every week. 'I don't like these things disseminated through the country simply because our class are landowners!'[16] It was annoying to be held up as an example of useless extravagance. Besides, there had been many quiet country people present. In short, Daisy was playing down the grandeur in a way that was hardly consistent with descriptions of the evening that came from other sources. Yet she was adamant that, as far as the ball had affected the town and neighbourhood, it had been 'a godsend to the tradespeople . . . as it has brought money directly to them, and given employment to many'[17] at a time when it was scarce. Was all this wrong? Would Stead advise her to reply to the press in writing? Or would he, *could* he be her champion?

If coverage in the radical press so far had been irritating, Robert Blatchford's piece in *The Clarion* hit much harder. He began by quoting the rapturous *Leicester Daily Express*: 'The brains of many an artist in dress must have therefore been actively employed in studying and their fingers in reproducing the garb of an age in which love of gaiety and ornament was everywhere visible . . .'

Blatchford's response was scathing. It was intolerable to mention love of gaiety and ornament 'while the gaunt and ragged artisan creeps shame-faced by the palace wall, begging as if he asked for charity to be allowed to work! Thousands of pounds spent upon a few hours' silly masquerade; men and women strutting before each other's envious eyes in mad rivalry of wanton dissipation . . . a vulgar saturnalia of gaudy pride . . .'[18]

The dispossessed – men, women and children – were huddling in ragged hovels, without the bare necessities of food, clothes or fire. There was no respite in their suffering, and no prospect of it coming to an end. There were references to 'meagre flesh', 'winter's cruel sting', and souls crushed. Blatchford asked: 'which to pity most? The shrieking victims or the fiddling Nero?'[19]

If the torments of the dying were pitiful, even more so was the callousness 'which laughs and mocks at misery'. Such callousness by implication was attributed to the chatelaine of the castle; as Blatchford wrote in conclusion: 'I deeply pity the poor rich Countess of Warwick . . .'[20]

Blatchford's comments were an out-and-out attack on the entire aristocratic way of life, and at the centre of it was the condemnation of a person who epitomised all that was wrong with such a way of life. Angry and mystified that anyone should portray her as callous and decadent, Daisy fought back, took the early London train one morning, and made her way to the office of *The Clarion* at Mowbray House in Norfolk Street, off the Strand.

Recalling the meeting in her autobiography, Daisy remembered that it was at the top of a staircase in one of the older buildings. She entered unannounced, 'and there at his writing desk sat the man who had dared to attack us for indulging in legitimate amusement that had at the same time given work to so many unemployed. His coldly gazing eyes showed no surprise at the unexpected and abrupt vision in his dingy office . . . He made no movement of welcome.'[21]

There could have been no greater contrast between the surroundings of Mowbray House and her own accustomed milieu. It was a strange confrontation: Blatchford wearing a garment which appeared to be half coat, half dressing gown, the Countess dressed by Worth. With the offending article in hand, she was determined to have her say, and with the innate confidence of her position she began. How dare he level such terrible accusations of selfishness and decadence against her? Very calmly Blatchford asked her to sit down, and for the next three hours he lectured her on Socialist economic and political theory. He pointed out that any idea that her entertainment had generated work was a misunderstanding of the difference between productive and unproductive labour. Rather to his surprise, Daisy allowed him to make his case without interruption, but he would have been unaware of the influence he was exerting on this unmistakably aristocratic woman. Late that afternoon, Daisy walked out into the darkening street, trying to absorb all that Blatchford had explained to her. After all, less than a month earlier, she had portrayed herself as Marie Antoinette.

Although Blatchford had made a strong impression on her, it would be some years before she experienced full conversion to his ideas. To start with, she spent two hours sitting on Paddington station, getting over the shock of being talked to in a way she had never experienced before. 'During the journey home I thought and thought about all that I had been hearing and learning. I knew that my outlook on life could never be the same as before this incident . . . I was as one who had found a new, a real world . . .'[22]

Blatchford gave his own version of what took place that day:

We have a picture of me and my office and my undignified garment. That undignified garment was a pilot jacket of the best Russian cloth, very warm and soft and comfortable, and I was really rather proud of it. And my coldly gazing eyes misled her ladyship. The fact is I was very nervous and very tired. I had never before spoken to a Countess . . . I am naturally shy and I did not feel at all happy during the interview.[23]

He had probably been 'a bit of a bear'. The lady had thought him cold and unsympathetic; he had thought her proud and scornful: 'Had anyone told me that I had awakened "the hunger of her soul" I should not have believed it . . .'[24] Ultimately he considered that she had been very brave.

~

The influence of W.T. Stead continued to be important in helping Lady Warwick to discover a more positive outlet for her intelligence than mere philanthropy: 'There were amongst her friends a number of patricians who gave her a personal interest in politics. Stead was different. In this man from quite another background, she found an idealism, a visionary fervour, and an enthusiasm for good causes which proved quite infectious.'[25]

Stead kindled her enthusiasm either by his writing or, when they were able to meet, by his personality. She had confided in him, and they had even discussed her relationship with the Prince of Wales, a subject about which the great moral crusader was remarkably uncensorious, and in fact rather intrigued by it. The years when she was enjoying her greatest social success were also the years when Stead was giving her advice, and they met as often as their busy lives allowed.

Under his direction she had been thinking very seriously about her future. Just a few weeks before the Warwick ball she had written an article in the *Pall Mall Gazette*, decrying the growing disparity between rich and poor. It seemed, she wrote, that the world was getting brighter, more interesting, even happier for a comparatively small and privileged class, while for the toiling masses it was getting relatively, and perhaps even absolutely, worse: 'All of us today who love our country, in contradistinction to its cities, are dismal and dejected . . .'[26] Referring to rural Essex, where wages had fallen and any continuous employment was uncertain, she wondered:

> How can I do my social duties in a district poverty-stricken as this now is? And when, woman-like, I protest against labourers forced to live on 10s. a week, against the wholesale cutting of trees and the destruction of the landscape, then forthwith I am deluged with Adam Smith and Mill; with the inevitable results of unrestricted competition . . .[27]

In conclusion, her article was an affirmation of the future contribution that women might make: 'I believe that a Parliament of Marcellas would accomplish something at once. It is almost an argument for Woman's suffrage. We women would not be quelled even by the prosy dreariness of Adam Smith.'[28]

~

Daisy Warwick's ideas were evolving radically, but she was still enjoying her social role, and it would be nearly ten years before she joined a political party. By mid-February Daisy was planning her Easter, asking Rosebery to join her small party at Warwick with his sons. If he could not be with her at Easter, then perhaps Whitsun, when maybe they would hear an early nightingale? Rosebery probably declined more invitations than he accepted, but there does seem to have been empathy between the quiet statesman and the far from quiet hostess who wanted to include him. When they had last met at Dunrobin, Daisy had discussed some personal problem with him, and she recalled how kind he had been:

> I have often felt grateful to you for your friendliness when we had that little talk: I fear I was egotistical in the recital of my woes, but you were kind enough not to seem bored, and I appreciated your forbearance. May I say that your own personality teaches a lesson of strength and courage and sorrows overcome . . .[29]

Exactly what her woes had been can only be guessed, but it is quite likely that she had confided in him about her unsatisfactory marriage.

Millie Sutherland enjoyed entertaining an eclectic mix of people at Dunrobin. It used to be said that one was never sure who would turn up, but the party might include a parson or a poet as well as more fashionable guests. She too liked Rosebery, and solicited his help in sponsoring some good causes: knowing how fond of children he was, she asked him for a contribution to an orphanage and refuge for destitute or cruelly treated children.

~

On 29 December 1895 Dr Leander Starr Jameson invaded the Transvaal with a detachment of men from Cecil Rhodes' South Africa Company in support of the largely English-speaking opponents of the province's Afrikaner government, an adventure which was hugely controversial. At worst it was seen as a disgraceful military blunder, undertaken for gold and imperial glory. On 6 January 1896 the special correspondent of *The Times* filed his dispatch, which the paper published the following day:

> Dr Jameson's and Sir John Willoughby's column, numbering four hundred men, fought on Wednesday last a battle lasting eleven hours at Krugersdorp, a hundred and twenty miles from Johannesburg, against two thousand Boers, who occupied a strong kopje position. Failing to defeat the Boers, the column moved southwards, fighting hard on the road to Johannesburg . . .[30]

By the following morning, after desultory fighting all night, they had come within six miles of Johannesburg:

> The column fought stubbornly until 11 a.m., when the men, having used all their cartridges, and having had no food for twenty-four hours, were obliged to surrender to the Boer force, which was six times more numerous than Dr Jameson's column.[31]

It later transpired that anti-government reinforcements from Johannesburg numbering two thousand had been supposed to meet the Jameson brigade at Krugersdorp, but had failed to show. The white flag had not been hoisted by Dr Jameson's order, reported the *Times* man, but after fighting for thirty-six hours, both Jameson and Sir John Willoughby were among thirty prisoners taken. Several of their men had been seriously wounded, and many were suffering from fever and dysentery.

Daisy Warwick was a prominent supporter of Jameson's exploits. When opinion in some quarters clamoured for severe punishment to be meted out to him, she wrote to *The Times* in his defence. She asked Stead not to blame her for doing so, because all her patriotism had been aroused 'by the scandalous suggestions in our own press'[32] that Dr Jameson should face execution. Her letter, published in *The Times* on 7 January 1896, was couched in strong language:

Sir,

It passes belief that today the English Press is so far forgetful of its bright traditions as to discuss in cold blood, the prospective shooting or hanging of an Englishman by the Boers. To what is it owing that this nomadic tribe is encamped in the Transvaal at all? It is owing to the determination of our nation that unspeakable indignities perpetrated on the negro race and its traffic in African slaves should no longer be permitted in a colony under the British flag ... Would any Englishman worthy of the name and the nation have failed to act exactly as Dr Jameson and his gallant companions have done?

He is appealed to by the leading residents of Johannesburg ... to come to the assistance of their women and children, at a moment when a revolution is seen to be inevitable. On his way to succour his countrymen with a force of mounted police, and after having disclaimed every intention of hostility to the Boers, he is apparently attacked by their armed forces ... But whatever may have been his fate, there is not an Englishwoman of us all whose heart does not go out in gratitude and deepest sympathy to these brave men. They did their duty, and if they have gone to their death, even in a fair fight, so much the worse for the Boers ... if they have been taken prisoners, to be afterwards done to death in cold blood, then there is no longer room in South Africa for a 'Republic' administered by their murderers ... Are English gentlemen, personally known to many of us – are such as these 'land pirates' and 'thieves' because when implored by a majority of the respectable residents of an important town they attempt to police that town at a moment of extreme urgency?[33]

Was Britain so caught up in diplomacy and at the mercy of German intrigues, she asked, that it was a crime for kinsfolk to be succoured? If Dr Jameson had turned a deaf ear to their appeal, and they had later been at the mercy of a hostile community, 'so vividly depicted by the late Lord Randolph Churchill', then Dr Jameson would have deserved censure by the German Emperor. 'The one light in all this blackness' was the presence of an Englishman in South Africa, 'upon whose resolute personality our hearts and hopes rely'.[34]

The Dutch press had reportedly been jubilant at the lowering of British prestige, and quick to advocate the incorporation of Rhodesia with the Transvaal. Meanwhile Lady Warwick's letter to *The Times* caused Count Munster, the German ambassador in London, to say that 'ladies should not be jingoes'. Being implicated in Jameson's raid, Rhodes was forced to resign the premiership of Cape Colony. Daisy began working to reinstate him, and in this endeavour she had a powerful ally in the Prince of Wales, who admired Rhodes enormously.

In the spring of 1896 they were both in Paris, where as usual they enjoyed quiet dinners at Paillard's or Voisin's. Then they went south, to Menton, and from there Daisy wrote to W.T. Stead, telling him that the Prince was within reach and could possibly be of help in the pro-Rhodes campaign: 'shall I ask him to write the letters you require?'[35] By now Daisy was becoming ambivalent about her role as royal companion, admitting to Stead that the Prince made too many demands on her time, but she felt sure that under her influence he would be willing to assist. Despite his puritan background, her mentor always emphasised the good influence she could have. Certainly he could put any such letters to good use. He almost hero-worshipped Rhodes, though he was totally out of sympathy with Jameson.

~

That summer Millie Sutherland was again enlisting Rosebery's support, this time for the Scottish Home Industries Association.

She told him that at last they were within measurable distance of obtaining a monopoly of the tweed industry in the Highlands and Islands. A company was being started with a capital of £10,000, and besides very much wanting his name as a patron, she suggested he could take a stake of a hundred shares for £1,000.[36] In spite of the fact that she never dabbled in politics, Millie was sometimes referred to as 'the Red Duchess'. While she was indeed every inch a duchess, Millie's social conscience was very much alive, and she felt an 'almost overwhelming sense of responsibility'.[37]

A letter she sent to Rosebery from Bad Mannheim was, however, entirely social. 'What a lighthearted person you are dear Lord Rosebery – in storm or sunshine ever the same!'[38] She would be in London early the following week, from where the Sutherland yacht would sail,

and we ought to reach the Firth of Forth on 22nd. Do let us take you to Dunrobin . . . I really don't think you'll be able to refuse me when you see me again!!! . . . I am dreadfully homesick, but then I am never content wherever I am – I *shall* be however if you spend a fortnight in the Highlands. (isn't this subtle flattery)[39]

Rosebery accepted Millie's invitation, and Daisy also joined the autumn party at Dunrobin, as she did most years. There seems to have been no less empathy between the two, and, while still in the Highlands, she wrote in warm terms offering to serve his interests, if he would give her his friendship and trust her:

Most women have their ideals of great men – you have been mine . . . Since we met here I have had two more years to 'consider' you and to pluck up the courage to tell you that I should be proud to be of some use to you – ever! I don't mean that I could ever be the political platform woman, but there are other quiet ways in which one can work and influence, and though our acquaintance is but slight, I have a true sympathy with your ambitions.[40]

She confessed to being attracted by his personality, though it might be 'unbecoming and unnecessary to say so', but added that his friendship would be her most valued possession: 'I want you to be back in power again, free from the trammels and difficulties of your last ministry, and with a free hand too as the ideal "Liberal" leader . . . I shall be more than proud and happy to work for you . . .'[41]

It is unclear in what way Daisy imagined herself working for Rosebery, but her letter brought a quick response, in which the man reveals a good deal about himself:

My dear Lady Warwick

I received your letter late last night and was equally delighted and surprised. My personality has not attracted many people in my life, and so at this time of day a spontaneous offer of help-fulness and friendship from a brilliant and beautiful woman comes as a sort of miracle. What can I give you in return? My friendship in the usual sense is worth very little. I am a wretched correspondent, a solitary being, more and more rooted in lone-liness and destined it seems to be more and more solitary . . . If then you accept my friendship you must know the worst, for I must not sail under false colours . . .[42]

He was in no doubt that the real power of a woman such as Lady Warwick was in social charm and insight, 'which turns all men topsy turvy, and that has a force in these days that is almost alarming . . . When feminine fascination and spirit are thrown in the balance against a man, that man is doomed. I do not think that this is right or fair, but it is so!'[43]

Daisy must have loved this tribute. Some people thought that they discerned a love affair between the two, but in the absence of evidence the verdict on that must remain open. Soon after receiving his charming letter, she also received an invitation to Dalmeny, his home on the Firth of Forth, and what a pleasure she thought it would be to enjoy such congenial company on the way back from Dunrobin.

She was prevented from doing so by neuralgia, from which she suffered a week of great pain, and all she could do was remain in a darkened room. Once recovered, however, she was keen to keep the friendship alive, and told him that she would be content to stand at a distance and use her 'poor woman's wit' in his cause, believing that 'To idealise is not always to follow a delusion. There is a friendship that means sympathetic comprehension, and the understanding of a voice that the multitude never hear . . .'[44]

Rather extravagantly, she offered to lay all her womanly powers at his feet.

❦ 5 ❧

New Love

I N THE AUTUMN OF 1896 Daisy was thrown out of the saddle
while hunting, her horse rolling over her and hitting her head
with one of his hoofs. For several weeks afterwards she suffered
from terrible headaches, and had to rest a good deal. However, she
was still able to arrange a meeting which she had wanted to
happen for some time: Stead would be introduced to the Prince of
Wales on 8 December, at a luncheon to be given at 50 South
Audley Street. This was the house Daisy had rented from her sister
Blanchie, who had married Algernon Gordon-Lennox in 1886.

A series of articles written by Stead about the Queen had
pleased the Prince, so much so that he had asked for them to be
presented as a book. Even so, both men had reason to be nervous,
though perhaps if anything His Royal Highness might have the
greater cause. In the aftermath of the Gordon-Cumming case,
the Nonconformist press had been distinctly uncharitable about
the Prince, and he was sensitive to criticism, often feeling misunderstood. Besides, five years earlier Stead had written an
uncompromising piece about the Prince which had offended his
private secretary. Knollys had protested in a frank letter that the
greater part of it was 'most unfair, unjust and incorrect, with a

total misconception of his character', asserting that he had been described as 'a sort of Louis 15th cum George 4th, with the profligacy of the one and the morals and extravagance of the other'.[1] According to Knollys, the delineation of character, as perceived by Stead, was so unlike His Royal Highness that it would be useless to attempt making suggestions by way of correcting the picture.

Although no doubt relishing the opportunity that meeting the Prince would give him journalistically, Stead would have been more at ease in the company of someone like Hugh Price Hughes, an outstanding preacher of the time. Yet the luncheon proved to be a surprisingly successful occasion, with the two guests finding more common ground than either had anticipated, and consequently conversation flowed easily. It was a triumph for their hostess, and the Prince later confirmed that he had liked Stead much more than he could have believed possible. Their meeting gave Stead a way of continuing contact with the heir to the throne, using Lady Warwick as the intermediary.

Indeed, one of Daisy's strengths was her capacity for friendship with people of very different personalities. Her letters to Rosebery are lightly flirtatious, and at Christmas she expressed 'not the empty words of the conventionally "festive season" but the heart-felt wishes of a friend, that all your undertakings may prosper and all your desires may be fulfilled (or at least as many as are good for you!) in the future days and years'.[2]

There seems to have been some gossip within their milieu that she had been pursuing him 'to oyster feasts and then to Paris'.[3] Pleading guilty to the first, her subsequent pursuit had been less successful. In the pleasure capital, she had only been able to meet him once. If Rosebery had not been so elusive, she said, her stay there would have been more exciting, but there it was, she could never see enough of him. He compared her to Catherine the Great, and Daisy replied that if she had wanted to behave like Catherine, nothing would have deterred her; in fact, even though thinking of herself as a pagan, she claimed to have high ideals. Her carefully chosen Christmas present for him that year was a first edition of Robert Louis Stevenson's collected works, and she invited him to Warwick in January, to join a party that was to include Lord Curzon and the Marlboroughs.

~

In the spring of 1897 Daisy spent several weeks in Paris to sit for a portrait by Carolus Duran, in whose atelier John Singer Sargent had been a pupil. Apart from her long daily sittings in a stuffy studio, she enjoyed her freedom. 'I have daily got on my bicycle and sped away for air and exercise and all kinds of adventures,'[4] she told Stead.

She had enjoyed the company of Millie and Blanchie at the Hotel d'Albe; they had been invited to several dinners, and got to know Sir Edmund Monson, the British ambassador, meeting pleasant people when dining with him. Naturally, there had to be moments spent in shops 'dear to the feminine heart' in the city.[5] Even so, she had found time to read a lot of literature on Socialism, and had decided that she must meet key figures in the Labour movement, such as Tom Mann, leader of the railway workers. Could Stead bring them together? While in Paris she had become friends with Paul Deschamel, a rising young politician and Vice-President of the Chamber of Deputies – in her view a most intelligent man, with serious ideas and splendid oratorical powers.

It had been altogether a refreshing interlude. Daisy was feeling very well and looking young, which pleased her as much as the finished portrait. Now she wanted to get back to work, and she was looking forward to entertaining a party at Warwick which would include Lord Rosebery, the Asquiths and Arthur Balfour. Within a few weeks a number of prominent educationalists would be congregating at the castle to take part in a kind of informal seminar – 'all those interested in education in Birmingham and the midlands, beside those from London and Oxford', she told Stead jubilantly. Would he and his wife like to come? It would be a great pleasure to meet Mrs Stead. 'I feel deeply that very question of Technical Education in Rural Districts and am going to read a paper on the subject at the Congress in June.'[6]

One of her particular concerns was with children living in poverty, both urban and rural, who were cut off from education. In rural areas, the farmer and the squire were not on the whole favourable towards anything but the most rudimentary schooling. Some of them begrudged children secondary education, fearing that it might deprive them of servants and give their labourers the means to get better-paid work. The agricultural labourer for his part usually thought that what had been good enough for him was good enough for his children, whose earnings were important. An immediate shilling seemed a better bet than a possible future pound. Daisy wanted to do something to counteract that kind of retrogressive thinking, and the fruit of her inspiration was Bigods, a technical school for disadvantaged children from rural Essex. It opened in the summer of 1897 and was to provide a secondary education for both boys and girls, with an emphasis on science, agriculture and craft skills.

At first the school building was in one of the outlying farms on her estate, near Dunmow. Only small fees were charged, and there were some scholarships, which made it accessible to children whose fathers were small farmers or even farm labourers. The germ of the idea had come from Raphael Meldola, Professor of Chemistry at Finsbury College, whom Daisy had met while presenting prizes for the Barking Technical Instruction Committee. Thus began a long association between these two far-sighted people. Meldola had begun his speech by mentioning the need for Britain to compete in foreign markets, but it seems that it was Daisy's own idea to apply his ideas to north-west Essex, where agricultural depression had hit hard.

Bigods was imbued with the pioneering spirit. The school opened with twenty-three pupils, who were offered a combined secondary education. After fifteen hours a week of science for the first two years of the course, agriculture would be studied during the second two years, a subject for which the earlier stage was a solid foundation. Unusually for its time the school was co-educational, because its founder believed that boys became more courteous and gentle, girls more perceptive and understanding when educated together. Over the next ten years, this school was to cost Daisy around £10,000 in running costs, with additional bursaries.

She described her enterprise to Stead:

My technical and science school near Dunmow is answering so well that I have taken a large country house as a boarding school for boys and girls between the ages of twelve and sixteen. The house will hold fifty. We have a lovely garden and farm, and the agricultural and horticultural side will be developed with bees and poultry. Buttermaking will go on after lesson hours. It is an ideal colony.[7]

During this year another project was demanding her attention, but it was one that Daisy was pleased to do, although she rightly anticipated that it would bring out the hostile element within her own class. She had agreed to write the preface to an autobiography which was bound to be controversial, courageously linking her name with that of Joseph Arch. Founder of the National Agricultural Labourers' Union, Arch had fought his way from the ploughtail to the House of Commons, but in the 1860s, fiercely opposed by the established Church and landowners, he had spoken up for a large submerged class. Through sheer dogged determination he had organised the union, which had secured some fundamental employment rights. Her admiration for Arch was conveyed in the words of her preface, which summed up his achievement in these words:

A Warwickshire peasant, at first alone and unaided, started and led an organization which revolutionized the condition of the agricultural labourer.

From small beginnings – a handful of labourers, a hurried meeting under an old Chestnut tree in the gloom of a February evening – an agitation was set on foot, which rapidly grew . . . until it permeated the length and breadth of rural England . . . coincident with its growth was a visible improvement in the moral and material condition of those for whom it was organized . . .[8]

The union had been the herald of further progress, leading to enfranchisement of the agricultural labourer. While admitting that she was not totally in agreement with the entire text, Daisy was wholehearted in her recognition of 'an honest and good man'. Echoing the words of Cardinal Manning a quarter of a century earlier, she wrote: 'To couple my name with that of Joseph Arch gives me no displeasure.'[9]

Some of the impetus which gave Daisy her zeal for public work had come from her happiness with Joe Laycock. They had probably met during the hunting season of 1894–5, in Leicestershire, where they rode with the Cottesmore, Quorn or Belvoir. In an early letter, Daisy told him that he had made her understand love for the first time in her life. Joe gladly provided three scholarships for the sons of tenants on his Durham and Nottinghamshire estates, and furthermore equipped the school workshop. His enthusiasm was as welcome as his financial help.

Indeed it gave Daisy no little pleasure to play several different roles, from amanuensis to a former Warwickshire peasant to attendance in the Royal Enclosure at Ascot. In 1897 Persimmon won the Gold Cup for the Prince of Wales, and naturally Daisy had been in the royal party. Persimmon's victory led to an experience which the Prince described in his own expressive style:

My own lovely little Daisy,

I lose no time in writing to tell you of an episode which occurred today after you left – which was unpleasant and unexpected – but I hope my darling you will agree that I could not have acted otherwise, as my loyalty to you is, I hope, a thing that you will never think of doubting! Shortly before leaving Ascot today, Marcus B. came to me, and said he had a great favour to ask me, so I answered at once I shall be delighted to grant it. He then became much affected, and actually cried, and said might he bring his brother C. up to offer his congratulations on Persimmon's success. I had no alternative but to say yes. He came up with his hat off, and would not put it on till I told him, and shook hands. We talked a little about racing, then I turned and we parted. What struck me more than anything was his humble attitude and manner! My loved one, I hope you won't be annoyed at what has happened, and exonerate me from blame, as that is all I care about . . .

It was nice seeing just a little of you – my sweet love, and I was so happy that you could at last see a horse of mine win a good race . . . Don't forget, my darling, to expect me from five on Sunday next . . .

Goodnight and God keep you, my own adored little Daisy wife.[10]

The Prince's adored one was well into her relationship with Joe Laycock, and might even have realised at this time that she was pregnant by him. Hence it was probably of little consequence to her that Charlie Beresford had met His Royal Highness for the first time in seven years. The Prince's letter shows not only how much he still felt for Daisy, but also significantly that he was still visiting her in the afternoon. Nevertheless, she had found a greater love, a man who appeared devoted to her, and she had been spending several weeks at a time with him at Wiseton, his estate in Nottinghamshire.

There was now therefore the matter of what to do about the Prince. It is likely that their relationship had become platonic, although there is no firm date as to when that transition was made. The previous year, both Joe and the Prince had been guests in the same large house party at Warwick, and it seems quite possible that although in love with Joe, Daisy had continued for some time as the Prince's intimate friend.

Her pregnancy, however, changed things. Daisy maintained strict secrecy about her baby's father. Only one or two people were told, her husband among them; in the wider world people assumed that the child had been conceived within marriage, after a gap of thirteen years. But it was now clearly necessary to distance herself from the Prince, while if possible maintaining his friendship.

Taking the initiative, Daisy wrote him a clever letter, in which she told her royal lover that their interests now lay in different directions, signalling that she wished to withdraw from her role as mistress. This 'beautiful letter'[11] reached the Prince while he was staying at with the Devonshires at Chatsworth early in January, and he found it difficult to describe how touched he had been. When he gave it to Princess Alexandra, he said, she had been moved to tears. (Daisy had also written to the Princess, who replied through her husband that 'she really quite forgives and condones the past'.[12])

The Prince knew that his loved one could not help writing to him as she had done, though it had given him a pang, after the kind of communications he had become used to receiving for nearly nine years. No one could have received more assurance of devotion than Daisy:

> how could you, my loved one, for a moment imagine that I should withdraw my friendship from you? On the contrary I mean to befriend you more than ever, and you can not prevent my giving you the same love as the friendship I have always felt for you . . . we have that sentimental feeling of affinity which

cannot be eradicated by time, and we still have so many objects in common! . . .

You do not tell me how you are my poor little love?[13]

He hoped she was feeling better and trusted 'that by complete rest and quiet your health may not suffer and that all will go well with you till the proper time!'[14]

Later, the Prince was to find out more about the man who had replaced him in Daisy's affections, and it was a considerable blow to his pride. There were arguments, but in the end he forgave his adored Daisy. She usually got her own way. Thus assured of the Prince's continued friendship, and with her profile at court in no way diminished, she had managed her disengagement with consummate skill. At Chatsworth there had been after-dinner performances in the lovely private theatre: Miss Muriel Wilson (daughter of shipping magnate Arthur Wilson, owner of Tranby Croft) and A. Mensdorff had acted a short French play admirably.

Then Mrs Willie James and Mrs Leo Trevor had performed a short, most amusing impromptu piece. 'Everybody seems gone mad about acting here,' the Prince reported, 'a welcome change from gambling!'[15]

Daisy's pregnancy had been difficult, and during the later part she was unwell enough for her doctor to order complete bed rest, but Joe was supportive, and she looked to the future confidently. When at last the waiting was over, and her son, given the name Maynard, was safely born on 21 March 1898, Daisy felt the greatest joy. After the confinement, it took her several weeks to gain her strength, and to complete her recovery she took the baby to Clacton-on-Sea, with an entourage of nursemaids. From there she wrote to Stead that 'the wretchedness of the past months' had been forgotten, and sent him a cutting of sweet peas, hoping that he would plant them in Maynard's honour. She also thanked him for his 'kind, beautiful words'.[16] With his mother's blue eyes and blond hair, Maynard was a lovely looking child, and immediately became the centre of her world in a way that her older children had not been.

Cecil Rhodes and Lord Rosebery agreed to be godfathers, the latter being assured that he would not be expected to present any silver spoons or to hear her son's catechism.

~

With Maynard in his nursery, Daisy began to circulate and entertain as usual. She was also setting up an agricultural college for women, which would give them the skills to run a smallholding. Horticulture would be taught, because she herself had a passion for gardening. Originally based near Reading, the school had its share of teething problems, but once up and running it flourished. In 1902 the college would move to Studley Castle, near Birmingham, a huge mock Gothic building with 340 acres. Thereafter it was to prove something of a white elephant, which swallowed a great deal of money.

For many months Stead had been focusing on the importance of Anglo-American understanding. American involvement in the war over Cuba had prompted him to claim in the *Review of Reviews* that America had emerged as a great new power, and to express his hope that the result would be closer ties between the two branches of the English-speaking race. When Cecil Rhodes had pronounced that England and America needed each other, the May edition of the *Review* had given prominence to his speech.

Having begun 1898 with a survey of Britain's position in the world, Stead had seen it threatened by military weakness, commercial competition and diplomatic isolation. The best future course, he insisted, was an Anglo-American alliance, and when discussing the idea with Daisy had suggested that the Prince's influence might be useful in promoting the entente. Warwick Castle would be a rallying point, as it was already visited by so many Americans. Stead's long letter to the Prince reached him via Daisy, and he used her as intermediary when giving his reply:

I have shown Mr Stead's letter both to the Princess and Francis Knollys, and we *all* think that we cannot mix ourselves up in the scheme – as far as I am concerned I heartily wish for an 'entente cordiale' with America, but during this unfortunate war we *must* observe *strict neutrality* – and Chamberlain as a Cabinet Minister went *too far* in the recent speech he made![17]

Daisy called the Prince's reply 'absolute rubbish!'

While staying with Baron Ferdinand de Rothschild at Waddesdon earlier in the summer, the Prince had damaged one of his knees in a fall. His general health was far from good, so when Daisy accepted an invitation to join his party at Cowes in August, she referred to him as 'The Invalid'. According to the American press, Lady Warwick was acting as the Prince's nurse, a story which made him furious. While on board the royal yacht, Daisy had been able to ascertain the Prince's views about Tsar Nicholas, prompted again by Stead, who thought that a rapprochement with Russia would be politically desirable.

The Prince had said that although he personally liked his nephew, he was a young man, 'as weak as water', and entirely under the thumb of his minister Murienoff, 'a subtle intriguer of the old Russian school, his one idea to oppose and thwart England'.[18] As for Stead's editorial, calling attention to the Tsar's idea of disarmament throughout all nations, the Prince thought it 'the greatest rubbish and nonsense . . . France could never consent to it nor we!' No wonder Daisy added, 'This is of course *private* dear Mr Stead.'[19] In his letters to Daisy the Prince was often remarkably indiscreet.

Although Daisy and the Prince were no longer intimate, a letter written in the late 1890s from the Marlborough Club leaves little doubt of his continuing affection for her. After thanking her for two letters, one received in the morning and another in the evening, he explained that he had stood for an hour and a half at the levy that day, despite an aching knee, had just returned from a Guards Club dinner, and was in reflective mood:

I have not forgotten anything you allude to – I never shall – but has it been *my* fault that we have not met so often lately as of yore? Especially in the evenings? Will you not try and consider me *still* your best and most devoted friend? Have I deserved to forget it all? It is just *ten* years since we became the great friends which I hoped we were still. Many things have happened in that time, and we have had to put up with *trials* of different kinds, which has [sic] not fallen to the lot of others. Time and circumstances have doubtless produced changes, but they should be faced and not change a friendship, may I say a devotion, which should last till 'death do us part.'

If I thought you did not care for me any more, even as a true friend, I should indeed be the unhappiest and most miserable of men! My life seems an easy and a happy one, but though I have no right to complain as I receive so many benefits for which I cannot be grateful enough, it is not always 'a bed of roses.'

Anyhow I do not forget my friends – that my worst enemy cannot impute to me – but I have no virtues to extol . . . Goodnight my little Daisy wife and au revoir on Friday next at 5.30 . . . For ever yours, your only love . . .[20]

That year the Prince had met Alice Keppel, and the liaison which was to last for the rest of his life began almost immediately. Yet even now, nearly ten years from the beginning of her relationship with the Prince, the Countess of Warwick was still to him 'My own lovely little Daisy'.

~6~

Turbulent Times

THE FOLLOWING YEAR, 1899, was to be dominated by the outbreak of war half a world away from Britain. Conflict seemed imminent during the hot summer, as negotiations between the British and the Boers dragged on. Beyond the political sphere, however, life continued as normal. In June, the Prince of Wales won his second Derby with Diamond Jubilee. Writing in reply to her congratulations, he wished Daisy could have been there to see the race. He also wished she could have joined his Whitsun house party at Sandringham, instead of Lady Randolph.

As political tension mounted, there was intense patriotic excitement. Then came news that the Boer troops had taken the initiative and were advancing on Cape Colony and Natal. In London, General Redvers Buller was appointed Commander-in-Chief, the reserves were called out and the Army Corps ordered to Table Bay. At the beginning enthusiasm for the war spread far beyond military circles. There was much jingoistic fervour throughout the country, reflected in the London music halls.

Being still a great admirer of Cecil Rhodes, Lady Warwick endorsed his vision of South Africa's future and wanted to see British forces victorious, though she was far less bellicose than at the time of Jameson's Raid. Stead, however, was now a vocal supporter of the Boers, and turned all his invective against British 'aggression'. In the *Review of Reviews* he denounced the British nation for 'the pride of power, the insolence of wealth, the arrogance of the Pharisee' which had led to this war, 'as a nation . . . acting exactly as the Chosen People acted in old time, when their apostasy brought down upon them the burning invectives and solemn warnings of the Hebrew seers . . .'[1]

This was Stead as Old Testament prophet, and he hoped to do his part in bringing down Joseph Chamberlain, under whose tenure as Colonial Secretary the South African adventure had been executed. In the autumn of 1896, Stead had tried to get to the truth of what had happened in South Africa. Replying to a letter from Stead, Arthur Balfour, then Leader of the House of Commons, had asserted that there had been no prior knowledge of the escapade in government circles, but Stead continued to believe that there had been duplicity. Having read the documents given to him, he felt there could be no possible doubt 'that Rhodes, Jameson and co. had reason to believe from communications forwarded to them from London that the Colonial Office knew and approved of what they were after'.[2]

Now Balfour again addressed Stead on the subject:

> I believe I know or did know, all the facts about Chamberlain's conversations, telegrams etc. before, during and after the Raid, and I can assure you that the idea that he was in any way connected with or responsible for it is wholly illusory. I confess I think it is deeply to be regretted that so much of the discussion in this great national emergency has been coloured by personal distrust and dislike of the Colonial Secretary, which I am convinced he has done nothing to deserve . . .[3]

Daisy Warwick was an assiduous reader of Stead's periodical, and after reading his November edition she wrote to him, taking issue with his anti-war views:

It is a wrong war and a bad war, but it is too late to draw back. We have got to see it through and for the honour of our army we have got to conquer. Therefore, I fear no expostulation is of any avail now, but you might have done so much good had you published all this earlier . . .[4]

As for Joe Laycock, stalwart officer of the Nottinghamshire Yeomanry, he had left England in September 1899 to join the Imperial Light Horse, serving under General Sir John French, and he was to have a good war. A letter to his mother written from the General's House, Ladysmith, 'a miserable little town',[5] gave his résumé of the big battle of Elandslaagte, which had been fought three days earlier, starting at 3.30 am and continuing all through the following night. Only at noon the next day did the troops return from the field. Laycock had impressed the commanding officers by making his way down to the railway after the battle and reporting to them by telephone.

His letter contains a vivid description of some experiences on the battlefield: 'I had some narrow shaves, as I got a dead Boer's rifle and cartridges and went on with the Gordons. We had a rather beastly night, very cold and no shelter.'[6] The few Boer tents there were had wounded in them. Losses had been heavy on the British side:

> Our men behaved splendidly, and so did a few Boers who did really all the harm and shot so many of our men . . . Over two hundred killed and wounded . . . Some of the Volunteers, mounted infantry they all are, are very good indeed, and understand Boer ways. A lot of the enemy were killed . . . all their leading men and two guns – all they had there.[7]

The British had taken many prisoners, and the gallant wounded on both sides were now being well looked after. Joe had been mentioned in dispatches and was hoping to get some award, but thought that there may not have been enough men engaged to warrant his receiving one.

~

When war looked likely, seventeen-year-old Guy had left Eton precipitately and started cramming for the army. He bought a second-class ticket on a steamer bound for East Africa, but Sir Evelyn Wrench, an adjutant at the War Office, managed to persuade him to do some preliminary military training at Aldershot. Harry Rosslyn, educated at Eton and Magdalen College, Oxford, had succeeded his father as the fifth Earl, but soon showed that he had not inherited his pater's character. After he managed to gamble away a fortune at the tables in Monte Carlo, Dysart had perforce been put up for sale. Harry's commission in the Royal Horse Guards had come through early in 1890, and in the summer he had married Violet Aline de Grey Vyner, by whom he had four children. Always a very enthusiastic actor, in the late 1890s he had turned professional, appearing at the Court Theatre in *Trelawny of the Wells*. Then, with the outbreak of war, he found himself in South Africa as a serving officer attached to Thorneycroft's Mounted Infantry. In addition Rosslyn was a war correspondent for the *Daily Mail*. He was present at the relief of Ladysmith, and was awarded the Queen's medal with two clasps.

As for lovers and wives left behind, there were fewer entertainments in London. This, said the Prince, was just as well, seeing the scarcity of men. Daisy later claimed to have given up all social life during Joe's absence as a mark of her concern for his safety, not wanting frivolity when he was in danger. It seems unlikely.

On her thirty-eighth birthday, she received greetings from the Prince of Wales, and one of his usual lavish gifts. Even though his 'very warm feelings had under force of circumstances, and by her own wish, cooled down',[8] he still held her in the greatest affection.

In the spring of 1900 Guy sailed for South Africa, waved off at Tilbury by his parents. The Prince of Wales was sensitive about

Daisy's predicament, and wrote from the Marlborough Club the same evening how deeply he felt for her in parting with her son. In the circumstances he thought his parents had been right to let him go 'as he was so bent on doing so'[9] and they had been virtually powerless in the face of such determination. The Prince did, however, give his opinion that Guy was really too young to go on a campaign, and ought to have devoted two or three more years to his education. A further note, understanding how low his mother felt, was positive that all was for the best. 'It is impossible to say when the Boers will give in,' he wrote, 'but I hardly think they will allow Lord R to walk in unopposed!'[10] (Lord Roberts was commander of British troops in the relief of Kimberley.) There was some consolation for his mother. Attached to Sir John French as a galloper, Guy would probably be relatively safe, and Captain Douglas Haig had reassured the parents about that. Daisy herself was going over to Paris, which the Prince felt sure would do her good. Just as she had waited anxiously for news of Joe, she would now wait to hear about her son.

We gain some indication of the Prince's activities during this period from his letters to Daisy of early 1900. Not long after Guy's departure, the Prince and Princess were on their way to Copenhagen. When their train was quietly moving out of Brussels station, a young anarchist fired into their carriage, but did not find his target. The Prince gave his dear friend an account of what had happened:

> We were certainly surprised at seeing a young man mount on the step of the carriage and put his gloved hand through the open window, and then fire a couple of shots deliberately at me at two yards! If he had not been so bad a shot I don't see how he could possibly have missed me – so it was indeed a very narrow escape.[11]

None the worse in any way, the royal party had finished their journey comfortably. Putting the blame on certain people who were 'instilling such hatred in the Foreign Press against England',[12] the Prince said it was not pleasant to be an Englishman travelling on the Continent at that time: 'Civilisation and education avails little if the anarchichal propaganda finds such easy instruments to attempt the lives of innocent people – as it is obvious that I have no more to do with the Transvaal war than a child unborn.'[13]

A week later, the *Daily Telegraph* gave notice that Guy, Lord Brooke, had reached Bloemfontein and joined General French's staff. The Prince had seen the notice, and suggested that now would be the right moment for him to be gazetted into a cavalry regiment – perhaps the Seventh Hussars? Sir Evelyn Wood would be pleased to arrange it, because the Seventh was very short of subalterns, so many of its officers being specially employed at the moment, although the regiment was not in South Africa. In fact Guy was commissioned Captain in the First Life Guards. News had also come through that Harry Rosslyn had been taken prisoner; the Prince conjectured that he might put on some theatricals for President Kruger.

The Prince and Princess had made an unremarkable journey home from Denmark. The German Emperor had met them at Altona, 'which was really most kind and friendly of him, as he came the whole way from Berlin to do so!'[14] Daisy wrote to him about the assassination attempt, and the Prince said that her kind words had touched him so much. It was now lovely summer weather at Sandringham, such a welcome contrast from the intense cold in Denmark.

∼

Daisy's visit to Paris evidently refreshed her – the city was always a tonic. On her return she became 'wildly busy with matters agricultural'[15] and attended a Co-operative Conference in Leeds, where she was encouraged by the enthusiasm shown by north country workers. The Prince was wary of her involvement in what he felt to be a masculine world, but he did admire her intelligence, even while he warned her about engaging in public life.

Several of his letters to Daisy at this time refer to their special friendship. Daisy may have written to him about Alice Keppel; she had mentioned a certain lady who had allegedly been indiscreet: 'it is really very hard that I cannot see anything of a lady without the ill-natured remarks that are made. Honestly speaking I have become far too much hardened to care what people say . . .'[16] He felt himself to be the best judge of whom he liked, or did not. His feelings for his own lovely little Daisy, though, would never change. She was right in saying that people had talked a lot about their friendship:

> You were persecuted by my family, Society and the Press, to an extent that was never known before, and alas with my Family matters will I am afraid never come straight . . . Society is always jealous of a pretty woman if I have the misfortune to think her so. Then there are certain women I don't like, and do not disguise my feelings towards them, who are sure to attack her and me.[17]

He would be miserable ever to think he gave Daisy pain or sorrow, but it was rather hard if he could not prefer one lady to another without being thought to be infatuated with her.

Daisy likewise did not want to be too distant from her former lover, but she had clearly chosen Joe over the Prince. 'Why you should say that with my new friends I should not miss you, I know not,' he wrote soon after, giving further evidence of his special regard for her: 'you will always be my best and dearest friend whatever happens . . . If you will not allow me to be more it is your fault, not mine.'[18]

ᦵ7ᦵ

The Hero's Return

JOE LAYCOCK RETURNED FROM Africa towards the end of 1900, having covered himself in sufficient glory to be awarded the DSO. Within a few months he had embroiled himself in an affair with the Marchioness of Downshire. Kitty Downshire already had a record of adulterous relationships, and consequently did not enjoy a high reputation even among the hunting people who gathered around the Leicestershire town of Melton Mowbray each winter. She was pretty, and ten years younger than her rival. Despite hearing rumours, Daisy did not find it easy to believe that anything had happened to affect her life so profoundly. 'Please say it isn't true,'[1] she wrote. Slowly came the sickening realisation that it was indeed true, but despite the facts staring her in the face there was still an element of disbelief.

Over the succeeding year, Joe divided his time between his new and old lovers. Despite hating the situation in which she found herself, Daisy accepted this arrangement, perhaps hoping that by so doing she might eventually reclaim her man. When Joe sustained serious injuries in a hunting accident and came close to death, Kitty rushed to his bedside and tried to exclude Daisy. However, once Daisy arrived and took charge, it was she who remained close to

Joe at Wiseton during his convalescence. But if she had hoped that this devotion would make all the difference and win him back, she was sadly mistaken. Daisy's lovely figure could still excite him, yet he had proved fickle, revealing himself as a selfish creature who enjoyed living alternately with two women.

By Christmas 1900 she was unwell and miserable – she later claimed that she had been pregnant. Joe's silence was hurtful. Apparently without regret, he was living his usual round of sporting life, hunting and shooting all season, and hardly, it seemed, giving Daisy a thought.

Despite this, she had to manage the Christmas festivities. At Easton, the party for servants and children was usually held on Boxing Day in the ballroom, which was dominated by a huge glistening tree brought in from the park. It was a truly festive occasion, when all received carefully chosen presents. The village children, some of them rather shy, were ushered in to receive packages of lovely toys. At Warwick, people in the almshouses were not forgotten, and neither were the disabled children. They all had bulging stockings to open on Christmas morning.

In the New Year there were painful scenes when Daisy tried to reach a better understanding with Joe by having an honest talk. Their rendezvous at Melton Mowbray ended abruptly when he walked out. Unwilling to admit defeat, she tried again the following week. The second occasion was almost worse: on a bitterly cold night, she was left standing on a road, watching his receding figure as he returned to the comfort of home, where Kitty was living with him.

When rejected in so humiliating a way, why did she go on? Probably because, emotionally destructive as it was, this man had become her life – and he was the father of her adored little son. She felt sure his greater, more lasting attraction was to her, and that they could never finally separate.

In the spring of 1901 they were planning a trip to Paris, which held good memories of many visits when they had stayed in

Daisy's apartment in the Avenue Marceau. Joe felt that their old love could be reborn, and she would have liked to believe him. However, when he wrote that she had been 'a dear generous Daisy' and that things would be all right, she could no longer fully trust him.

Kitty was capricious and hard, playing a cynical game against her rival, and Joe knew his involvement with her to be a kind of madness. Was sanity ever going to return? Begging his old love to be patient, appealing to the goodness of her 'great heart', he attempted to re-establish his credibility in a rather cringing letter: 'Dearest, I shall always look to you as the best influence and most splendid character that has crossed the untidy track that I shuffle along. Perhaps when this folly is over you will be able to regard me as a thinking being again.' Contrite, he said that Daisy had been 'so sweet and good it would win the heart of a toad'.[2]

The last time they had met he had given the excuse of madness, and had confessed that he felt no passion for any other woman. Yet he was breaking up her life. As for her influence, what could she discern? Kitty Downshire was making him 'thoroughly bad, dishonourable and contemptible'.[3] If for no other reason, Joe owed Daisy loyalty for the sake of Maynard, their son, but he had abandoned both of them for his own gratification. 'I suppose in some measure you have satisfied your desires?'[4] she wrote bitterly. If they did cross the Channel to stay in Paris, the old magic did not return. But with her personal life in disarray, there was perhaps more incentive to sustain work.

~

Queen Victoria's death in January 1901 brought less change than might be imagined in Daisy's relationship with the new King. She still had considerable influence on him; according to one American magazine, it was incomparably greater than anyone else's. It had been the general impression that their friendship had waned, but not so: the correspondent of *The World* had been informed that the King entertained the highest respect for the Countess of Warwick's ability and sagacity, frequently consulting her on difficulties he encountered in guiding his public conduct. He held the highest opinion of her judgement in such matters.[5]

The war in South Africa had started with an appetite for a fight, both among the military and civilians, but news of the early reverses had been received with utmost gloom and considerable recrimination. Then there was wild euphoria in Britain at the relief of Ladysmith in late February 1901, and of Mafeking on 17 May. Daisy did not share the mood, and made a distinction between true patriotism and the appetite for reckless imperialism. In her view, the war had been a distraction which Lord Salisbury's government had allowed to overshadow the deep social questions facing Britain. By June 1901, Lady Warwick saw fit to give public support to an actual opponent of the war who was standing as Liberal candidate for the Stratford constituency in Essex. Lord Warwick was appointed Lord Lieutenant of Essex that same month, and the publicity attracted by his wife's unusual political position was not helpful to him. Undeterred, she carried on, even when it meant breaking with family tradition, and in the autumn general election she did not campaign for the Conservative cause.

Although her political creed was still far from consistent, Daisy's mind was far-sighted about the importance of education. In that field her credentials were strongest and her involvement deepest. Her campaign for longer and better schooling in the late 1890s had arisen from a belief that education was important to the future of all, but vital as a means of improving opportunities for poor children and in working-class emancipation. The Cockerton Judgment of 1900, by ruling the use of such monies illegal, had prevented the London School Board from continuing to provide higher grade secondary education funded by ratepayers. Faced with the likely cessation of higher education throughout the country, in the spring of 1901 the Conservative government had passed an interim bill allowing the schools boards to continue their work for one year only, subject to permission from their county councils. The government intended to introduce a comprehensive education bill in due course.

Lady Warwick, who had taken the chair at a protest meeting held in Leman Street, Whitechapel, developed her ideas in an article written for an edition of *The Nineteenth Century*. If their century had proved one thing, she said, it was 'that men will not rest content in the positions in which they were born'.[6] She pointed out that the scholarship ladder which theoretically enabled a poor boy to win his way to university was partly an illusion. The child of impoverished parents did not have a fair chance. He might have to be a wage earner out of school hours, or there might be no scholarship class in his school. Such children were terribly handicapped.

Sir John Gorst, Conservative MP for Cambridge and vice-chairman of the education committee of the Privy Council, was singled out for not sticking to his belief, which had caused him to condemn the present system in the past. His bill had done nothing to remove the caste system, 'the curse of education in this country'.[7] Her article concluded with a rousing call to the British working man to demand a thorough overhaul of the education system. Until that happened all political leaders, however democratic and advanced they claimed to be, would simply be tinkering with reform and nothing of substance would emerge.

When the government produced its Education Bill in 1902, it did not go far enough to meet with Daisy's approval; it was not, she thought, the means of inaugurating a fundamental equalising of society. But the scope of her ideas put her far ahead of her time.

~

The summer at Warwick was exceptionally busy. The Countess took her local duties seriously as well, extending hospitality to large numbers of people. In one week there were visits by five hundred Freemasons and two hundred crippled children from

Birmingham. In addition she had opened five flower shows, a workhouse fete and a police orphanage. In her memoirs, Daisy reflected on the opportunities she had enjoyed in being able to meet a range of people from many countries:

> The privilege was ours as hosts with such a background, to have the joy of assembling the best in our day of men and women of mark socially, politically, and artistically in the widest use of the word, and no joy in my life has been more keen than that of being able to throw wide the doors of Warwick and share with my contemporaries the beauty of a dwelling-place that will outlast us all.[8]

The personal friends she invited were always an interesting mix. She held a house party with 'such a delightful and clever young architect, Lutyens and his wife ... Pamela Plowden and Lord Kenyon (who will propose to her for the 100th time and be refused!)'[9] and Alfred Parsons, the garden painter and botanist.

More surprising was the inclusion of Lady Colin Campbell, ostracised by Society after a sensational divorce hearing in the 1880s, but according to the hostess 'such a charming woman'. Lady Colin, refusing to be an outcast, had become a journalist, and was at one time arts editor for *The World*.

On 22 August King Edward wrote from Marienbad concerning a mysterious unresolved issue, the exact nature of which is difficult to uncover in the absence of Daisy's letters to him. A recent letter of hers had touched him very deeply, he said, but there were other remarks which he thought very severe. He was in complete agreement that the great friendship and deep affection which had existed between them for the last ten years entitled them to have no secrets from each other. However, there were things difficult to say, even harder to write, and he could not always be answerable for his feelings, or able to convey things as he wished. 'Men are but mortal, and in many instances poor creatures in comparison to the fine sense that women possess.'[10] At their next meeting, he wanted to talk over the very important matters about which Daisy had written.

Their substance seems likely to have been at least partly the terms of their friendship, possibly with regard to his attachment to Alice Keppel and Daisy's to Joe Laycock. The King admitted that through force of circumstances he had changed in certain respects. Daisy had also changed, he thought, since Maynard's birth. She had become more serious, more independent, and he had felt for some time that he could not be of much use to her in her life. However, in spite of what he called his many shortcomings, her continued devotion had astonished, pleased and touched him: 'Though I should hate more than anything in this world to have any disagreeable discussion with you, still I cannot shrink from it now, and hope an opportunity in the autumn may enable me to have a good long talk with you.'[11]

Daisy gladly accepted Millie's invitation every autumn to spend a few weeks at Dunrobin. That year, Cecil Rhodes had also invited Daisy to join his house party at Rannoch Lodge for a few days. Regardless of his failure to keep a previous appointment with her at Stafford House (one of the Duke of Sutherland's London properties), she was delighted to have his invitation, her admiration for him undimmed. Most of her fellow guests were business tycoons, and they included Alfred Beit, who had made a fortune from South Africa's diamond mines. Young Winston Churchill, who was also present, may have found an audience for after-dinner stories about his experiences in South Africa.

Rhodes was too ill for sports, so he and his admirer went off together on to the moors, mounted on hill ponies. With Loch Rannoch stretched out in the distance, against a backdrop of heather-covered hills, he talked beguilingly. His death, early the following year, was to make Daisy reflect on the force of his personality: 'It was impossible to think in limited terms when one came under his influence . . . Life assumed vast dimensions, as though invisible barriers had yielded to his touch, and one found oneself on a larger plane.'[12]

∼

On 17 December 1901, Joe received his DSO from King Edward. Daisy was not with him at the Palace but proudly imagined him there in his uniform. That night, Lord Rosebery made a much anticipated speech in which he appeared to be seeking the leadership of a reformed Liberal Party. It was impressive, and newspapers which varied in their political allegiances all agreed that Rosebery had fulfilled expectations on this occasion. Daisy wrote a letter, saying that she was full of hero worship. Members of her household were at his feet with admiration, she reported: the French governess thought his oratory equal to Mirabeau's, and the Irish music teacher had compared him to Burke.[13] It was somewhat gilding the lily, but certainly the speech had been something of a landmark. A divided party since Joseph Chamberlain's decision to support the Conservatives over Home Rule, the Liberals had been out of power for nearly fifteen years.

Joe had been thinking vaguely of a political career and had been impressed by Rosebery's speech, seeing hope for a Liberal revival. On the latter topic, Daisy commented: 'You say "we all agree", but has the country shewn it had these sentiments when it returned to power the present wretched and effete government?' At the last election, she pointed out, people had shouted themselves hoarse for Chamberlain, but maybe England was now beginning to realise that 'the Birmingham merchant' could not run either 'the England that we love or the Empire we are so proud of'.[14]

Daisy was never a person to pay much attention to political labels, but her continuing pride in Empire sat increasingly oddly with her leaning towards Socialism.

❧ 8 ❧

Coronation Year 1902

RALPH WALDO EMERSON CONSIDERED Society to be 'a masked ball, where everyone hides their identity and reveals it by hiding', and in respect of Daisy Warwick's personal life his appraisal had resonance. In 1902 certainly much had to be hidden. As an old woman Daisy was to describe the kind of morality that had prevailed in her social circle, of which the Prince of Wales was master of ceremonies: 'Everything was all right as long as it was secret, hushed up, covered.'[1] During this Coronation year Lady Warwick's secret would nearly kill her.

Joe Laycock had been central to her life for more than five years. On 1 January Daisy wrote to him late at night:

Please believe me, my Joe, that I am not feeling badly about you, and that I *will* not think badly. You know me well enough to know how deeply things go with me, and that to love really means 'for ever' – and that I am your wife from the body I gave you . . . that you used to kiss all over . . . to the heart and *soul* that beat inside me, and all the biggest grandest thoughts and feelings that my mind is capable of! My poor darling you are enslaved at this moment . . . I know some day, you'll hate to think of all the meanness you have said and done to *me*, your little one . . . who has so often crept into dear arms for safety and trust and comfort . . . I know my Joe will come back to me . . .[2]

She believed him to be in love with a shadow, and dared him contemptuously to go on loving it. It would not hurt her any more. Despite Daisy's intention not to let Joe see her sorrow, she did so a great deal.

Over the winter, Melton Mowbray as usual became the focus of social activity. Every winter relationships started which had often burnt out by spring, but during the hunting season potential scandal provided a frisson of excitement no less potent than jumping those large fences in Leicestershire. There was much pursuit of the 'Quorn kittens' and the 'Cottesmore cats'. In mid-January another discontented person became a player: Artie, Lord Downshire, wrote to his wife from Hillsborough Castle, warning her about rumours and gossip. He addressed her as 'My *own* darling', and stated quite simply that he did not like her 'going about with Laycock so much . . . and for good reasons too'. He wanted to stop people talking about her:

This I absolutely will not have, and my own darling I may be the greatest and most absolute idiot on God's earth, but mind nothing *more* than this . . . It has nearly broken my heart to hear your name coupled with Joe Laycock as if he was your husband. You *I don't believe* grasp what 5 out of 6 of the people in that part of the world *do* and to hear you accused in the same way as the rest of them . . . is *more* than I can stand.[3]

In fact, so far from not knowing how the Melton hunting set behaved, Kitty fitted well into their world. Everybody except Artie Downshire had known about Kitty's reputation. Nevertheless, he continued: 'Darling the only way to make them believe that this *is* not and *has* not been the case is *not* to have him staying in the house any longer and also to *cease* being so awfully familiar with him . . .'[4]

During January there had been occasions when Joe and Daisy were together, but she realised how much their relationship had changed. No longer was she worshipped, although Joe told her how beautiful she had looked in bed at Ingarsby Lodge, her hunting lodge. Kitty at Leesthorpe was the alternative attraction, and it was Joe's prolonged visits to her which had disturbed Artie Downshire. In her own remarkably frank letters at this time, Daisy revealed her most private thoughts, the *leitmotif* being fear of loss:

> *You* know how your touch affects me – you know all the love you taught me, and how my whole self vibrates to you, and even now here, sitting in pink dressing gown, I remember even the feeling of last night. I would give all my life for one long love-kiss, as I sit lonely over fire here! Well God grant we may come back to each other again, for I see *nothing* ahead but sadness . . . I must just take up the wreck of my happiness, the *only* happiness of my life and bury it all . . .[5]

Despite her unhappiness she realised how favoured she had been in her life – affection, admiration, respect, interests, career had all been hers – but she was still unsatisfied.

~

That season Joe planned to leave the hunting field for India, where the Maharajah of Cooch Behar had invited him to enjoy some of the best sport anywhere in the world. Daisy put together a selection of books for his voyage out, which would take about three weeks. There were also prospects for his consideration when he returned. For instance, he might stand as a candidate for the proposed Imperial Liberal Party, if that should materialise. It was something Daisy had already discussed with Lord Rosebery, who might take on the mantle of leadership. However, before Joe was due to sail, Daisy impetuously went to Windsor and ambushed Artie Downshire at the White Hart Hotel, where she divulged details about his wife's adulterous relationship. When Joe got to hear of this he was infuriated, and his anger was enough to wither Daisy and make her ill. Sleepless nights followed miserable days, during which she brooded on what she had impulsively done. Forgiveness was what she craved, so that she could wave him off to India at peace with herself, knowing that their relationship had been restored. She needed reassurance when Joe was going six thousand miles away, but it was not forthcoming.

He sailed for Bombay on 2 February, and no doubt was relieved to get away. There was royal hospitality waiting for him in India, a sportsman's paradise. Besides, he was leaving behind the raw English winter, with enough snow that year to bring down the telegraph lines. Daisy went to Paris with Brookie. It was snowing there too, but she enjoyed hearing plenty of political gossip from the British ambassador, Sir Edmund Monson: she reflected that he was 'the most *indiscreet* of Diplomats',[6] clearly enjoying the insider's view, even while admitting that he had no business to talk confidentially. Paul Deschamel and his wife also called on her, to give her the *dessous des cartes* of French political life, which was always intriguing: Irish Home Rulers had apparently infiltrated the press in Paris, and the Anglophobe papers were obviously influenced by them.

Brookie was occupied in a way entirely to his taste, trying out a Charron motor, with the manufacturer driving him obligingly all over Paris. Consequently, he placed an order. Meanwhile, his wife continued to enjoy stimulating conversation. In a letter written to Joe, addressed care of the Maharajah, Daisy was, however, still fretting and anxious: 'I can never forgive myself for seeing Lord D and denying it to you, others making you believe *all* I said was untrue, and indeed I had far more to say only you were not in the temper to listen to anything . . . I *will* not let my mad love for you ever master me again . . .'[7]

However, she did, and compounded her first foolish action with a second. Joe never reached India. Instead, he received a wire at Marseilles, which informed him that Lord Downshire intended to file a divorce suit, naming Joe as co-respondent. That telegram was destined to change completely the course of his life. He sailed on as far as Port Said, maybe intending to enjoy the East in spite of bad news, but decided against that plan, and made the return trip from Egypt.

Once back in England, Joe faced a situation which put him in an invidious position, where his name would be openly linked with Kitty Downshire's. Such piquant scandals delighted certain sections of the press, and they made the most of their opportunities. Scurrilous publications like *The Candid Friend* relished the gossip:

We are likely to be startled next week by one of the prettiest scandals that have amused London society for a good many years. It is the story of a countess, a marchioness and a man. The countess, who is one of our most beautiful women, was in love with him first, but he had the bad taste to weary of her and attach himself to the marchioness, who is rather a commonplace young person. Then, the other day, he must needs start off for India to shoot things with a Rajah friend of his. He, however, got a wire at Marseilles which brought him post-haste back to London. When he got back there he found that his old love had been to his rooms, ransacked his drawers, found the other lady's letters, which, *par parenthese* were very badly written, and sent them off to the noble marquess, her husband. They say nothing will stop the latter from bringing divorce proceedings.[8]

∾

Early in March, while hunting, Daisy had another heavy fall, but once again she was lucky, suffering nothing worse than concussion, a broken arm and bruising. Fripp, the eminent orthopaedic surgeon, set the arm, but the accident kept her out of action for several weeks.

Many people wrote to her, expressing their concern and sending good wishes: one letter from old Professor Meldola addressed Daisy as 'Our Lady of Warwick', and continued: 'There is nobody among all your vast roll of inferior beings who heard of your accident with more concern than we did . . . it is the horse and not your brain which ought to be concussed.'[9] A general helper at Lady Warwick's home for crippled children sent a very affectionate note. Lizzie, an orphan, had learnt needlework at the Easton school, and then found an occupation which she loved. Having a genuine affinity with handicapped and deprived children, Daisy would have been very pleased with Lizzie's enthusiasm. Amos Mills, a mechanic at Glovers Works in Birmingham, described himself as an uneducated working man, but assured her Ladyship (who had lent him books) that the working classes had expressed sorrow and sympathy about her accident. Far removed from the working classes, holidaying in Rome, Elinor Glyn also sent her good wishes.

As Daisy gradually regained her strength, she returned to an active life. The newspapers noted that her first engagement would be at a meeting for the scattered homes of workhouse children, a scheme whereby such children would be placed in one of a number of ordinary houses in towns and cities. Having discharged this duty, she had to decide what to do about Kitty and Joe. She considered making a visit to Binfield Grove, Berkshire, where the barrister Sir Robert Wilmot and his wife were giving Kitty refuge and where, since his return from Port Said, Joe had paid all too many visits.

In the end Daisy decided against confronting her rival. But she intended to do everything possible to stop the divorce, and might well have felt repentance for her part in precipitating it. Some at least of the gossip reported in the press was true: by sending Lord

Downshire his wife's love letters she had created the present situation, which was infinitely worse than before. It was proof of Kitty's infidelity which had determined Artie Downshire to file his petition. Impetuosity had been costly.

Although it was in Daisy's nature to make her own rules, she also had a powerful awareness of convention. The social code of her time made it unthinkable that Joe should marry a divorced woman, who would be the mother of his future children. His self indulgence did not alter the fact that he was bound to Daisy through their much loved son. Joe would be cited as co-respondent, and Society punished those who found themselves in the Matrimonial Division, with all the often lurid publicity that accompanied proceedings. Yet if, as seemed likely, Lord Downshire was granted a decree nisi, Daisy feared that her Joe might do the unthinkable. Society would think it incumbent on him to marry the woman he had seduced. For Daisy, his marriage to Kitty would be disastrous.

A private detective must be engaged, to find any possible evidence against the Marquess of Downshire. The sleuth carried out his assignment admirably all over Berkshire, where servants from the Downshire estate at Easthampton were loquacious. Passing himself off as one of the lower servants, the detective spent a night at the Duke's Head with several of the Marquess' employees. No sign emerged that Lord Downshire had been even remotely attached to any woman other than his wife. All the servants thought well of him, a down to earth, if slightly eccentric nobleman. As the sleuth reported:

He is a most remarkable man, and amongst other things goes round to his tenants in a butcher's smock and cap in his donkey cart after having a sheep killed and sells it at so much a pound to them.

He also works with them digging etc., and eats bread and cheese and bacon with them and in fact makes himself one of them.[10]

This unspectacular information was duly sent to Charles Russell & Co. of Norfolk Street, the Strand, the law firm run by the son of the Attorney General. Daisy had been meddling, and when talking to Sir George Lewis (knighted in 1892 for his services to the Prince of Wales in, among others, the Tranby Croft case) had encouraged him to think that Joe might defend, just to keep the opposition guessing. Sir George had said that, once divorced, Kitty could get pretty well all she needed from the Downshire family. If that were true, perhaps Kitty would release Joe.

But Joe's attitude was dismissive. He had to make the best of an inevitable marriage, and wrote to Daisy vaguely that he might see her someday. From Warwick came her indignant reply:

> I cannot believe you to be so utterly callous, heartless and *crooked* as your words denote . . . After all the years of love and unchanging loyalty and devotion I have given you, that you can sit down and write to me that off hand note . . . Do you know how ugly the thing looks to me? That you and this woman have *combined* to make a fool of me since your return from Egypt – that you wished to *exploit* as much of my generosity and love as could be of use to you in saving the situation, that you spoke of love and affection – and *more* . . . *only* to work me for your ends – and the moment you see I can be of no more use, you go down to this woman for two days, and the result is the letter I receive this morning . . . I was to risk and compromise myself, *believing that you wished to get out of this horror*, and have been simply the dupe of you and Lady Downshire![11]

Joe had made use of her, she believed, and the theme of betrayal is constantly repeated.

Unable to face being in England during the divorce hearing, Daisy was looking for some means of escape, maybe to Paris or Venice. Lord Rosebery understood things as few others did, making him an ideal companion, if he would accompany her.

Feeling insecure, Daisy had also contacted Charlie Beresford, and received the warmest letter from him saying he would love to see her again, or do any mortal thing he could for her. He had travelled the world, he wrote, and had never met anyone to equal Daisy. Such an affirmation must have felt comforting: 'I don't know why but when I see your handwriting all the old thrill and mad excitement fill my brain and body, and I dream of all the mad wild happiness we have had together . . . Bless you dear . . .'[12]

Even the King's considerable personal influence, and every other effort to stop the Downshire divorce proceedings, had failed. When the case was heard in April, it was prominently reported in *The Times*:

ARISTOCRATIC DIVORCE SUIT

Millionaire Co-Respondent

The presiding judge, Sir Francis Jeune, had before him the case of Downshire V. Downshire and Laycock. This was the petition of the Marquis of Downshire for the dissolution of his marriage on the ground of adultery of his wife, the Marchioness of Downshire, with a co-respondent named Mr Joseph Laycock, described as a captain in the Yeomanry. The Marquess and Marchioness had been married in 1892.

. . . Mr Bargrave Deane, K.C., who appeared for the petitioner, outlined the course leading to the filing of Lord Downshire's petition. Captain Joseph Laycock of the Yeomanry, was a gentleman of large means, and first became acquainted with the petitioner and respondent during the hunting season of 1899–1900 in Leicestershire. The first time Captain Laycock visited the petitioner was at the end of 1900, and from that time the friendship became more intimate . . . visits became more frequent, so much so that the Marquis had reason to protest.

Evidence was given concerning the date January 12th 1902, when Lord Downshire had left a shooting party on his estate,

East Hampstead, one morning and gone to Windsor. Immediately following his departure, Captain Laycock had come to the house, and had spent that night with Lady Downshire. His bedroom, adjoining hers, had not been used. Further occasions of adultery had occurred, and Lord Downshire had discovered his wife to be sending telegrams to Laycock. In addition he had found a large bundle of letters from Mr Laycock to his wife at East Hampstead.

Counsel read a letter from Kitty to her husband, pleading for his forgiveness and hinting that she wanted to save their marriage. She promised never to wrong her husband again, and ended 'I shall always love you.' It had no impact on the case.

After hearing evidence from the Marquis and a servant, the Judge granted a decree nisi with costs, and the custody of the children was given to Lord Downshire.[13]

Socially, Kitty was now in the wilderness, stigmatised by divorce, but as a man Joe would fare considerably better. And despite rumours in Society and hints in the press, Daisy had not been publicly linked with the case; the code practised by her inner circle would ensure that she never was. Invitations continued to pour in for every dinner and ball held in London to celebrate King Edward's coronation. Her own invitations to her London residence, Brook House in Park Lane, were eagerly awaited, and she would greet her guests as usual, wearing the Warwick diamonds. Good old Brookie would be at her side. Her unassailable position in Society remained, and she probably enjoyed more influence than the Queen who was soon to be crowned.

Daisy's elder son, Guy, was enjoying time in South Africa, with all the opportunities it gave for outdoor life: trekking, buck shooting, and sometimes sleeping under the stars. 'I feel so well here,' he wrote, 'and like the free and easy life which is also full of excitement.'[14] His comment on the divorce was one of commiseration:

Poor old Joe ought to have known better than to get involved with someone like Lady D.

∿

Lady Marjorie Greville, known as 'Queenie', would be coming out that year. Mother and daughter got on well, but being on good terms with one's debutante daughter did not mean that it would be right for her to know everything, certainly not the sophisticated life of a married woman. So Queenie almost certainly never knew about the events that in the following weeks were to bring her mother close to death. At the end of April, Daisy sent a telegram to Joe in Scotland, where he was trying to put the recent inconvenient proceedings behind him. It read:

GOING CHESTERFIELD STREET TILL THURSDAY THEN PARIS WHERE SHALL BE FREE SEVENTH TILL ELEVENTH IF YOU MANAGE BUT I AM SO ANXIOUS NOT TO BE SELFISH ONLY SITUATION DREADFUL FOR ME.[15]

Once arrived in Paris, staying at the Ritz, she wrote a letter that belied her inner panic. It was 1 May, and she began as radiantly as the season: 'Darling, the day was so lovely and journey from Calais lovely with all the country green and lilac and blossoms all out – and sunshine – you would love it, and it makes one's spirits better than in the nipping East winds at home!'[16]

The Ritz was too crowded for a discreet meeting, so in anticipation of Joe's arrival she thought the Elysée Palace would be better. She thought of lovely days, motoring out to Chantilly or Fontainebleau, and having supper at the Madrid, their favourite restaurant. Queenie, who had accompanied her mother, would be sent home, to get her out of the way and maintain her innocence. Daisy was gradually facing a great crisis, and anxiously asked Joe to let her know which day he would be coming over. With care, they could meet unobserved. Then she came to the point:

The big worry we won't talk of, dear one, and about *my* condition – I must do something but think I'll leave it till we have talked it over, and I don't want to make a fuss *before* the great Rosebery function 15th and the Court 16th, as it would attract attention – Perhaps I'd better come out here *after* that, again, *alone?* Only it makes me shudder![17]

Daisy was once more pregnant, and the child was Joe's.

He did not reply. Perhaps Daisy believed that he would show the same loyalty as he had demonstrated when their son Maynard had been born four years previously. Now, however, he was blatantly snubbing her. He went to Paris, but did not make contact. At the Ville de Lyon he was kept informed by Daisy's maid, Clarke:

BAD NIGHT. GREAT WEAKNESS. BUT WORST OVER. SENDS FOLLOWING MESSAGE. BE SURE NOT WORRY. DETERMINED GET WELL. WRITE HERSELF SOON BUT KEPT UNDER MORPHIA PRESENT. SO SORRY BEEN SUCH TROUBLE YOU.[18]

There is no reason to believe that Joe was in the least worried. Three days later, he received a wire at Fontainebleau from a mutual friend, Willie Low:

SHALL BE IN PARIS FOR THE DAY. MUST SEE YOU. MOST IMPORTANT. LET ME KNOW HOTEL LIVERPOOL FIRST THING IN THE MORNING.[19]

Willie Low of Wellesbourne House near Warwick was a popular fellow, whose wife Juliet was a Southern belle. He was often one of the guns in parties which included Brookie and the King, the latter being especially appreciative of the dinners provided at Wellesbourne by a Creole cook. Sympathetic and cool headed,

Willie was the right person for Daisy to confide in, and he was to play an important part in coming events.

Those events can be traced through the next few weeks. Daisy had returned to London briefly, and stayed for those few days at 7 Chesterfield Street, the house near Berkeley Square belonging to her sister, Blanchie Gordon-Lennox. She probably consulted a doctor and tried to find someone to perform an abortion, a delicate and professionally risky task for a registered practitioner. By not responding to her, Joe had in fact given a cruel answer. If she did try to find a doctor in England who would risk his career, her search was unsuccessful. Daisy then returned to Paris alone, as planned. Much of her harrowing description of what happened survives. The memories of those days in Paris and the following weeks would not fade quickly.

She had not been able to lie up and testify to the world what had happened. She did not feel able to tell Brookie, and one line to Joe summed up her state of mind: 'I am utterly heartbroken and yet I don't suppose you even care.' Dr Pozzi, a fashionable gynaecologist, recommended a woman who might help, and so on Friday 9 May and the next day as well, Daisy had gone to try and get the pregnancy aborted:

> She applied local treatment ... There being a railway accident that day, all passengers were obliged to walk nearly a mile on rough stones on the line, and this fatigue upset the 'arrangements'. Still on Sunday morning 11th there was good hope it was succeeding and I was going to Warwick and to bed, feeling desperately ill. You arrived London. I stayed – you know the rest.[20]

Joe had visited her the following afternoon, when she had continued to feel dreadfully ill, hardly able to speak. Later, while carrying out an engagement in Essex, she had caught a chill. Instead of appearing at court alongside Brookie, she had been suffering almost unendurable pain. Those of her circle who had attended the evening reception must have wondered why Daisy Warwick was absent.

That evening Joe suddenly arrived at her house again and persuaded her to go with him. At his house they spent the night mostly quarrelling, and the following morning, cold and exhausted, Daisy took a hansom to see a Dr Bennet, who could be trusted. After what she described as 'unspeakable pain and suffering', she somehow managed to make the journey to Warwick Castle:

> I tried to crawl about Sunday but had to go to bed and Monday night the 'thing' happened. On Tuesday I was very ill, blood poisoning, followed by inflammation of the kidneys and only my strength of *will* has brought me through the most awful time of pain I have ever known . . . Willie was so good in managing Brookie and helping me . . . That's why I told him all. Please burn this at once. It is awful to have to write it but your denial made it necessary.[21]

The night after Willie Low's telegram to Joe, Daisy suffered a relapse. It was septicaemia. Doctors were summoned immediately but they did not have the means to do anything much in the face of blood poisoning, and Daisy hovered between life and death for several days. Clarke wired Joe the following day, mentioning 'great pain'.[22] When, miraculously, Daisy was eventually pronounced to be out of danger it seemed unbelievable to her that somehow she had pulled through.

She owed her recovery to the best medical attention – Halliday Croom, an eminent kidney specialist, had been part of the team attending her – her natural resilience, and a great deal of luck. When strong enough she wrote to Joe, still addressing him with undimmed affection:

> *My dearest dear – My dear only love* . . .
>
> I have been so ill – Tuesday night I might have died . . . the haemorrhage and the morphia have made me so weak and

lightheaded I find it difficult even today to put words together so as to reach your heart my darling. Willie has promised me to go to you and find you . . . he has managed to get Brookie away and keep things straight for me, as all this happening at home was so dreadful. But I have an absolutely devoted doctor and old Clarke, and then when the violent *kidney* trouble came it was all put upon *that*, and I have got out of it somehow – at least I don't know *how* . . . Don't let's ever mention 'love' again. It has brought hell to us both . . .[23]

It was some time before Daisy completely recovered, and she must have wondered what her future could be. Surely Joe did not love Kitty enough for marriage; he 'must be honest with her', Daisy suggested, forget any sense of obligation, and go abroad till everything was forgotten. Newspapers noted that the Countess of Warwick had been confined to her bed for several days. One even mentioned septicaemia, another said that she was far from well. Yet if any reporters ever suspected the real nature of her illness, their suspicions were never aired publicly. Even the more sensational news sheets relied on hints and innuendo when writing up their stories. And any idea that Daisy might talk about Joe even to mutual friends made him furious. She told her sisters simply that she and Joe had parted. Thus, by dissimulation and silence, could appearances be maintained and the unwritten rules of Society kept.

Daisy's brother-in-law 'Strath' Sutherland had been on board his yacht *Catania*, moored off Venice, when news had reached him of Daisy's illness. He was puzzled, having seen her in Paris where she had apparently been so well. Equally in the dark was Violet Manners, Marchioness of Granby. The former Violet Lindsay, still one of Daisy's closest female friends, asked whether it was true that she had been ill as the newspapers had said.

One of the few people who had been trusted with the knowledge of the recent terrible events was Mary Hunter. Mrs Charles

Hunter had become one of the most successful Society hostesses, and luminaries of the artistic world as well as the court circle were to be seen at her lavish parties: Mary used to say that she considered it her duty to spend Charles' money. As one of Colonel Smythe's five daughters, she had been introduced to Society by Sir William Eden of Windlestone, a sportsman and, like her husband, a coal magnate. Sir William was also an acknowledged watercolourist, and an early patron of the New English Art Club.

Being a woman of the world, Mary Hunter had gone to the Paris studio of Auguste Rodin, where the master had sculpted her as Pallas Athene. She had also sat for Sargent, with whom she had developed a deep friendship. Charles and Mary had known Joe for many years, so it was natural for Mary to write to him:

> I too was very glad dear Joe, to have a word with you – you have had a difficult part to play. I shall go on trying to make D realize that she must stand aside completely – go right out of your life – She never showed me your letters or telegrams until I doubted her veracity – so don't blame her for that.
>
> I have said all I can to make her realize that you *wish* to be left alone – and also that unless Lady D of her own free will sets you free you are bound to marry her . . . I don't want to judge you. No one can tell but yourself what the complications have been, and certainly you and D have suffered! She had internal inflammation and when I was at Warwick was kept on Barley water and fish, but the necessary operation was successful and she will soon get over the physical trouble and she must live her life without you.[24]

It would make all in their circle happier if Joe was given his freedom, but equally none of them would wish him to evade the inevitable, unless Kitty were willing to let him go. Soon afterwards Mary Hunter wrote to Joe again, thanking him for some vintage wine and flowers received for a dinner party at Hill Hall, her country house in Essex (which contained an entire room from a Venetian palazzo). To this letter she added further thoughts:

> I saw D yesterday and told her that you begged her to stand aside and leave you alone to follow your course independently. I also told her that the only way to retain your love and even your gratitude and interest, was to pass out of your life. It is only when she is generous and unselfish that she can have any hold on your heart . . .[25]

Not in the least a sentimental person, Mary Hunter's heart ached, having never seen a woman so abjectly miserable. She was trying, she said, to be perfectly rigid, impartial and scrupulously honest to them both, but she felt that the extraordinary inventions and downright lies being circulated made it impossible to see the truth: 'it is very difficult to reconcile such different statements . . . Don't marry in a hurry and don't be quixotic . . .'[26]

Joe had been masquerading as lover both to Kitty and Daisy, but although disparaging his once adored but now inconvenient mistress there were times when he returned to her with all his old ardour, putting a construction on events which was most favourable to himself. While Daisy herself had not been entirely innocent, most of all she was the victim of self-deception.

∽

By the summer of 1902, nearly six months had elapsed since Lord Rosebery's impressive speech, but he had not made a move. The ailing Lord Salisbury had resigned as Prime Minister, and in a private conversation with Daisy the King posed his dilemma: 'How can I send for Campbell-Bannerman? I shall have to if R won't take this opportunity, and I can't do that. Why does he hang back?' His Majesty thought he knew: 'He is a Conservative at heart!'[27]

Daisy had denied that Rosebery was anything of the sort, replying very plainly that he was 'a Liberal of the best and strongest type and of the clearest conscience'. Perhaps the King had intended his thoughts to be passed on, but anyway Daisy had been haunted by his words and had been prompted to write to Rosebery, knowing, she said, that he would not abuse her confidence. She urged him not to wait any longer, and though he had got everything in the world and had no incentive to work, a great opportunity like the present was given to few:

> no personal enjoyment is so great as to feel oneself the *leader* of others, you yourself being the inspiration of a party . . . You have all those grand Liberal traditions of the past to inspire you to make a policy now, and no political Napoleon will ever score as you will . . . I seem to see your cynical smile as you read! But I don't care! I wish I lived in your house as secretary or charwoman and could give you a good talking to twice a week!![28]

She reminded him that he had devoted friends, and that staunch Liberals such as Sir Edward Grey, Herbert Asquith and Richard Haldane would serve him till death, but he must do something to justify all the admiration people felt for him, 'all who spend our lives in "'hero-worship"'!'[29]

~

The King's Coronation had been planned for June, but the onset of appendicitis and consequent surgery had caused it to be postponed till August. There was a slight feeling of anti-climax, but the usual London season continued. Showing no signs of her recent ordeal, Daisy Warwick looked radiant.

One invitation among many she accepted was to Violet Granby's first dinner at 16 Arlington Street, Piccadilly. The Granbys had just acquired this imposing William Kent mansion, located between Green Park and the Ritz. Violet had added a note: 'I can't bear to think we never met the last time you were in London – I *long* to see you dear sweet Daisy.'[30] After returning from Arlington Street at midnight, she was too tired to attend a late reception at Lansdowne House, but she wrote to Joe in the hope that they could meet. With all the season's activities, it would not be easy to arrange, but she needed to see him. There was a one-day trades union conference in London which could serve as an excuse to leave Ascot, and perhaps that would be a good time.

But the outcome was disappointing, even though they spent the night together. By the time Joe left Brook House at dawn, she knew that there was no hope of a future for them together. For some reason Daisy had believed that Joe was going to choose her over Kitty. When she saw that was not the case it brought her to the point of hysteria: 'I feel absolutely certain now that it must be a future *together*, or Death for *me*.'[31] She was threatening to take her own life quietly at Wiseton. Despite his worldliness, such an enormous potential scandal must have given Joe some uncomfortable moments.

Obviously Mary Hunter had not made much of an impression, for Daisy continued, pleading for them to go away together. Her final direct appeal was:

> let us go and *live* and see the world and defy 'convention' and live for each other . . . Is it not *I* who have been deceived and treated by *you* with cruelty and meanness . . . shame and misery such as you and the woman you left me for, can never understand in your narrow shallow minds . . . For indeed Joe she has dragged you down to her own level . . .[32]

In her own estimation Daisy had given him love, devotion and complete loyalty, despite his unfaithfulness with women in London and Paris.

Kitty Downshire meanwhile was soon to leave for Schlagenbad, a German spa. Since her divorce, the atmosphere with Joe had not been harmonious, as a letter to him signed 'Blue Eyes' shows:

In case you are still thinking of coming to see me on Thursday, I am writing to ask you not to, as I would rather not see you – as time goes on it would be easier – but just now it could only lead to hot and bitter words on both sides, which is so painful – you must know I could not mind your going to shoot, then of course I was disappointed not to see you – but what I do mind is your having broken your word to me, and flaunting yourself in public with the woman who has spoiled my life – and is being discussed and commented on by everyone – I suppose you are going up to be with her tomorrow night – if she is enjoying her triumph she is welcome to it – I wish you both joy – but surely we never made a greater mistake than to think the feeling we had for each other could possibly be love.[33]

Daisy and Joe were being seen together in town, and she had asked him to accompany her to *Victory*, Ethel Smythe's new opera; perhaps that night at the opera accounts for Kitty's outburst. Whatever the reason, she hated the position in which she found herself:

It is useless to try and disguise the fact that we would both give anything we have or years of our lives to undo the past – and the future seems so hopeless – I think now I am to be pitied more than you – the dreadful longing I have for my home and my children and the right to hold my head up amongst my friends . . .[34]

Joe did not keep away, and when he went to see Kitty the atmosphere, as predicted, became heated. Her subsequent letter was repentant about what she called 'the folly and madness of the cruel and hateful things'[35] she had said to him that day. No reparation could ever atone for them, she said, and her previous unhappiness had been as nothing compared to the bitter pain she now felt. She was tortured by the knowledge of having hurt the very person whom she claimed to love, and was afraid that she might have killed any love Joe had felt for her. Afterwards, Joe was magnanimous; he even gave her a present from Paris.

In July, while Kitty was preparing for her visit to Germany, the triangle of relationships continued. Daisy and Joe spent what she called 'our heavenly night at the Russell Hotel', and a few weeks later she told him that she was yet again pregnant, 'stunned and numb and miserable'.[36] The issue gave rise to surprisingly little comment; there is a strange silence about it. Whether Daisy dared to put herself through another abortion or whether the pregnancy ended naturally, cannot be known. However, her mind was busy, determined on a last-ditch attempt to prevent Lord Downshire obtaining his decree absolute. That just might be possible through the intervention of the King's Proctor, but it was difficult to know what the grounds for such an intervention would be. If a way could be found for reconciliation between the Downshires, Joe would then be free. It seems that tentative offers had been extended, but that Kitty had turned them down.

Millie did all she could, inviting the King on board the Sutherlands' yacht, because he wanted to discuss matters with Daisy in privacy. Daisy herself, when she wrote to Joe in August, was full of fighting talk:

> As to *myself* I will be frank now – I have sat still about *her*, said nothing, *feeling sorry for her if she loved you* . . . I am going to let all the world know the sort of woman she is . . . she chooses to stick to you for your money, and *everyone* shall know it . . . I shall injure her absolutely, entirely, irrevocably . . .
>
> I am so thoroughly disgusted with all she says to her men, her family, her friends, that I have no feeling for her but contempt and disgust . . . I am at an end of patience and gentleness and forbearance. It shall be war to the knife . . .[37]

⚜ 9 ⚜

Late Summer 1902

THE VICEROY OF INDIA, Lord Curzon, had arranged for loyal Indian princes to attend the Coronation, and during the summer various government receptions were given in their honour. Some leading hostesses issued them with invitations for the sheer glamour of their national dress. The princes from Hindustan were entertained at the India Office, but *The World*'s report was not entirely glowing:

> Too many people were invited and the really interesting ones were rather lost in a sea of minor politicians and unknown Government clerks . . . the long wait was so dispiriting . . . the Royalties did not come until twelve and by that time . . . even the much-bejewelled Princes were beginning to pall. The Princess of Wales had the greatest success, she looked so well, and bore herself so bravely among all her Royal guests . . .
>
> It was difficult to distinguish people in so great a throng, but two of the loveliest women were Lady Warwick, in pale green, with a beautiful tiara, and the Duchess of Sutherland who . . . wore sapphires with her lovely diamonds; they came together.[1]

Less than five miles away from the mansions where such events took place were Jack London's people of the abyss: a starving, threadbare mass, living either in stinking hovels or the workhouse. The American had embedded himself in the East End that summer, disguising himself in the shabbiest clothes he could find. His experience among the underclass was turned into a classic account of that other London, a city containing some of the worst slums in Europe. Daisy had gained some first-hand experience of lives lived on the margins of society, and would have known something of the sights Jack was observing.

While Daisy was in London, Brookie wrote to say he was very lonely without her and missed her so much. At Warwick in July they entertained four hundred and fifty Colonial troopers, who had arrived for the Coronation. Whatever her depths of private disappointment, Daisy had her formal role to play. Under the direction of Sidney Greville, lord-in-waiting to the King, the day was a brilliant success. Four-year-old Maynard was lifted shoulder high, and received a collection of regimental insignias. His mother also took him to see the review at Buckingham Palace, which he watched from the Household stand. The little boy was having quite a busy season: dressed in white satin, he had recently distinguished himself in the role of pageboy.

Edward VII's Coronation finally took place on 9 August. Daisy was seen resplendent, but Queen Alexandra, in a dress of golden embroidered gauze, eclipsed all her rivals that day. Changed out of his shabby clothes for the occasion, Jack London watched the Coronation procession from Trafalgar Square. The burly Life Guards lining the route seemed to him like an insult to the dwarfish, malnourished bodies in Mile End. Powdered footmen escorted coroneted dukes and gorgeously arrayed duchesses. It was a vision of people who seemed to own the earth, manifested by an endless procession of black and brown Imperial troops in turban, fez and helmet. To the accompaniment of crashing bands and wildly cheering crowds the parade marched past. Even Jack

London was almost carried away by the surge of excitement when the King's gilded coach appeared, drawn by 'the creams' – the Hanoverian Royal Cream horses which had drawn the royal coach for almost two hundred years.

Yet, despite his response to such an impressive display, he thought the whole show an aberration of pomp and circumstance. From what he had seen there was no hope among the underclass. While the frail Archbishop, Frederick Temple, crowned the King, hordes of his subjects were celebrating the day in meaner streets, some drinking themselves into oblivion, others dossing down wherever they could. The police were otherwise engaged, and did not disturb those prostrate figures who were to be seen from Spitalfields to St James' Park, sleeping like the dead.

~

When Kitty arrived in Schlagenbad in the middle of August, there was a wire from Joe waiting at the Hotel Katrina, wishing her well. She was naturally delighted to be in his thoughts and responded: 'It is quite heavenly here – lots of lovely walks in woods, and the waters so good to drink and wash in and the air delicious – I am perfectly happy, at least as happy as it is possible to be away from you . . .'[2]

In her first letter from Schlagenbad she also confided:

everyone and everything sinks into insignificance compared with you. My one thought alone is of you darling – and I am only a worry to you loving you so well. It is my jealousy of that other woman that prevents me from behaving genuinely to you and giving you up. Also the horror of having no name and no man's protection that makes me shudder for myself – and then the joy of knowing that we shall belong to each other predominates all . . . but to you it must only mean a drag on all that constitutes a man's love of freedom, besides the degradation of your being married to an utterly stupidly hopeless woman with a past . . . I want you to realize all my unworthiness, but not to cast it back at me afterwards . . .[3]

While at the spa she visited Dr Pagenstacher. His diagnosis pinpointed several ailments, including eczema, nervous prostration, anaemia and exhausted brain power, which would make it necessary for the patient to stay several weeks. He was very thorough in his approach, and gave his patient confidence that all would be put right, wrote Kitty after the first consultation, for which the fee was £2. For her part, she intended to stick to the regime for Joe's sake, and felt it would all be worthwhile. She was not lonely, having made friends with a certain Lady Grove, 'good looking and clever . . . altogether most fascinating'.[4] Lady Grove had written books, and from time to time was a reviewer for the *Cornhill Magazine*. Her sister-in-law Edith Fox Pitt was also there, and insisted on staying on at the spa because Kitty was alone. 'She doesn't bore me and is very large minded about things, also has a sense of humour which is a blessing.'[5]

Kitty had never had a female friend before, and it was rather a comfort. She appreciated Joe's letters: 'You are an angel about writing, and it does help to make the time pass.'[6] She was so sorry to have written Joe what she called a stuffy letter, and called herself 'a miserable jealous little idiot',[7] but he must know that it was only because she loved him so much. Had he been angry or amused? she asked. Kitty had few inner resources, and certainly lacked the means to create an independent life for herself.

When Kitty returned from Germany towards the end of September, she realised immediately that something was wrong. Her dreams of a sweet future quickly faded. Having been such a faithful letter writer, Joe's attitude towards her was now noticeably distant. In her absence he had become closer to his former lover, and had been having second thoughts about marrying Kitty – thoughts which Daisy had no doubt done everything possible to encourage. At his reunion with Kitty he was cold, calculating and spoke not one word of love, while she accused him of having worked up lustful feelings so as to mask the truth. Finally she dragged out of him that he had been plotting with Daisy Warwick to banish her. The facts were ugly. Though she lost a lot of sleep, she had to fight.

From the Hans Crescent Hotel, Belgravia, she wrote that not only did Joe's cruelty and want of understanding hurt her, but that downright brutality would be far kinder: 'Why won't you be honest and straightforward and tell me that you can't bear the sight of me?'[8] The reassuring letters he had sent to Schlagenbad now meant little, and she was totally disillusioned: 'Should you not succeed in vilifying Artie sufficiently to stop the divorce – this intended marriage between us will *now* be as hateful to me as it is to you – what I know now has shattered my soul in the intensity of its horror.'[9]

Jealous and afraid, Kitty was willing, she said, to accept any terms, even the possibility that they could separate immediately after their wedding. In what by now was something of a routine when finding himself in a tight corner, Joe apologised.

There were moments when Daisy seemed to perceive Joe without illusions, but she failed to realise the implications of her perception, and would always resume a self-destructive course. If she had acted on her instinct instead of ignoring it, her future would certainly have been different, and possibly less painful. At the end of September, Kitty appeared without warning on her doorstep, having impulsively decided to confront her rival. It must have been a tremendous shock for Daisy when the footman announced Kitty's arrival. In the conversation that followed, the two characters revealed something of the truth behind the conventional appearance of their lives, rather in the style of an Edwardian playwright. Daisy spoke first:

'Why have you come?'
'To talk about Joe . . . I suppose you know that I have you and Joe completely in my power now if I choose to speak.'

'You cannot hurt Joe, and as for me I am too broken hearted to care for any of those pricks and stings.'

'That baby you were expecting . . . I never believed it . . .'

'You too have loved Joe, and of what use is love unless it can rise above suspicions and jealousies . . . You are young and pretty, I am not surprised he fell in love with you.'

'You are beautiful.'

'No, I am old.'

'He has behaved badly to us both.'[10]

'Blue Eyes' sat gazing at her rival, somewhat overwhelmed by everything that Daisy was saying in praise of Joe. Then, as if experiencing a revelation, she said, 'You *do* love him.' She kissed Daisy's hand and departed, leaving her hostess dazed and apprehensive.

In a long letter she wrote soon afterwards, Daisy triumphantly remembered how her rival had lapped up all those cunningly contrived compliments. Kitty was described as 'absolutely selfish and hard, with a narrow little soul inside a childlike little body . . . one looked in vain for any spark of bigness or generosity . . . what a shallow fool! With eyes like flinty steel, and ideas like those of a third housemaid . . .'[11]

Kitty for her part had conceded that Lady Warwick was a wonderful woman who deserved a better fate. But she wanted some kind of revenge, and her terms were unequivocal. If Daisy was prepared to risk all in a divorce, making herself equal in disgrace, Kitty would give up Joe. Otherwise, she claimed him. Brookie meanwhile was not asking for an end to his marriage, but had gallantly said 'I will only divorce you if you wish it.' Daisy would not entertain the idea. She had too much to lose.

As the time for a decree absolute approached, there was an atmosphere of deepest mistrust between the three principals involved. Joe and Kitty had profitless meetings during which they quarrelled violently; on occasion he taunted her about her past, the very thing she had begged him not to do. She felt betrayed:

My Joe, how wrong you were to lie to me so from the very beginning – and so wreck three lives – yours and mine, and the woman who loves you and is loved by you. Why didn't you throw yourself on my generosity, and just tell me all! That you could never give her up! But you lacked the moral courage, as she so rightly says . . .

I would then have struggled and fought my way back to Artie – but believed that you loved me, and as you had told me, had parted from Lady Warwick, and so I let myself go – and now I can't *can't* give you up and love you in the mad reckless way that is so near to hate at times . . . [12]

Joe's cover of honourable behaviour was blown away when he told a friend that he had been bound to hedge in his attitude to Kitty, because if he had to marry her it would be worse if she hated him. Could anything be salvaged from this wreck? The course of their relationship seemed to confirm Oscar Wilde's dictum: 'Between a man and a woman there can only be passion or enmity.'

Daisy believed more than ever that the best course would be for Joe to break away for several months until the whole affair was forgotten. She did not mind if her relationship with him became public, and if necessary they could defy the world together. Probably sometime in the future Joe would marry, but let them live for the present. The bachelor felt himself hounded, and expressed his reservations to Robert Wilmot, who had assumed the role of Kitty's protector. Wilmot thought the marriage should go ahead, because the scales were weighted in favour of social conformity.

The decree absolute was granted, and Kitty and Joe were finally married in a quiet civil ceremony on 14 November. It was almost inevitable, but hardly a triumph. Daisy suffered silently, and felt very tired. Brookie showed himself to be the soul of generosity, saying that he was so sorry for all that his wife was suffering, unable to understand why Joe had behaved in such a way. Guy attempted to console his mother, saying that he was sorry for Joe, *having* to marry that sort of woman. When out in London Queenie had glimpsed Joe and Kitty as they passed by in a hansom. She was puzzled, saying in all innocence: 'Fancy, I saw Mr Laycock this morning and he stared at me and didn't know me. I expect I've changed a lot, and there was some lady with him!'

⚜ 10 ⚜

A Journey South

DAISY NOW HAD TO be strong. High on her list of priorities was Queenie's coming-out ball at Easton. Caryl Craven had been commissioned to create a splendid décor, and an army of workmen took a week carrying out his plans. Four hundred guests were given a night to remember. *The Onlooker* devoted an entire page to describing the scene:

> The whole county of Essex was turned inside out for the occa-sion, and from all parts people flocked to be present at the brilliant occasion which took place on Friday night . . . The ballroom itself was a work of art. Passing through the French windows of the salon was a white pillared hall, all trellis work entwined with roses and ivy.
>
> On the left side was the supper-room, gay with yellow silk hangings, while each of the innumerable small tables was done in different flowers, one in Parma violets, others in yellow or pink roses or poinsettias, and in the middle a larger round table was exquisite with orchids, mauvy-pink and white.
>
> On the white walls of the ballroom were clusters of lilac and roses with mirrored walls, and in a curtained recess the band

played delightfully all through the night. The belle of the ball was, of course, little Lady Marjorie, the sweetest picture in her soft, white dress with delicate embroideries of silver . . . Lady Warwick was the queen of the evening and wore the loveliest dress, supposed to represent the rays of the sun and moon, worked in silver and black, with silver and black stars on the graceful falling leaves. She carried in one hand a bouquet of gardenias and with the other clasped the hand of her little son, Maynard . . . A Russian tiara crowned Lady Warwick's hair, and in her dress she wore a large knot of diamonds . . . and a large rope of pears twisted twice round her neck . . .[1]

During the summer Daisy had commissioned Harold Peto, who had made his name as a garden designer in the Italianate style, to carry out major work on the gardens at Easton. His labour force was none other than a contingent of about seventy men from the Salvation Army colony at Hadleigh in Essex, for whom wooden huts were built in the grounds. They worked well, stayed sober and were heard singing hymns every evening. Occasionally they received game from the estate, and as further evidence of her Ladyship's bounty the workmen celebrated Christmas with a feast, in which she joined them.

Having launched Queenie in style and survived Christmas, Daisy felt exhausted. Her life was essentially unresolved, and the darker aspects of her existence had to be concealed. She could only be honest in her secret letters to the man she had not yet given up as lost:

My darling,

It was dear of you to write I was unhappy at having written so *miserably* when I got back here, and felt I had perhaps been selfish again in telling you how all these memories make me suffer. In the night I wake and every way I look I see your face!

I *must* put the photos away – and I haven't had the courage to
do so yet and wherever I am I meet your eyes, and when I shut
mine I seem to feel again your arms and your kisses and all is
forgotten for 2 minutes . . .[2]

In Daisy's mind they could still live together, but she seems to have
been oblivious to the fact that no amount of wishing could undo
the fact of Joe's marriage two months earlier. It was typical of her,
however, to disregard any inconvenient obstacle which stood
between her and what she wanted, and so she set out the terms of
a possible future:

I can never be divorced or marry you . . . Unless B. dies, but I
should be quite content . . . and we should be so rich, you and
I together, that in doing great things for other people, we should
forget *ourselves*, and a life full of interests and usefulness could
always be ours . . . and we could do *so* much together for those
who are sad and want helping . . .[3]

In a bid to get well and escape from her loneliness, she had decided
to take a holiday in Sicily with her small son. Joe would be yacht-
ing in the Mediterranean for several weeks, and Daisy wondered
whether they might arrange to meet, whether in Palermo, Naples
or Rome. Anything might be possible if he were willing. She
described her reasons for making this journey in a letter addressed
to Joe at the Cercle de l'Union, Cannes:

I have been very unwell as you know for months. I cannot get
strong, and I can never describe to you the strain it has been
that on top of the greatest misery given me by you, I have res-
olutely had to face my work, my life, and to keep all the threads
in my hand. I have won – however I don't choose to lose my
health and my looks for any man! But eight days of work in
every week when one is physically weak from an awful shock

has made hunting impossible, as I get so dead tired. So I am going away for a month's rest ... Villa Igiea (Ritz Hotel) Palermo, and arrive there on March 9th.[4]

Would Joe meet her? She begged him to wire just 'yes or no'.

Millie Sutherland would be staying in her own villa at Taormina, but despite their warm relationship, Daisy had decided not to stay there, because she wanted 'absolute rest and quiet from the family to begin with'.[5] Maynard would be going with his mother, because his throat had been a problem during the damp Essex winter, but even without that excuse Daisy would not have wanted to be apart from him. He was so important in her life, and she was very much the fond mama:

> He is growing so tall and is so sensible and clever, you would hardly know him. Yesterday in London, he said to the King 'Mummie and I are going to Sicily to live close to a volcano', but he added 'If you like to come with us we will take care the lava does not cover you!' Then he sidled quietly to the door and I said 'Where are you going?' He said 'To tell Nannie about the King' and departed! . . .
>
> Dear one, there is so much that can only be talked over by you and me and I am writing to suggest this one chance, as *you yourself* have made it impossible for me to see you or speak to you in England . . .[6]

Their meeting would be 'absolutely secret'. No one would know his name at her hotel, if he were to call there, and he would be living on his yacht. The third week in March would be ideal. Joe wired that it would be difficult, but he would try.

.~.

Daisy spent some time in London before her departure, and was very busy receiving visits. Among others who called were Balfour, now Prime Minister, Winston Churchill (to discuss his next important speech in opposition to plans for reform of the army proposed by St John Broderick, Secretary of State for War), and George Wyndham, Secretary of State for Ireland. The King too was a regular visitor to Brook House; he enjoyed discussing the world, and sometimes even confidential Cabinet matters, with this most worldly of women. She was not in the least envious of Mrs Keppel, now firmly established as Edward's mistress.

Many people in public life besides the King admired Daisy Warwick's intelligence, and the use to which she was putting it. With the backing of Sir John Gorst, she had been active in trying to establish the provision of free school meals. The scope was immense and the need urgent. Daisy had undertaken research which showed that thousands of children were too hungry to learn; empty stomachs made for poor concentration. The poverty endemic in parts of all major cities meant that deprived youngsters were effectively disqualified from education. Besides malnourishment, the children in many board schools suffered from disease, through no fault of their own, but because the standards of hygiene were often appalling. This major problem was one of Lady Warwick's primary concerns, and she had what was then a Utopian vision of healthy, well-fed children in clean, attractive school buildings. In that environment they could receive an education to give them a chance of adult lives better than those of their parents. Gorst had allied himself with her, and when he spoke about her in the House of Commons, it made her enormously proud. She described herself to Joe as 'the only woman whose name has been mentioned as to her *work* except Florence Nightingale . . .'[7]

She was gradually becoming more active politically, and was the only woman who had been asked to speak at a major conference on unemployment held at the Guildhall in February. The day after, looking tired, she made a speech at the Co-operative Union Conference in Braintree; it was a strain for her to get through it. She was very run down, and after doggedly carrying out all her

Frances Evelyn 'Daisy' Maynard, at the age of nine.

Daisy (on horseback) with her younger sister Blanchie at Dysart in Fife, the home of her stepfather the Earl of Rosslyn. (Painting by Aster Corbould, reproduced by kind permission of Caroline Spurrier.)

(*Above left*) The rejected suitor: Prince Leopold, youngest son of Queen Victoria.

(*Above right*) The man Daisy married: Francis Greville, Lord Brooke, heir to the Earl of Warwick.

Daisy, aged 19, in her wedding dress on the eve of her wedding at Westminster Abbey, April 1881. (Reproduced by permission of Caroline Spurrier.)

(*Above left*) The married lover, naval commander Lord Charles Beresford; Daisy claimed in later years that he was the father of her daughter, Marjorie.

(*Above right*) Joe Layock: the faithless lover who fathered two of Daisy's children – and broke her heart.

The royal lover: Edward, Prince of Wales (leaning on the balustrade) during a visit to the Maynard family home, Easton Lodge, in June 1886. Daisy is standing in front of the Prince. (Reproduced by permission of Caroline Spurrier.)

(*Above left*) Daisy dressed as the Queen of Assyria, circa 1890.

(*Above right*) Daisy, now the Countess of Warwick, dressed as Marie Antoinette for her spectacular *bal poudre* at Warwick Castle in 1895.

(*Above left*) The Countess of Warwick, the Queen of Society.

(*Above right*) Daisy's sister, Blanchie.

Daisy at Warwick Castle in 1899.

The grand staircase at Easton Lodge in Essex, Daisy's favourite home.

The gardens at Easton Lodge; Daisy commissioned Harold Peto to re-model them in the Italianate style.

Daisy with her daugher Marjorie, riding her favourite hunter at Warwick Castle, 1891. (From the painting by Lynwood Palmer, reproduced by permission of Caroline Spurrier.)

Daisy riding a gig at Warwick Castle. (From the painting by Lynwood Palmer, reproduced by permission of Caroline Spurrier.)

The Prince of Wales pays another visit to Easton Lodge, November 1891: he is standing in the centre, with Daisy on his left, and the Earl of Warwick seated in front of him.

Daisy on horseback in front of Easton Lodge, with her dog and pet goat; her love of animals remained strong to the end of her life.

public engagements must have looked forward to some time recuperating abroad. Spring in southern Europe would be the ideal atmosphere in which to restore herself.

~

Daisy left London with Maynard on 4 March and two days later arrived in Rome, where they were to stay at the Grand Hotel. From there she wrote to Joe again immediately: 'This morning at 7 o'clock Tiny One and I went by Genoa. I suppose your yacht was there? I heard you were going there. But I suppose no instinct told you that your Little One and your Tiny One were passing close to you – who have betrayed and deserted them – for what??'[8]

Daisy now badly wanted to 'talk life out', as she put it, and meeting abroad would be much easier. At heart she would always be torn between her instinct to observe Society's rules, and her other self, which could be reckless. Now she was asking Joe to cast aside convention and meet her. Once she had arrived in Palermo, they could be safely alone. Would he take this great opportunity?

Journeys across Europe, though long, were comfortable for first-class passengers, and Daisy's entourage included Maynard's nanny and a footman. Protected from incidental annoyances, travelling was delightful. After a few days in Rome, they boarded the train for Naples, and then crossed the straits to Sicily. In the South at last! There was a lot to see in Palermo, a town on which Arab, Saracen and Norman invaders had left their influence. Strolling round the harbour, five-year-old Maynard begged his mother to buy a baby donkey, which came complete with a traditional harness and a cart painted like a gypsy caravan. Shipment home had then to be arranged for this equipage.

Often, as they walked around, the aristocratic woman and her lovely child drew admiring glances. Despite feeling some relief in the warm spring weather, Daisy's chances of restoring her former health and high spirits were undermined by uncertainty. She was not a person to accept defeat, but she found it difficult to deal with her feelings, and spent several hours every day looking out to sea for Joe's yacht. Having believed that her hold on him would last as long as she wanted, she had not recovered from the shock of recent events. Desperate to make contact, she sent him a wire:

ALL RIGHT TILL MONDAY, BUT OBLIGED TO LEAVE MONDAY NIGHT. DO TRY SATURDAY. TALK WOULD BE DELIGHTFUL.[9]

On board the yacht *Louise* Joe's response was indecisive:

WISH I COULD ARRANGE. WILL WIRE IF I CAN. IMPOSSIBLE COME PALERMO. PARIS EASTER BETTER BUT ALL SO DIFFICULT.[10]

Daisy was in suspense for three weeks, but finally faced humiliating disappointment. Her feelings were expressed in a letter written at the Hotel Villa Igiea:

My darling

I wonder if you despise me as much as I despise myself for ever having allowed myself to think that you would do something good to me at inconvenience to yourself . . .

If you had written at once saying you are completely ruled, and that it was impossible, it would have been kinder to me – but you suggested it was possible – though difficult, (and all difficulties are only made to be got over *if one wishes*). I have stayed on and on Tiny One's birthday, 21st, an English yacht came into the Harbour, and I stupidly made sweet thoughts around it, and waited all day feeling it must be you! And that you would give me one pleasure . . .[11]

She reproached herself for having been foolish enough to suggest seeing him and for suffering the consequent rejection. It was utter folly, she said, to believe that love, forgiveness and fidelity could win against the influence which had coerced him into bondage. Though he may have been regretting his marriage, Joe seemed to have no more freedom at sea than he had at home, and had deliberately kept her in cruel suspense:

> I think you love to hurt me, just as you treated me all last year, living with me, loving me in your arms, all the time meaning *to do what you did*.
>
> When I was *mad* with your cruelty and treachery and your utter loss of the sense that you owed me more than you could ever owe *anyone* else . . . I suppose I was less expense than a woman in the streets would have been all the year.[12]

Sometimes – too rarely – she saw Joe for what he was, but she would then deny these moments of recognition. They never seemed to lead her to appraise him or her situation truthfully. The sensual attraction between the pair made her extremely vulnerable, and she was always carried along by her emotional impulses. More than once she called Joe the love of her life, and detaching herself from him was more than she could bear: 'You were my world. I cared for you, thought of you, schemed for you, loved you for your dear self, and for all I know in you lying under the selfishness . . .'[13]

Joe had given no proof that he possessed such hidden depths of unselfishness, yet she blamed the bad influences, 'toadies and rotters male and female' surrounding him, as an excuse for his behaviour. Her ideals had been projected on to the wrong man, and no amount of loyalty on her part could alter his character. Nevertheless she later wrote abjectly: 'My whole self lies at your feet for good or evil and for ever, and I can't I *can't* get free, though I try hard!'[14]

Without consolation, it was time to leave Sicily and set off for Rome once more. Perhaps they would be reunited there, or perhaps in Naples? Joe did not turn up in either city. The one success of the holiday had been enjoying Maynard's company, and seeing him look so well. He had learnt a few words of Italian, and had shown himself to be adaptable as well. The maps he always enjoyed at home had come to life. It was his best adventure. When his mother informed him that he would be travelling back to England, he remarked that he would much rather travel to 'nowhere', and went on to explain: 'I want to travel to "nowhere" because then we could never get out of the train, but travel on for ever!'[15]

Always full of fun, he was very observant: 'I said to the footman yesterday, "give me a rug for my legs", and Maynard said: "Why do you say that Mummy? You should only say 'a rug'. Because it can only be for your legs. It isn't a cloak!"'[16]

A brief stay in Rome was all that time would allow, to the disappointment of many in diplomatic circles who were eager with their invitations. Queenie joined her mother in Rome. Ambassador Frank Bertie had been a friend of Daisy's for many years; she had used her influence with the King to secure the British Embassy for him when the Foreign Office had favoured other candidates. There was a dinner at the Embassy, and when they took their leave Bertie saw them off at the station, accompanied by several members of his entourage, who presented bouquets.

Maynard was to go straight back to London with Nanny Wilby, accompanied by a courier, while mother and daughter travelled on to the Riviera. Faithful Brookie was waiting for them at the Hotel Cap Martin, Menton.

Brookie loved the South of France, and that year they were going to look at a villa on which he had set his heart. However, when Daisy arrived in Menton there was something much more important than a patient husband awaiting her. A telegram from

Joe had been forwarded from the Paris Ritz. He had carelessly sent it there, confusing it with her hotel in Palermo, also known as the Ritz. It meant that Joe had been thinking of her after all, and his silence had been due to a silly mistake. She chose to believe that he had not been treating her with deliberate cruelty, but in his slap-dash way had mistaken the address. With this message in her hands, Daisy's mood became one of relief and excitement.

Only later did she discover from a notice in the *New York Herald* that Joe's yacht had entered Palermo harbour after her departure. Ruffled and uncomprehending, she wrote:

> I can't believe that you only waited till I left to go to Sicily? No. I *won't* believe it – for you would have *hurt* me more than I can say – and you told me it was 'impossible.'
>
> Please say you understand how unhappy I was when I got no reply, only a telegram saying you were 'sailing' and that I felt hurt and angry. You know how impetuous I am . . . and I had to keep the Sutherlands away by main force with every excuse, so as to be free, and then I thought you were heartless and did not realize how much I was risking too.[17]

Everything she had written in her angry letters had been prompted by his intolerable silence. She would be at the Paris Ritz in mid-April, and would look for his response then.

In the meantime, Queenie would accompany her parents to visit several friends whose cards had been left, with invitations to lunch, dine and 'automobile'. Churchill had telegraphed from Cannes that he would come over for lunch. What a surprise! Daisy had thought him attending to parliamentary business in London.

Almost the entire fashionable world descended on the Riviera for three months every winter. The King himself was in his element in the relaxed atmosphere that attracted other European royalty and a sprinkling of Oriental princes. Lord Brougham had pioneered the British exodus to this playground as far back as the

1860s. Forty years later, aristocrats mixed with American millionaires, and even with certain sophisticated ladies whose background did not bear close scrutiny. Gradually, the fishing villages, Nice and Cannes, had become towns, and palatial hotels had been built, although some of the Mediterranean coast was still *au sauvage*; almond blossom, lemons and the scent of mimosa were everywhere.

After the freedom of Sicily, Daisy was back in a more formal, intensely social life, one which she did not entirely relish. One was obliged to dress for dinner, and many evenings were spent at Ciro's, the stylish restaurant which had been bought by James Gordon Bennett, proprietor of the New York *Times Herald*. On a whim one night he had paid 40,000 francs for the establishment, and had then handed it as a tip to a waiter. The lucky man, Ciro, had made it so fashionable that only the most influential people could get a table.

The Mediterranean gardens were a world apart. One belonged to a villa owned by Ralph and Daniela Curtis, American millionaire expatriates. Originally from Boston, they travelled widely in Europe, and could also be found at the Palazzo Barbero in Venice, where Henry James was often their guest. Daisy was impressed by the Villa Curtis garden, as she wrote to Joe:

> I longed for you to be with me, because it was *ideal* and shows what *can* be done with *good* gardening here . . . My friend Peto has laid it all out, part *wild* garden – part Italian, part tropical, and a winding 'river' of Iris and Narcissi of all kinds made a blaze of colour, and *roses* blazed as in our June gardens in England – and every sort of glorious flowering creeper and shrub covered the walls, and in one corner a real 'garden of the Hesperides' was laid out, with orange trees etc – *only* lacking the lovely ladies in orange draperies!![18]

After having plenty of rest and sleep over the past few weeks, Daisy was feeling like her old self again: 'It is glorious to feel *well* isn't it? I do hope you are the same my darling, on your ship. How I should *love* to see you on the Bridge, in your oilskins, and muddling over your charts! And the wind blowing! I should *love* it!'[19]

She took her daughter to Monte Carlo for the first time, as a kind of initiation into the adult world. Lord Savile accompanied them into the casino, and gallantly gambled for Queenie as well as for himself, after which another friend gave them a strawberry tea.

A visit to Fitzroy, her brother, was always a comfort. He lived mostly on the Côte d'Azur, and his villa at Eze, a little hill-top town, had one of the finest gardens in the area. He was a very gentle man, whose health made it necessary for him to live in the south. Knowing all about his sister's ill-fated love affair – it seems that Joe had paid him a visit, as he was to do again – he was very concerned about her. That evening with Fitzroy made a deep impact on Daisy, and her subsequent letter to Joe beautifully evoked the spirit of place:

My dear one

I must write to you of how I spent last evening, because my every thought has been 'saturated' with you all night, ever since – I told Fitzroy I would dine with him quietly and alone at his little place at Eze, and I got a man to drop me in his automobile on his way to Beaulieu at Fitzroy's gate. (By the way how terrifying motors are on this road with all the corners! And what awful accidents are happening.)

We dined in his little room, and then sat out in such heavenly moonlight all evening talking – He smoked – I lay in hammock and the sea softly splashing, and the wonderful moon, and the scent of the stocks and carnations and mimosa, all mixed was heavenly – Oh Joe, if only you had been there with us! We talked of life and all its difficulties, and its few joys and its deep sadnesses, and then of the poor lady whom Fitzroy loved and who died – and whom he never forgets.

And then of *you* Joe. And he told me of your coming to see him and loving his garden (and the sense of your having been there seemed to bring you *close* to me), and I lay there while Fitzroy talked on, *feeling* you near me, and in the dark shadows I brought your face and your eyes and your *dear hands* as an image before me, and I *felt* you were there, and I said 'Joe, Joe' softly to myself – and oh the yearning and longing just to hear your voice and touch you. How *can* I tell in writing all I was longing?[20]

Fitzroy seemed to be more in sympathy with his sister's love affair than any other member of her family, but even he thought the uncertain life she was now leading would kill her. Did she now feel any different towards Joe? he asked. She answered that nothing would ever change the fact that Joe was the one love of her life, and she cared for him more deeply than ever. If drowning herself would do him a service, she said, she would walk right out to sea.

They talked for several hours till she was able to bear it no longer, feeling that the garden was full of the lover whom she had summoned in her imagination. It was a rush to catch the last train back to Monte Carlo. On the drive back along the coast to Menton she was in a reflective mood, noticing 'the smells of the flowers, and the croaking of frogs, and the little glow-worms besides the road'.[21]

~

Daisy planned to spend Easter among several of her circle. There is no indication from her letters whether Brookie went too. In her next letter to Joe she reported that she had found the villa of Brookie's dreams, but she made no mention of her husband at all:

. . . We have nearly bought such a pretty little villa and *lovely* garden – down by the sea, at Roquebrun [sic]. I could make it lovely, and the garden is a dream – and I think it would be nice

as a haven of rest and refuge – perhaps for 'us'?? and I'm
arranging to buy it – (it isn't expensive). It is right off that dusty
road . . .[22]

Her silence about Brookie is eloquent; if he was there, his presence
was too shadowy to merit a mention. But Guy and Queenie were
both in Paris for Easter. Among the familiar group were Gladys
Ripon, who would later be Diaghilev's patron, and Lady Dudley,
one of the King's former companions. 'Here, in Paris, I am lonely
as ever in the midst of a "crowd" . . . there are heaps of men about,
so I suppose it is cheery . . .'[23] she wrote to Joe.

If Queenie were to fall in love and marry, then it might be easier
for her mother to choose what to do with her own life. At the
moment it felt somehow unreal, as if she were on stage giving a
performance. How could she uproot herself from the love that
meant everything to her? She called herself 'wild, free and impetuous'. Hers was not an easy nature to control. That season, she
indulged extravagantly in shopping. Queenie was having a dress
from Worth, which she would wear to make her curtsey to the
King in the summer. He too was in Paris, and his presence had
aroused great interest.

∽

Even though Daisy had chosen to join the old crowd, her more
serious interests set her apart. She talked about lives 'bounded on
one side by Worth and Cartier and on the other by King Edward's
Court and Bridge'.[24] Unsatisfying as it might be, she was still part
of that circle, buying her clothes at the most exclusive shops in
Paris. But she felt that she had been lazy long enough, and wanted
to get back to doing things which were important, such as meeting
her Labour friends for stimulating discussions.

John Burns, the Labour activist and MP for Battersea, was
engaged in drafting a bill that would facilitate land transfer – a
subject that was to become increasingly close to the heart of a

landowner such as Lady Warwick. Daisy was to make her own contribution to the Labour Party's manifesto, on their education programme. She returned to London feeling renewed, and could be seen driving her famous equipage of chestnut horses around town. Taking up residence at Brook House, she began inviting groups of young Tories to luncheon each week, a slightly odd gesture given her increasing involvement in left-wing politics. She also entertained every Wednesday evening, and compared her 'salon' to the bygone glories of Lady Palmerston's: 'Literature, politics, art, all come to talk to me. Then the boys and girls dance, and the older frivols play Bridge or billiards. There is dinner for thirty, and we go to bed at 2.30 a.m.!'[25]

As always, Daisy spent Whitsun at Warwick with her husband. That year, Balfour, George Wyndham and other young Tories had been invited, as well as some of her Socialist friends. There would be lively discussion, and plenty of disagreement between political adversaries, but the atmosphere would be cordial. Motoring excursions round Shakespeare country and luncheon with Joseph Chamberlain were on the programme. Some idea of Lady Warwick's status as a reigning beauty can be judged by a paragraph from *The World* sent to her by George Wyndham, and on which she scribbled 'Alas, how little the World knows':

The Beauty of the Day

Who is the greatest beauty of the early part of the twentieth century, is a question which was discussed a little while ago by a number of well-known people. After the claims of many of the most noted women, including Princess Henry of Pless, the Marchioness of Londonderry, and Hon. Mrs George Keppel, Miss Muriel Wilson, and Mrs Langtry had been advanced by their friends, the decision was finally given in favour of the Countess of Warwick. Her beauty, coupled with her charm of manner, her exquisite sympathy allied to bright wit, which is never ill natured, all combine to give her that position which in the old days would have been held by the queen of the tournament, the woman who not only satisfied those who knew her but struck the imagination of those who were only privileged to gaze on her.[26]

George Wyndham and Winston Churchill were two men in her circle who remained platonic friends. Wyndham, Secretary of State for Ireland, was remembered by his niece, Lady Cynthia Asquith (née Charteris), as:

all that a Renaissance Prince could possibly have been – brave, cultured, gifted, and good to look on, a scholar who was modest about his learning, a warrior modest about his courage, an orator and writer almost unaware of his extraordinary command of cadence and vocabulary, and a statesman whose only ambition seemed to be to serve the State.[27]

With her usual energy, Daisy moved frequently between her various houses: 'I motored from Warwick to Easton last Sunday – heavenly – 100 miles in 4 hours, lunched Easton, gardened all afternoon, dined there and motored back to London, through Epping Forest, a lovely summer night . . .'[28]

Harold Peto's redesigning of the gardens at Easton had been completed, and showed why his reputation stood so high. There was now a croquet lawn, bordered by rose pergolas, and new borders which were giving a marvellous show of colour. A superb Italian garden had also been created. The men of the Salvation Army colony had done excellent work.

~

More than six months had passed since Kitty and Joe's marriage. Daisy still perceived Joe's wife as a woman who had shamelessly dragged Joe to the register office, and she thought that he had acquiesced because it would make him appear like a gallant knight who had come to the rescue. It was no good, she told him, trying to appear as a hero, when in reality he was wounding the woman who had been far more important to him for far longer. Despite that, she still clung to her illusion, calling him 'the one glorious best man'.

During the summer of 1903 Nellie Melba was at Covent Garden, and Daisy would often be there. When Madame Melba sang Berg's 'Night' at a gala concert, Daisy had been unable to stop her eyes brimming with tears. She was observed by her old friend, Prince Francis of Teck, who told her that never had he seen more sorrow in a woman's face. Yet her mood could change quickly, if she let her imagination loose. She would dream of a new existence, sailing with Joe in his yacht all over the world. They would go big game hunting and ride horses in deserts, but would naturally not do without deliveries of all the merchandise needed for existence. These probably included food parcels from Fortnum and Mason and even dresses from Worth.

Wild, impossible fantasies. Daisy Warwick had moods when she might wish to escape the constraints of Society, but she was too much of an insider ever to detach herself completely. A certain way of life was all she had ever known, and even her Socialist beliefs never completely changed it.

That summer there was duty to fulfil, taking Queenie on outings with her friends, and on weekend visits, so that she could circulate among eligible men. There was also time to enjoy Maynard, who loved going on nature walks with his mother. She had taken him to his first opera, a big treat: 'He knows all the Carmen music and the story,'[29] she proudly told his father.

Guy would soon be celebrating his twenty-first birthday. Daisy was amused that he condescended to live with her at Brook House that summer, in expectation that she would gather together all her important friends, 'the best worth-knowing great men . . . He arranges all this himself and I obey!' According to his mother, Guy was 'eaten up with ambition', but so far his main achievement had been to leave the Household Brigade with an MVO, giving her 'a nice job with King Edward getting him to realize that Guy did not think his beloved Household Cavalry good enough to remain in!'[30]

Now he had various plans, including a possible secondment as aide-de-camp to Lord Curzon. India might be as mind-expanding as South Africa had been invigorating. He was confident that he could become Colonial Secretary by the time he was thirty. Besides career ambitions, Guy had fallen in love with Elinor Glyn, amusing to his mother and scandalising to Essex.

Daisy meanwhile still held the belief that her own destiny lay with Joe Laycock. Enclosed with her letter inviting him to see her newly designed gardens was a poem, casting herself as the redeemer of a lost soul:

> . . . wistful, content to wait
> To wait, that should you falter on the stair
> And wander into twilight of disgrace,
> She may be with you in that outer place,
> The sadness and the solitude to share;
> The burden of the discipline to bear;
> To woo you to a vision of God's face . . .

But no amount of idealism could change the fact that by this time Joe had written his life's script, and it was irreversible.

Joe had been spending a good deal of time on his yacht *Valhalla* that summer, but once back at Wiseton he received a note by messenger, in which Daisy suggested that they should meet. Joe was irritated and asked her not to write to his home address in future, because it caused scenes with Kitty. Daisy's response was made with customary directness:

The creature who married you in order to hurt me has no place in my thoughts, but as I have had experience of how her temper quells you I certainly should not risk it. Neither have I any desire for secrecy, and if you know me at all you know that only my past great love for you makes me submit in any way to conventionality for your sake . . .[31]

At least, however, she had persuaded Joe to see her before the end of summer.

⋐ 11 ⋑

Reunion

THE COUPLE MET AT Easton, an idyllic place for them. Their mutual attraction was still powerful, and Daisy yielded to Joe. With renewed confidence, she suggested a visit to Paris, where the two of them might relive their earlier life together. Before that, there was a large weekend party at Warwick, and her great friend Violet Granby would be there. Soon afterwards, just when life seemed to be settling down, everything changed, as a terse note explained: 'I am ill and waited on purpose to come to you. I am going to have your baby too. I have to see you.'[1]

When they met, Daisy derived no comfort. As indicated by her next letter, Joe was furious, and made it difficult if not impossible for her:

> As the whole thing seemed to annoy you so much we will not talk or write of it again. I have so little in my life left that to have something of you left with me is something not easily parted with! I am quite heartbroken and in despair about everything . . .
>
> We can never meet again, as you have willed to wreck my life at the expense of another woman . . . You have sacrificed me to her in everything, and yet you told me and tell me, that you love me . . .

You are mine as I am yours, and if you choose to treat me as you do, risk nothing for me, sacrifice nothing for me, probably I am not worth it and probably you are a coward . . .

You tell me to be patient for a summer, an autumn, a winter. Darling, have you ever thought that what it means to me is a whole life and a whole eternity?[2]

Could he be trusted at all, or was he so hard and worldly that he could do nothing for her? She knew the answer, and had probably known it for a while, but could not break the pattern. When Joe turned up at Easton there was tension and recrimination, and the hot afternoon ended angrily when he walked out. In the silence afterwards, Daisy lay sobbing her heart out.

That day was both an end and a beginning. From the autumn, when she had thought they might have been in Paris together, Daisy was very much alone. The summer encounter at Easton had shown that the old attraction could still be reignited, but Joe wanted to run away from any consequence. Once again, he regarded this pregnancy as something for which he was not responsible, and so he distanced himself from her.

Maybe Daisy half wished to forgo passionate love herself. It had been so costly. Yet little of her marriage now remained beyond the formality. Brookie was often away, symbolising the absent emotional tie, and after Queenie's wedding he had arranged to go abroad for six months. By mid-November, rather earlier than usual, Daisy's pregnancy was visible, and gossip was rife in Society about the possible father. The King had heard the rumours, and wrote to say that if they were true he could never see her again; it was an uncharacteristically harsh judgement.

❧

Over the New Year of 1904 Daisy's spirits were low enough to keep her in bed. Joe spent the festive season on the Riviera, where he visited Fitzroy. Daisy's brother, as he wrote to her, had come to the conclusion that she must try and forget:

> he said that he was very miserable about you but that consid-
> ering what people in Society were saying and considering what
> he owed to his wife forsooth! He thought it much better not to
> see you. I asked him if he knew the state you were in and he
> was quite casual about it . . . Darling you must bury him out of
> your thoughts and life . . . he is not worthy of you . . . You
> know how I feel for you but you must be brave . . . [3]

Fitzy's perceptive and dispassionate letter was not one to make easy reading for Daisy. Unable to accept its implications, she chose to ignore it. In her weak and depressed state, it hurt her to be at the centre of rumours. There were days when she simply broke down in tears.

There was one more meeting between the pair, at which a final decision about their future had to be made. Joe felt a duty towards Kitty and their son, who had been born the previous winter. It was impossible for him to break away, flout convention and live openly with another woman, even though he loved Daisy more than his wife. Destiny had conspired against them. There could be no compromise, and it was better not to see each other again. After they had parted, Daisy went straight to Arlington Street, where Violet Granby saw that she was heartbroken.

～

During the remaining months of the winter, Daisy's health gave cause for grave concern. Mental strain and physical weakness combined, and she contemplated suicide, proposing a date in March that would mark her ninth anniversary with Joe. She could derive no comfort from anything, and although she drew back from suicide, the next few months were the bleakest of her life. Yet even at her lowest ebb Daisy had to maintain some structure in her life, something notoriously difficult to do in depression. The main event occupying her mind was Queenie's wedding, and she spent time helping her daughter prepare for the big day.

When Queenie had become engaged to Charlie Helmsley, heir to the Earl of Faversham, her mother had been very pleased. Charlie had been Daisy's favourite as a prospective son-in-law, but she had not attempted to influence her daughter's choice. A Conservative MP at the age of twenty-five, Queenie's future husband was also parliamentary private secretary to the First Lord of the Admiralty.

Palms, lilies and other hothouse flowers decorated St Mary's Church in Warwick, where the wedding took place on 19 January 1904, conducted by the Bishop of Oxford. Six months pregnant, the bride's mother had to appear in a disguising outfit, and chose cream silk, cleverly cut along flowing lines. Queenie made a radiant bride in *peau de soie*, with a long train of Alençon lace, accompanied by fourteen bridesmaids and two pages. A thousand guests had been invited to a reception at the castle, but only two hundred and fifty sat down to a wedding lunch in the Great Hall.

There were hundreds of presents on display, including lots of exquisite jewellery. Daisy and Brookie had given a diamond and turquoise tiara, the King a diamond and ruby brooch. Many other friends had been equally generous. The town was *en fête* with flags, and banners spelt out good wishes to the young couple, who were given a tremendous send-off when they left to catch their train to Staffordshire. Among the crowd were disabled children from Daisy's own foundation. Once arrived in the north, the newly-weds were given an equally warm reception by tenants of Lord Faversham. They were to spend their quiet honeymoon at Ingestre Hall, a Jacobean mansion near Stafford lent by the Earl of Shrewsbury.

Queenie was soon introduced to the gentry at a ball given by Charlie's mother at Duncombe Park, and Lady Helmsley was evidently appreciative of her daughter-in-law: 'Last night she looked lovely in the prettiest white gown with a silvery zone, and wearing *the* turquoise tiara. She was immensely admired, and charmed everyone by her magnetic manner . . . It is a constant delight to me to watch her, and hear her speak! She is blossoming like a rose . . .'[4]

Very soon after the wedding, Daisy suffered a collapse. The doctors were particularly concerned about her heart, and she had no choice but to take Queenie's advice that she should rest. It was during this period that Daisy wrote to Joe one of her most poignant letters, containing words of utter despair:

> In a few weeks more I have to go down to the brink of death to have your child. My darling, if you can remember the hope and courage and joy there was in our Tiny One's birth, you will think now of what *this* means to your Daisy, who loves you as no woman ever loved a man, and whose life you are taking inch by inch by your desertion. My Joe, think . . . of all your tender words, when, after all the suffering of the past, you took me in your arms last summer and all my great love for you killed jealousy and resentment in the passion out of which another child will be born. Will you realize that *we* have this one more tie that makes parting impossible . . . I gladly welcome death which will end a suffering that I cannot bear longer . . . Not death or eternity can kill the love that is yours . . .[5]

As the weeks passed, Daisy gradually found some of her equilibrium and strength restored. Her family and close friends could only offer their loving support. Millie, while hoping that her sister's cup was not quite so bitter, posed the age-old question 'Why do women always lean to the worthless in men?' She also said something about casting away good men, perhaps a hint about Brookie.

Some friends believed that the best support they could give was to write and tell Joe that he must see Daisy. Violet Granby was among them:

I saw *her* today looking very lovely and wonderful – and sad
and good . . . don't *ever* tell her I have written this . . . I would
not for worlds that she should know . . . but, if you feel inclined
– if you yourself feel a little hunger for her society – or if you
feel it would be sweet for her – *don't* because you have come to
an arrangement together *not to meet* refrain from doing so . . .

She is better, a little, in health, but death is so busy just now
– and I was thinking if she were to die when the baby arrives –
I should be sorry not to have just suggested this to you . . .[6]

Joe's reply from White's was a little softer, but he remained essentially unmoved:

Dear Lady Granby

Everything seems very difficult. It is difficult for me to refuse so
small a thing as one hour's talk with her who for years was my
one friend and who through my own fault to a large extent, I
lost . . . It is better that we have no meeting. We couldn't now
agree . . . I have never been considered and I may have got
obstinate and hard but I have been driven to it and attach now
no blame to myself . . . I feel very sad and hurt that things
should have come to this and please tell her so, and how sadly
I think of it all.[7]

He knew that his decision would appear hard, but he must hold
to this course; Daisy was to be told that he had decided to be obstinate. This caused Violet to reply the next morning:

I *can't* believe it!!! Forgive me – but it sounds *so* horrible that
you refuse – no one *in the world*, not even your wife could
object to such a friend of 10 years, as you say – who may die!
seeing you! It binds you to nothing – It does not (to the *world*
even if it should know) show that you have anything to do with
this 'event.'

Your keeping away would accentuate it – not disguise it – I think – But oh surely you will not visit on *her* these friends' cacklings? *She* is not responsible for their vile talkings, and so she at this moment might be soothed and forgiven the worry you may have been having because of her existence.

Please, I entreat you – be gentle and fearless. It is your duty – I cannot see how your heart – or head can let you be so 'obstinate' as you call it. *I say horribly cruel*. Poor little thing – Remember there is really a chance of her dying. That is your excuse, and mine for troubling you. And believe me I swear she will *never* breathe it to anyone but me . . . and for God's Pity sake – let her have just even a *handshake* from you – to let her know you are feeling kindly and gently towards her. *Do. Oh! Do*.[8]

Helena Clarke, Daisy's personal maid, wrote saying she had to 'soothe my lady like a child', and Joe wrote to Elinor Glyn, acknowledging some sadness, wondering if any action of his could do good. He doubted it. He would like to write, he said, if it would be any comfort, but what could he say:

everything is so hopeless and I must just be put down as heartless. I suppose I have most bad qualities . . . but oddly enough do feel . . .

I only write as I do as one longs to communicate with someone who knows, even if they don't see more than one side, probably the right one – It is sad, very sad, and I wish I saw brighter times coming . . .[9]

Mary Hunter also tried her best. Although by no means a sentimental person, she felt disturbed by the depth of Daisy's suffering, and with that incentive urged Joe: 'For Mercy sake see her – it *must* be right – it is too ghastly to leave her as she is – I consider murder would be a less crime and I feel I must use all my influence, persuasions, arguments what you will, to save her from what seems to me absolutely brutal . . .'[10]

Joe was not persuaded, and left England for several weeks as the birth came nearer. Soon after Queenie's wedding, Brookie too had gone abroad as planned, in a deliberate separation from his wife. The King, knowing that Daisy now had neither husband nor lover, wrote a characteristic note, his gruff kindly voice almost audible: 'Do take care of your dear self and get well quickly, then everything will be better again. You *must* come back to us all – your old friends – just as you used to be, your bright brilliant self – and for God's sake get that heartbreaking look out of your eyes.'[11]

Daisy rallied sufficiently to spend some time taking Maynard on outings in London and interviewing no less than twenty prospective governesses for him. A woman from France was already teaching him her language. News from the outside world came from the many politicians who dropped in to Easton Lodge, and sympathy was given by all her stalwart friends, Millie, Violet, Mary, Jennie Cornwallis-West (wife of Randolph Churchill) and Willie Low among them.

Looking ahead to when the baby had been born, she considered going to an International Women's Congress in Berlin. Herr August Bebel, founder of the German Social Democratic Party, would be there along with all the leading Socialists, and she visualised herself among their number. Her chauffeur, Rabett, would motor her to Berlin in the Mercedes. She also dreamed of having a wild time in the German forests with Joe, living on love and strawberries.

The date of her confinement was now very near, prompting Violet to try once again with Joe. Having failed to change his mind, she commented that he was 'Obviously frightened out of his wits . . . Fool!'[12] Violet understood Daisy's experience, and she urged her friend to have courage. Daisy responded:

Violet darling,

Indeed I think it kind and good of you to have written to my Joe, but perhaps he would rather not see me now my outside self is ill and suffering, only it would mean such *comfort* to me . . . I think my friends mean well – but won't forgive him all my sorrow . . . *you* know all that my Joe is to me . . . I long for a sight of his dear face – only as I said before I am perhaps not looking nice enough for him to want to see me, and now I may die without seeing him again, and he has been my *world* for 10 years . . .

Thanks darling for your kindness and your sympathy, *you* understand that Joe is part of myself for ever . . .[13]

On 10 April at Easton Lodge Daisy gave birth to a daughter, to be named Mercy. She looked astonishingly like Joe, with big brown wide-apart eyes, and lay beside her mother 'big and strong and cross'.[14] Queenie received the good news by telegram, and wrote the same day from Nawton Grange, her home in Yorkshire: 'I am *too* delighted that everything has come off so well and that you are feeling alright. I am *so* envious to think that you have another daughter – horrid little thing to put my nose out of joint!!! I am more than jealous of the baby sister.' She reassured her mother that Maynard had not only lost his cough but had gained apple red cheeks in the good Yorkshire air, and was in raptures about the baby, signing herself 'the dislodged Middle One'.[15]

Violet Granby had been away in Italy, but she too had received the news, and while on the train from Verona to Paris, she wrote: 'My darling – I long to come and see your little Easter egg baby, and to know you are glad of it! But perhaps you are too sad. My dear – darling – I do think of you in your quiet misery and *mind* it so.'[16]

~ 12 ~

Comrade Warwick

AFTER MERCY'S BIRTH DAISY recovered well, and soon she was plunging vigorously into an active public life again. The tempo of her political work increased as she took a greater interest in the international dimension of Socialism. Guy had gone to Russia, accompanied by the journalist Maurice Baring, to report on the Russo-Japanese war for Reuters. Daisy's son might be half a world away and the war he was covering of great political interest, but at home life followed its usual course. She had taken Sir John Gorst and his Conservative colleague Sir William Hart Dyke to Bigods, which was flourishing: of particular interest had been a recent experiment using several different manures, which had proved extremely beneficial to the crops.

At a court ball in midsummer, Daisy had encountered Charlie Beresford. Although she had travelled a vast distance intellectually since her association with him, emotionally she was still in turmoil. The rejection she had suffered during the affair with Beresford was as nothing to that which she had experienced with Joe Laycock. Her thoughts turned to Laycock constantly, but he had distanced himself and would never relent. In the early summer, when staying in Paris, Joe and Kitty were involved in a car accident, and so serious were Kitty's injuries that one of her legs had to be amputated. This trauma seems to have had the effect of making the reluctant husband decide that whatever his misgivings, loyalty to Kitty must mean a final break with his old life.

Daisy immersed herself in the cut and thrust of politics almost as a refuge from her unhappiness, and although such a dynamic interest did not entirely remove the pain, it occupied her mind to a large extent. Increasingly it became the focus of her life. In mid-August 1904 she attended the International Socialist Conference in Amsterdam. It was there that she first came into contact with Henry Myers Hyndman, the gentleman revolutionary who had taken on leadership of the Social Democratic Federation, a seminal Marxist party in Britain.

Hyndman was from an upper middle-class family, and after a private education had gone up to Oxford, where many future states-men had been among his friends. Convinced by Socialist theory, his political stance had naturally distanced him from the class into which he had been born. Nevertheless, he was always impeccably dressed, and nothing like the popular picture of a revolutionary. He could well have been taken for a City banker when he stood on his pitch in the Strand selling *Justice*, the Socialist paper.

As far back as 1886 Hyndman had been one of the leaders of major demonstrations against poverty held in Trafalgar Square, in which assorted Marxists, Socialists and Anarchists had taken part, including Bernard Shaw and William Morris. There had been violent clashes with the police, and one particular day had been referred to as 'Bloody Sunday'. Protesters had broken through police cordons, marched up Pall Mall and attacked some of the gentlemen's clubs. This agitation had caused consternation in government circles, and fear that the militant action might undermine the nation's stability. During the following years, the Socialist movement had grown steadily worldwide.

Lady Warwick arrived at the conference in Amsterdam without the credentials of an official delegate. She soon solved the problem by sending her name in to Hyndman. He came out to receive her, saying 'You need not introduce yourself. I know all about you – and you are all right and always welcome to us.' She was flattered when, as she wrote in a long letter to Joe Laycock, Hyndman introduced her to August Bebel as 'a Comrade, working for the children's enlightenment'.[1] Bebel replied, 'I have heard of you. You have courage. God bless you.'

There were other outstanding people from the Socialist International present: French Socialist Jean Jaurès, Frau Liebknecht, wife of the founder of the German Communist Party, and eighty-year-old Sarojini Naidu, awaiting freedom for India. In his memoirs Hyndman recorded that the effect produced by Lady Warwick's appearance was 'almost startling amid the rather sombre surroundings of a Socialist congress',[2] and she soon knew everyone worth knowing at the gathering. Writing after one of the conference sessions, she conveyed her enthusiasm, describing 'This wonderful assemblage of men and women of every nationality, all with one great *creed* of Humanity, all giving their lives to a *cause*, which whether right or wrong, is an inspiration of how characters are formed. You see it in their faces, their eyes, their voices, the great "cult" of the "Brotherhood of Man".'[3]

On the opening day, there was 'a great dramatic coup'. A Japanese delegate spoke in English for an hour, proposing a resolution deploring the war. This was seconded by a Russian who made a speech in French, a gem of oratory. Following the resolution, 'Ten thousand men from all over the world held up their hands in favour and unanimously. The Jap and Russian gripped hands for a moment, and such a roar went up as nearly blew the roof off the great Concert Hall of Amsterdam.'[4]

Some of the delegates were already known to her: founders of the British Labour movement such as Keir Hardie, Pete Curran, Ben Tillett, Dan Irving and Will Thorne were all there. In the evenings she would sometimes go downtown with them to eat in a 'slummy restaurant' which offered basic cuisine: 'a bit of bread, meat and a glass of Pilsner'. Unaccustomed as she was to anything remotely 'slummy' in her usual milieu, Daisy thought it worth accepting, so as to be in on the discussions after each day's conference agenda had been concluded. Comments she made about those occasions show that she was aware of the social distance between herself and her companions: 'I'm rather glad I'm good looking! For it is my best *asset*! And counteracts the excessive handicap of my class!! . . . I really find a pretty hat and a sweet smile opens the doors of even Socialist hearts . . . A very plain "Countess" would, I feel sure, have had to beat a retreat!!'[5]

One evening there was a big open-air meeting, when several of the prominent delegates spoke, and Hyndman recalled how Lady Warwick walked round listening to each of them, taking notes. When she did retreat, it was to the Grand Hotel Amstel. Hyndman was in the habit of subjecting people to a barrage of talk, and owned up to having done so one evening at the hotel. His monologue on Socialist dialectic during and after dinner would have been off-putting to any but the keenest listener – he had no light touch – but Daisy succeeded in interrupting to ask a few pertinent questions and even to raise some objections. She was obviously well-informed, Hyndman thought.

Daisy's first experience of international Socialism had been positive. In her letter to Joe she asserted that there was 'more attraction in helping however little, to right the world's wrongs, than in flirting and racing and gambling, with the sop of blankets and soup, and charity and *heart* and *intellect* counting for very little'.[6] In fact she was underestimating the value of her own charity work, but now she had moved on to a different level. The Socialist movement seemed unstoppable, she felt: the one 'religion' or 'creed' that did not separate into factions, that bound all together of every nationality, 'and therein lies its strength, the hand grip of brothers all over the world'.[7] It was an idealistic view, but at this stage the Socialists' tendency to dissipate into splinter groups was not something of which she was aware.

~

After returning from Amsterdam, Daisy took Maynard to Frinton-on-Sea, where they rode ponies on the sandy beach. While there she received a note from Joe, dismissing her and saying that in the circumstances they must not meet: 'I am sorry if this all seems hard, and if you think I have no feeling . . . it is all very very sad . . . Don't you understand that it is hard for me to write like this?'[8]

It seems that they had spent August Bank Holiday together and talked about their situation; she thought that they had come to an agreement to communicate about their children principally, and occasionally to meet. She begged him to show some kindness, some sympathy, and not to drive her to despair.

Only Daisy was capable of misreading the situation so totally. Joe replied that in future, should there be cause such as serious illness, any communication would be through solicitors.[9] He would not open her letters, and though this decision might seem 'the refinement of brutality', nothing would induce him to change it.

~

Lacking emotional fulfilment and now approaching her mid-forties, Daisy's energies would in future be devoted to politics and to her two young children. She planned to speak in no less than seventy constituencies in support of Labour before the next general election. To begin with, an autumn tour would include Glasgow, Sunderland, Jarrow and Newcastle, then Manchester, Burnley and Accrington. She had a particularly good meeting at Hebburn, where she had gone to speak in support of former Glasgow blacksmith Pete Curran, now one of the leaders of the Gasworkers' Union and a prospective parliamentary candidate. The miners received her enthusiastically. When the vote of thanks was proposed, her reply was: 'I want to come back to Hebburn. I want to stand on this platform with Pete Curran *MP!* and listen to the band.'[10] She had hit the right note and brought down the house, for the local brass band had just won a big competition. Daisy was almost mobbed and could hardly get out. When she finally did she was followed all down the street with shouts of 'Come back soon.'

Her political insight was increasing. She was gaining a feel for the grassroots movement through her accumulating experience at public meetings. Her conviction was growing that the interests of workers could only be advanced and safeguarded by having a strong Labour Party in the House of Commons. Ultimately, only men of the workers' own class could articulate their needs, despite the good intentions of others like herself who were socially distanced from them. The best men in skilled labour were fully able to discuss questions relating to their welfare on any platform. Those honest working people were an inspiration: keen, strenuous and well read. She preferred bread and cheese up in the north with them to luncheons and dinners at the most expensive restaurant in London – although she still managed to participate in both.

One gratifying outcome of this northern tour was a letter from Hyndman, congratulating her for putting 'life and spirit into the disinherited classes', something he felt was an uphill job. The trouble lay, he thought, with the mood of British workers. If they chose to go on giving their votes and their interests to any capitalist party, they would get nothing: 'In class warfare there is no really effective weapon but *fear*.'[11] People who behaved like sheep, he said, could expect to be fleeced. Only when, if ever, they were roused or kicked up to a higher level would the revolution begin. He doubted that it would come in his lifetime, though he did not doubt at all that it *would* come.

That hectic northern tour had taken a lot of her energy, and Daisy chose Aix-les-Bains as the ideal place for a holiday. From there, she wrote a long confessional letter to General Sir John French, inspired by her surroundings: a great lake and the Alps. It was a letter tinged with bitterness: how much more easily, she considered, people get through life when they have no soul. Gazing into the clear lake, with white sand and pebbles visible on the bottom, she was reminded of the nymph Undine, who was happy until she wished to possess a soul: 'What a pity some world-wise well informed person did not enlighten poor Undine, and tell her that of all possessions that of a Soul can most easily be dispensed with . . .'[12]

It was of course a metaphor applicable to her own recent past. Why, she asked, was she being denied the human affection and companionship that every woman needs?

Daisy wrote of her gratitude for the affectionate letter Sir John had written her. He understood her, and took a wide view of life, without mean or paltry thoughts, but he was strong enough to be master of his own destiny, whereas hers had belonged to another: 'The enchanted garden is closed, the years go by, wasted in the hope of that which never comes back.'[13]

~

In November 1904 Daisy Warwick made one of the most important decisions of her life in choosing to join the Social Democratic Federation. Launched by William Morris in 1881, the SDF was not at all interested in a comfortable brand of Socialism. Favouring direct action, it aimed to bring about a revolutionary change in society, in fact the end of capitalism. Her choice of the SDF may have had a good deal to do with H.M. Hyndman, its urbane leader. It also showed that Lady Warwick was not a person to be content with half measures. She plunged into the organisation with zeal, and during the first two years took on an enormous number of public-speaking engagements. One of the first with which she showed her credentials was on 10 December 1904 when she went to speak at a meeting of the Gasworkers' Union in Canning Town, in the depths of London's East End. She often entertained several hundred members of the SDF at Easton, where

Hyndman vividly remembered her distinctive figure crossing the lawn to meet the guests on perfect summer days.

In January 1905, after staying with Charlie Helmsley and Queenie in Yorkshire, Daisy left early one morning and travelled to Grimsby in bitterly cold weather to speak for an Independent Labour Party candidate. Hyndman had the measure of Comrade Warwick and was full of praise, writing of her to Gaylord Wilshire, the American millionaire Socialist: 'She is a beautiful, charming and generous woman filled, I believe, with genuine enthusiasm, and she can do an enormous amount of good, is doing it now in fact.'[14]

However, it was not long before her good intentions proved controversial. On the eve of the Opening of Parliament, 14 February, Daisy gave a dinner party at Easton Lodge for trades unionists, Socialist MPs and prospective Labour candidates. It was evidently not the kind of event approved of by some members of the Independent Labour Party, Labour's radical wing. Although the evening had ended with the singing of revolutionary songs, including 'The Red Flag', she came in for scathing criticism. It was hardly a crime to give a party, but all the same a hostile article appeared in the *Labour Leader*: 'Do they realize that it [Socialism] is to us a religion, and that the parading of wealth or vanity or even sympathy – is hardly less to some of us than blasphemy?'[15]

At the State Opening that year, Daisy, wearing her emeralds, was the most conspicuous woman listening to the speech from the throne. The same month, an announcement was made that Lady Warwick and Mrs Bridges Adams (co-hostess of that Easton dinner) would tour the country in Daisy's luxury car, specially painted red. They would be visiting all seventy constituencies that were putting up a Socialist candidate, and they would also be campaigning for free school meals. But even this dedication was provocative to the *Labour Leader*, which thought that 'Socialism and starving children are to be made the occasion of a Countess' holiday.'[16]

Perhaps a flamboyant red Wolseley was too much for the sober-minded, but no one could deny that Daisy Warwick reached out to all strands of the Socialist movement. Differences of emphasis seemed less important to her than the overriding principles which all held in common. The unforgiving *Labour Leader* article must nevertheless have opened her eyes to the fact that Socialists could be as intolerant as anybody else.

Yet if comradeship was sometimes forgotten, Hyndman's support did not waver. As he told Wilshire: 'That her preaching of Socialism, which becomes more and more definite, not to say passionate, every day is doing us an immense amount of good can not be disputed . . . People would come to see and hear her who would never come to see or hear you or me.'[17] In a country where rank was important, a Countess was a great prize to have gained, and he was determined that the SDF should keep her. She was the star attraction at their meetings, which were currently drawing large numbers. There had been an occasion 'on a frightful night' when the Memorial Hall had been packed with over two thousand people, most of them from the well-to-do class. It was crucial, in his opinion, to convert the rich and educated classes in Britain to Socialism, rather than concentrating exclusively on the proletariat. His reasoning was based on a blunt assessment of English workers *en masse*, whom he had described a few years earlier as 'ignorant, conceited, apathetic, addicted to gambling and drink, and for the most part indifferent to their own welfare'.[18] If even a few of the well-educated people in Great Britain could be converted to the revolutionary Social Democratic movement, it would be a great advance.

Daisy was equally full of praise for Hyndman, regarding him as *the* great Socialist, and she had no doubt that his ability ensured him a brilliant political future, perhaps even as the first Socialist Prime Minister. He tended to agree.

∾

Daisy with her beloved son, Maynard, who was born in March 1898.

(*Above left*) Maynard Greville, Daisy's son by Joe Laycock. He had his mother's blue eyes and blonde hair, and quickly became the centre of her world.

(*Above right*) Maynard at Easton Lodge, demonstrating his early love of horses.

Maynard takes the reins, surrounded by the menagerie at Easton Lodge.

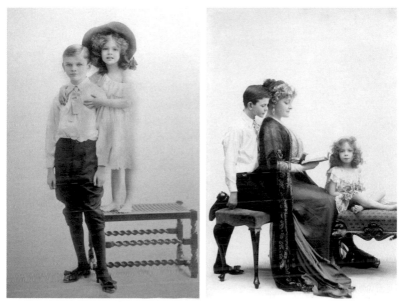

(*Above left*) Maynard and Mercy.

(*Above right*) Daisy with Maynard and Mercy, her daughter by Joe Laycock who was born in 1904 when Daisy was 42.

Maynard posing at the wheel of the family's first automobile at Easton Lodge.

(*Above left*) Frank Harris, the louche Irish writer who offered to help Daisy write her memoirs – and sell her love letters from Edward VII for a large sum.

(*Above right*) Maynard in adulthood; he was to inherit Easton Lodge after Daisy's death in 1938.

'Brookie', now the Earl of Warwick, who remained touchingly loyal to his wife to the end of his life, despite her infidelities.

Mercy, Daisy's youngest daughter (far right) in an amateur play; it was to further her acting career that she met the distinguished theatrical producer Basil Dean – later to become her husband.

After divorcing his wife, Basil Dean married Mercy at Strand registry office in July 1925. The Countess of Warwick (on Basil's left) does not look very happy about the marriage.

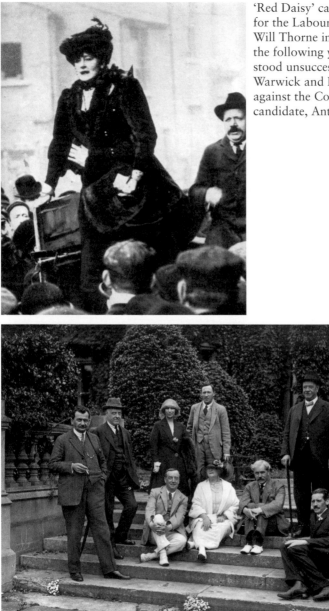

'Red Daisy' campaigning for the Labour candidate Will Thorne in 1923; the following year Daisy stood unsuccessfully for Warwick and Leamington against the Conservative candidate, Anthony Eden.

The Socialist Countess; Daisy with members of the Labour Party at Easton Lodge in June 1923. Leader of the party, Ramsay Macdonald, is sitting on Daisy's left.

Easton Lodge after the disastrous fire in 1918; it cost £30,000 to repair the damage.

Daisy at Easton Lodge in the 1930s, with her herd of retired circus ponies.

In the gardens of Easton Lodge in 1937, with her granddaughter Tessa, Mercy and Basil's child. (Reproduced by kind permission of Jane Clargo.)

Daisy at Easton Lodge near the end of her life; she was chairman of the Essex branch of the RSPCA.

For some time Daisy had been thinking about the problem of how to help the thousands of children who regularly went hungry. The report of the Duke of Devonshire's Committee on Physical Deterioration, published in July 1904, had contained evidence that malnutrition was widespread. In September, a meeting of the Trades Union Congress in Leeds had unanimously passed a resolution demanding at least one free meal a day for children attending State-supported schools, while at a conference which followed, held in London's Guildhall, delegates supported the SDF policy of full State maintenance for deprived children. The campaign to 'Feed the Children' was widely supported: some Liberals and some Conservatives allied themselves on the issue with trades unionists and the SDF.

One of the campaign's leaders was Sir John Gorst, who had been one of Daisy's strongest supporters in her work for children. Several mass meetings were held to maintain momentum, at which Daisy was one of the principal speakers, and in March 1905 Gorst, Dr T.J. Macnamara MP, and Dr Hutchinson of Great Ormond Street Children's Hospital went with her on an unannounced visit to the Johanna Street Council School in North Lambeth. The situation there provided excellent publicity: in Standard One, twenty boys had been told not to go home to dinner because there was no food; sixteen had been given breakfast by a private charity; two had not had any food at all. In Standard Two, Dr Hutchinson found, forty-five boys were suffering from habitual under-feeding, six had not breakfasted, and thirty-four would not be getting a meal at home.

The visitors went hot-foot to the Lambeth Board of Guardians, where Gorst put the case that those starving children should be fed immediately. Immediate relief had to wait while the Guardians passed their resolution in favour and drew up their report, which was forwarded to the London County Council and then to the Board of Education. Bureaucracy never moves with lightning speed, but it did act without long delay. After two months, education authorities were empowered to apply to the Poor Law Guardians to feed the children.

It was a step forward, but though it represented some advance, it did not go nearly far enough for Lady Warwick. For one thing, she did not like the involvement of Poor Law Guardians, believing that the taint of pauperism would stick. In an article carried by the *Fortnightly Review* in March 1906, she was to state forthrightly the case for taking seriously the cause of deprived children: 'One looks wistfully for a general recognition of the fact that it is exactly the poorly fed, ill clad, and therefore imperfectly educated children of today who become the ignorant, stupid, slovenly parents of tomorrow.'[19] She firmly believed that children should receive full-time education till the age of sixteen, and condemned the use of children as workers.

The great commitment Daisy had given to the 'Feed the Children' campaign was to achieve results, and she could take credit for the success. Although not alone, she had been one of the prime movers, and had done a great deal to sustain the movement. Largely thanks to her publicity value, the issue had been discussed in the press, and awareness raised all round. The Liberal government that came to office after the 1906 election, headed by Sir Henry Campbell-Bannerman, was to take action to initiate the first provision of free school meals, as well as medical inspections of schoolchildren.

~

In March 1905 Comrade Warwick went on a tour of Lancashire's cotton towns, where she visited mills that still employed some child labour. Three thousand weavers and spinners attended the meeting at Accrington. Burnley and Blackburn were also on her itinerary, followed by Swinton's miners. After one day's rest, spent at Warwick, she was again travelling north, this time to Sheffield, where she took the chair at a great Labour and Socialist meeting held at the Empire Theatre.

Lady Warwick's attendance at such meetings attracted considerable press attention, but this focused rather more on her personality than the political issues. While admitting her sincerity, reporters found it hard to believe that an aristocrat could have dedicated herself to the Socialist cause. Daisy brought distinctive glamour to the campaigns, and the press got good copy. Although many fellow Socialists knew her value to them, however, her platform appearance in stylish, expensive clothes was enough to make some diehards suspicious and even antagonistic. Being an aristocrat through and through, she wisely never pretended to be one of the proletariat. Neither was she one of the plain-living intellectuals who espoused Socialism. Members of the Independent Labour Party, influenced by their Nonconformist upbringing, nevertheless censured her in the manner of somewhat puritanical chapel-going folk. Hyndman told Gaylord Wilshire that both Keir Hardie and Ramsay MacDonald had written letters to Lady Warwick which he would have hesitated to send to a discharged housemaid.

After committing herself to a heavy programme of political meetings throughout the winter, Daisy was back at Easton for Mercy's first birthday in mid-April. Much of the bitterness surrounding her birth had seemingly been forgotten, and the little girl was already showing herself to be a character. After this brief spell at home, there was a holiday in Paris, which Daisy always found refreshing. From the Hotel Vendôme, she sallied out to enjoy a private view of art objects and gems at the Petit Palais. She also met fellow Socialists, politicians and literary people. It was, she said, a wonderfully instructive time.

Towards the end of April, she was with Hyndman in Northampton for an SDF conference, and made a speech that came from the heart:

Up and down the country I have gone in the cause of children, and everywhere I see that Socialism lies at the bottom of the salvation of our country. Those whom you and I meet very often, those who occupy the seats of power in the government of this country may jeer at us, but Labour will win. In Northampton you have thought that salvation lay in advanced Radicalism. I know that phase of thought well, because I myself have passed through it.

Does it much matter if a Liberal government or a Tory government is in power? I am quite sure that all in this room have come here knowing that there is only one way out for the workers of this country . . . I feel personally that I owe no apology for having joined an organization which, whatever may have been its faults, has always been known for its strict adherence to principle.[20]

She claimed to be no stranger to her audience, having spent some of her childhood at Passenham, the Maynard estate near Stony Stratford. She was speaking to them not just as a Socialist, but as the owner of no less than three thousand acres in Northamptonshire. Until the law of entail was abolished she had to accept her role, but she made it clear to her audience that she did not wish to be a landowner. The capitalist press, she said, had made great fun of her, drawing attention to her clothes and her red motor car. The said car was on offer to any genuine Socialist candidate, and she felt that at the next election it would show itself to be speedier than the blue or yellow cars of Tories or Liberals.

The climax of her speech was a brief utopian vision, just the kind of rash statement that her critics held against her: 'Slowly the earth's disinherited are awakening. The storm is gathering, but the storm will pass, and the rainbow of Socialism will encircle the globe with its message of peace and plenty and happiness.'[21]

Hastening away from the meeting late at night, Comrade Warwick availed herself of a special train. Hyndman did not regard such action as a good advertisement for Socialism, but like everyone else he had to accept her idiosyncrasies. It is only fair to add that her own record states that she made the long return journey by public transport.

Despite the fact that they genuinely admired each other, the relationship between Daisy and Hyndman was not always smooth. There was almost bound to be friction between two such strong personalities. By nature outspoken, he knew that care was needed so as not to antagonise her, and she too wanted to maintain a cordial atmosphere. Gaylord Wilshire had expressed doubts about Lady Warwick's durability, but Hyndman had no fears on that score, telling him that she was 'exceedingly plucky, and adventurous and generous'.[22] With those qualities, he believed she would stay the course, her only drawback being, as he saw it, that she rushed her fences. Generous she certainly was, and during the spring she offered the SDF a professional organiser, whose salary she was prepared to pay for six months.

Now that she was working in a much more influential sphere Daisy felt her position as a Poor Law Guardian to be superfluous, and sent in her resignation letter. In the autumn she joined Sir John Gorst again at Hanley, a town in the Potteries, to speak about children's welfare. Soon after that September meeting, she took herself and Maynard off to Paris, where part of her time was spent visiting municipal schools and workshops for the unemployed. All such first-hand knowledge would come in useful for subsequent winter lectures. Daisy enjoyed a reunion with Jaurès, and a luncheon with Clemenceau and other members of the government in France. She called them 'stodgy', but her old friend, Frank Bertie, now at the British Embassy, and with whom she went to the theatre one night, was a delightful companion.

～

Dasiy's first year as a member of the SDF had been full of experience, and it had extended her. However, apart from fulfilling speaking engagements, her time was spent in much the same activities as before her conversion: entertaining and hunting. Her links with the court circle were unbroken. Although many of her friends would consider the embrace of Socialism eccentric, maybe even a little mad, very few dropped her. Margot Asquith was credited with having first called her Comrade Warwick. Some people thought that her Ladyship had been motivated by boredom, and considered her latest enthusiasm just a novelty. And as if to emphasise that her life was very much as before, in November a large shooting party was held at Easton. The guns included the Duc d'Albe, Prince Francis of Teck (Mercy's godfather) and the Count Benckendorff, Russian ambassador at the court of St James.

Two members of the family were about to go abroad. Guy was sailing for India, where he was to spend six months on Douglas Haig's staff, and afterwards would travel in other parts of Asia. Brookie was going to spend four months in East Africa, visiting Kenya and Uganda for shooting and also in order to pursue a possible timber concession, about which he was optimistic. Brookie was ever the optimist about business ventures, but he did not have the Midas touch. Like many other landowners of the time, he had realised the need for additional income to make up the shortfall as agricultural rents dwindled, and all the better if a business opportunity could be pursued in some exotic location. As far back as 1887, he had travelled to Mexico in association with Moreton Frewen to investigate a 'gold crushing' machine for use in a remote Mexican mine. The undertaking had been a disaster from beginning to end: conditions had been rough, and weeks of manual labour had only showed how profitless the new-fangled machine actually was. Much worse, Brookie had failed to seize his opportunity to acquire the mine, which was later valued at £1 million.

On the East Africa expedition Brookie's party discovered a timber forest on the slopes of Mount Kenya, later valued by experts at the Colonial Office at £20 million. Great disappointment followed for Brookie when he returned to London. The government was unwilling to grant the concession on terms that made it possible for him to raise the finance necessary for development. It was typical bad luck, which he accepted with his usual grace.

While her husband was away, trying to make their fortune, Daisy spent the winter with her two young children. Queenie and Charlie with their baby son would join her for Christmas. Fitzy had at last found a pretty wife, nice and gentle, who won Daisy's approval when she entertained the couple at Easton for a few days. They lived happily at Eze until Fitzroy died in 1914.

~

By the winter of 1905 the Conservative government was in disarray, and it was obvious that a general election could not be far off. Hyndman and Daisy believed that the Socialists could well gain a great many seats, enough to make them a significant force. Optimism ran high that a widespread change in society was imminent. The trigger for this scenario was the expected fall of the Tory government. Balfour in fact resigned on 4 December, Campbell-Bannerman took office the following day, and the election campaign started soon afterwards. The SDF needed their star attraction, and naturally she was ready to serve whenever and wherever they called on her. Hyndman himself was their candidate at Burnley, which would be his second attempt in the constituency. Daisy found herself paying several visits, along with other leading Socialists who were making a concerted effort to secure Hyndman's election, among them Bernard Shaw and Robert Blatchford.

On 11 January, the day before polling, she made an all-out effort for Will Thorne, the Gasworkers' Union activist who was standing as Labour candidate in West Ham South. The first meeting Lady Warwick addressed on that eve-of-poll day was held at the dock gates near the Customs House. The platform was a wagon, on to which she climbed up steps of stacked ginger beer boxes. There was a crowd of about two hundred dockers, to whom she made a speech with all the power she could muster, though she admitted afterwards to having been nervous. They must have thought her like a figure from another planet. The *Daily Express* reporter summed up the scene: 'One glance at the beautiful Countess sitting on the kitchen chair in the potato cart made Socialists of all the waverers. They needed no invitation to step up closer. They closed round the cart, and whichever way the lovely Countess smiled she found a sea of admiring faces.'[23]

She made a second speech from the steps of Thorne's committee rooms in the Barking Road, where a huge crowd had gathered that included many children. The crowd was large enough to obstruct the traffic, and unfortunately the police arrived to break up the meeting on that account. All told, it had been 'an interesting and extraordinary experience' for Lady Warwick, and the hungry-looking, ragged children had wrenched her heart. When she mentioned them to Thorne, he told her that there were thousands more all over the East End. Seeing them for herself must have confirmed, if any confirmation were needed, that the work she was doing was of the utmost importance.

The climax of the campaign must have been exhausting. On the last day, she was due in Northampton to endorse two SDF candidates, Jack Williams and James Gribble. Would the results prove all the effort worthwhile?

Polling started on 12 January 1906, but the results took several days to come in. When they did, it was a landslide Liberal victory. The SDF had not won a single seat. However, Labour had gained fifty-four seats, including West Ham South where Thorne had been elected. Although far short of total victory, it was a crucial change in the political landscape, with significant Labour representation in the House of Commons for the first time. The Conservative and Liberal parties no longer had the field to themselves.

Apart from her tireless endorsement of left-wing candidates, Daisy had also made a modest contribution to funds, amounting to £500, for which she had sold a few diamonds. Gaylord Wilshire

released a private letter of hers to the American press, and unfortunately the British papers took it up. It was not the kind of
publicity that either she or the Socialist movement wanted, but the
record was put straight when the *Daily Chronicle* sent a reporter
to interview her Ladyship. Men and women were making far
greater sacrifices for the cause than she had ever done, the reporter
was told, and he was kind when writing up his piece: 'It is clear
that Lady Warwick regards the sale of her jewels as the least of the
sacrifices she has made for Socialism.'[24]

During the interview she had expressed the opinion that in the
conventional world a left-wing philosophy was still regarded as
dangerous in Britain: the word Socialism could not be spoken in
the universities or drawing rooms, whereas in other countries men
of all classes were found in the ranks of Socialists. Reflecting on
the election several months later, she felt in contrast that on the
whole there were grounds for optimism that the Labour Party
would become the major force working for Socialism in Britain.

But her commitment to Socialism in general, and to the SDF in
particular, had not been popular within her family. Guy, a conventional man, thought his mother's ideas idiotic. Queenie's
husband, Charlie Helmsley, was an ambitious Tory MP, the
member for Malton and Thirsk. His mother-in-law's politics, with
all the attendant publicity, cannot have been something that he or
Queenie found easy to accept. Brookie, on the other hand, with
the utmost tolerance gave his wife complete freedom. He helped
to entertain the Socialists his wife invited to Warwick Castle, and
they found him charming. But he too, by nature and tradition,
stood for everything opposed to Socialism.

✺ 13 ✺

The King is Dead

B EFORE THE 1906 ELECTION, Daisy Warwick had given more than a year of sustained effort to politics, and her contribution had been of value. During that period she had given little thought to her personal finances. With the benefit of a vast income, there had seemed to be no need to question expenditure, but her previous financial security was no longer something to be taken for granted. There was a reckoning to be made. In 1907, after years of extravagance, debts were piling up.

One of her most pressing creditors was Sir John Willoughby Bt., one of Jameson's raiders, from whom she had borrowed several thousand pounds. Willoughby had been a close friend of Daisy since the early days of her married life, but although he must often have enjoyed her hospitality, their friendship did not now deter him from insisting on repayment. Having failed to persuade her, he resorted to legal action and, under a writ of execution, the Sheriff of Essex seized property from Easton Lodge.

This humiliation was not something the chatelaine could tolerate, and that it was done at the behest of an old friend made it all the more bitter. But, apart from her personal feelings, Daisy had grounds for contesting Willoughby's action. By the terms of her grandfather's will, the Easton estate, including portable property such as china, silver and linen, was all entailed. Therefore, after the Sheriff's seizure, the estate trustees immediately claimed the confiscated goods. A complicated lawsuit, unwelcome to both sides, seemed to be looming.

An out of court settlement was eventually reached, by the terms of which Willoughby was repaid substantially from the sale of certain articles, and the trustees were able to buy back some others. At least the matter had been settled in a dignified way without publicity, but the position was dangerous, and there was a pressing need for financial retrenchment.

Daisy and Brookie realised that their continuing outlay for Bigods School was beyond their means. For some time, Essex County Council had been giving signals of its unwillingness to continue supporting the school, and it was becoming a financial burden. Lord Warwick wrote a letter to the chairman of Essex County Council, supporting his wife's sterling work but also mentioning 'the want of cordial support'[1] from the board, which had not helped the school's progress as it had deserved. Although the chairman replied that no one in the county undervalued Lady Warwick's zeal and insight, there was no mention of restoring the county grant. When urged by Sir John Medd, the rural educationalist, to keep Bigods going, Essex Council did not respond, and the decision was taken to close the school in August. A dismal sale of excellent equipment followed, and the children's carefully cultivated plots soon became overgrown.

The venture had been the realisation of an ideal, and the thought which had gone into creating it mattered every bit as much as the money invested. It was therefore deeply disappointing to the founder that her unique establishment could just disappear, leaving Dunmow without a secondary school. Three years after the closure, Daisy wrote to Professor Meldola lamenting the state of education in rural Essex. Many former pupils of Bigods acknowledged the benefits they had derived from their education, which had paved the way for successful careers.

By the 1920s, the need for secondary education had been acknowledged, whereupon the Essex County Council chairman wrote: 'If only we had your school now. You were twenty years too soon.'[2]

The agricultural college at Studley Castle, also very expensive to maintain, was, however, saved by Daisy's timely intervention. As the minutes of a meeting recorded: 'Lady Warwick stated that she did not think it desirable that the College should any longer remain a comparatively private matter of her own . . .'[3] A board of trustees and management was set up to administer the establishment, which from then on ceased to be her responsibility.

~

In September 1907, Daisy sailed for New York on the Cunard liner *Campania*. Attempting to escape attention from the press, she travelled as 'Mrs Greville', which fooled no one. While in New York she intended to enquire about some wonderful business opportunity. With creditors pressing, she certainly needed something lucrative, although in a letter to Joe Laycock, written on board, she did not explain further what the possible business might be.

Days of enforced rest at sea brought on a reflective mood. In a recent conversation with the King, he had talked intimately about his own life and said that he was feeling old. Referring to the way that Daisy had broken off their old intimacy, he was reconciled: 'Time softens things,' he had said. For Daisy, however, time had not done much healing in respect of Joe Laycock, and it never would.

Despite her money worries, Daisy was naturally travelling first class on a luxury liner, and the captain, whom she thought to be in love with her, ensured that she enjoyed the best service. When the *Campania* reached New York, there was a huge crowd of reporters waiting at the dockside, but after hiding in the captain's cabin for a while 'Mrs Greville' allowed herself to be escorted ashore and driven to the Webster Hotel. News of the Countess' arrival precipitated many invitations, and it was all very flattering, even if she did decline most of them. Her name had appeared in the American press so frequently that she was treated as a celebrity: on the far side of the Atlantic newspapers did not hide stories about her connections with the Prince of Wales and her other lovers.

From New York, Daisy moved on to Virginia, to stay with friends there. It is unlikely that the anticipated wonderful business materialised – she was no luckier than Brookie in financial matters.

However, Daisy usually had some scheme in mind, and once back in England, she began thinking about launching a Socialist newspaper. Why should the capitalist press go unchallenged? In her view, the distortions published by those newspapers amounted to a crime, and the only way to get even was to offer an alternative. What she had in mind was a periodical, which might be called 'The Outspoken Review', estimating that it would cost £50,000 to launch. Not having much idea of the newspaper business and its complex financial structure, she envisaged that her periodical would have sufficiently high circulation figures to dispense with capitalist advertisers. That much was clear, but far less clear was how it would be financed.

Until the middle years of her life, there had been no need for Daisy to understand money or to have anything personally to do with financial markets. Her bankers had done the work, while she had simply used her fortune to provide herself and her guests with every luxury. At an earlier stage in life she might well have been able to raise the capital, but now of course that was impossible.

Then came what seemed like an answer. Several publishers made very tempting offers for her memoirs. They mentioned sums of money which sounded fabulous, and would mean that the Socialist review could be launched. For the past twenty-five years she had known most of the prominent men in Britain, some of them intimately, and had heard many secrets. If she was willing to break the conspiracy of silence that prevailed, it would be easy to produce an autobiography full of indiscreet revelations. However, she resisted the temptation, mainly because of the difficulty in writing about close friends, including the King, who were still alive. What she had to gain had to be offset against the reaction to such a volume in Society, which would probably close its doors against her for ever.

What alternative way could she legitimately raise a lot of money? The answer appeared to come when, in 1909, she was introduced to Ernest Terah Hooley. A land speculator and stock market manipulator, Hooley had become a millionaire by the age of thirty-five. He had also become a friend of the Prince of Wales, and was about to receive a baronetcy in 1898 when he went bankrupt. By the time Hooley met Daisy he had fallen from a great height, in fact from something approaching £100,000 a year. Now, with much more modest wealth, but still wheeling and dealing, he found an easy dupe in the impulsive Countess.

Apparently offering the answer to her money worries, he told her that all she had to do was invest in one of his companies. If she took out £50,000 worth of shares, her expected return could well be double that amount. No money upfront was required, just her signature on bills of exchange. On presentation of those bills for settlement, not only would payment be no problem, she would have made a clear £50,000 profit. It was so enticing, and Hooley was a past master at the plausible fast talking that now mesmerised another victim. Without reference to her solicitors, bankers or trustees, Daisy signed. It all seemed so easy. In fact she had signed bills which represented Hooley's debts to various third parties, and in due course, when the bills came in, the folly of her action became all too apparent. Far from enjoying a bonanza from the shares, they were worthless. But the face value of the bills had not altered; she had acquired further massive debt, and creditors would pursue her ruthlessly. Daisy had behaved rashly, and blamed herself for having been duped, even though Hooley had not only been accepted but lionised in Society before his bankruptcy.

William Carter, a Dorset landowner, was one of those creditors, and he sued Lady Warwick in the High Court for non-payment of bills of exchange worth £10,000. Hooley, with previous courtroom experience, was co-defendant for a further £5,000. The following year, Hooley was prosecuted in another case and found guilty of irregular business methods; when he was sentenced to a term of imprisonment, the only surprise was how long he had managed to evade conviction.

Following this debacle, Daisy was involved in three years of litigation, harassed by creditors. As a first step towards redeeming her position, she decided to sell some land. Twenty-eight lots in all were sold, including a plot of twenty acres in Dunmow, but the total sum realised was only £3,132, nothing like the amount she needed to pay off those crushing debts or even to reduce them significantly. The dream of launching her 'Outspoken Review' had to be abandoned, and there was never any question of reviving the idea.

Daisy's personal annual income was now much reduced, to around £10,000 a year, and the attempts she made to increase it seemed doomed. Twenty thousand shares she had bought on the American money market, from which she had expected a profit of $80,000, had yielded nothing as yet; the US market had not been flourishing recently. Yet somehow, despite the enormous stress of her financial position, she managed to stay afloat without appearing to alter her lifestyle. Daisy had an aristocratic contempt for creditors and was eternally optimistic. But over the next few years, the crisis would deepen.

❧

While managing to sustain a more or less cordial relationship with H.M. Hyndman, Daisy was also capable of being on good terms with people whose views did not in the least chime in with hers. Ralph Blumenfeld, American-born editor of the *Daily Express*, was certainly not on her political wavelength. Yet when he came to live at Little Easton their friendship flourished, despite many ideological arguments. Daisy enjoyed sparring with Blumenfeld, who had founded the Anti-Socialist League, and whose views were mirrored so perfectly in the *Express*. When he invited her to submit an article for the paper, he was carrying out its policy of giving a platform to the opposition, and as a celebrity contributor, Lady Warwick had value. Controversy, the life-blood of popular papers, did not come much stronger. When she sent in her first piece, a covering letter made her point: 'although you may think my pen is dipped in strong ink, yet you will admit that our provocation from the Daily Express has been and is great . . .'[4]

So it would always be. But her articles continued, and many were the luncheons at Easton when Daisy Warwick tried to convert Ralph Blumenfeld. Many of her articles were in fact written by S.L. Bensusan, as Daisy lacked the necessary discipline for sustained work. A successful freelance journalist, Samuel Bensusan was a useful channel through which to express and polish her ideas, and he earned a percentage of the fees. His all-round career was successful enough to enable him to move into a fifteenth-century manor house on the Easton estate.

However, a short but well-written biography of William Morris published in 1910 was very largely Lady Warwick's own work. Morris, the Utopian Socialist, was a man with whose ideas she completely identified. Although the treatment she gave her subject was somewhat over-romantic, she made a creditable attempt to portray Morris as artist, politician and individualist. She had written her study 'in the hope that his life may be an illuminating picture of what mankind might attain to if environment were only more rationally considered'.[5] One unattractive side of Morris' character was, however, omitted, namely his tendency to dominate meetings, when he would ring a handbell to drown out dissenting voices. The book was dedicated to Conrad Noel, a Christian Socialist priest in whose career Daisy was about to play an important role.

~

On 6 May 1910, the King died. Bells tolled, and Britain was plunged into mourning for a monarch who had been much loved. A stark announcement hung on the railings of Buckingham Palace simply read: 'The King is dead.' Readers of *The Times* were given an obituary fulsome with sorrow and praise:

> King Edward VII is no more. After an illness which was not known even in London to the public until six o'clock on Thursday evening, and which was not pronounced to be grave until yesterday, he died last night a little before midnight. The loss of a ruler so respected and so beloved would have been heavy in any circumstances. The suddenness with which it has fallen upon us makes it the more overpowering to us all . . . To the last he had shown the courage of his royal race . . .
>
> It was his sincere devotion to the cause of peace and his labours in its behalf which did most to secure for him the high place he held in the good opinion of foreign peoples, as indeed they added very greatly to the love his subjects bore him . . . They loved him for his honesty and for his kindly courtesy to all. He was to them not merely every inch a king but every inch an English king, and an English gentleman. He returned their love, his patriotism as steady and ardent as their own.[6]

The King had been prevented by his last illness from meeting Queen Alexandra on her return from abroad, but she had been at his bedside. What *The Times* did not mention was her generosity in inviting Mrs Keppel to join her vigil.

Large crowds stood outside the Palace participating in the drama, and the widowed Queen asked the Salvation Army band to play hymns in the Palace forecourt. Substantial congregations gathered for commemorative services at many London churches, and the Bishop of London, preaching at St Paul's, pronounced that nothing could have been 'more Christian' than the King's passing: few men had been able to maintain the perfect dignity of kingship as he had done. Later, preaching from the same pulpit, Canon Scott-Holland said that King Edward had fitted his post like a glove: 'By his happy nature, by spontaneous manhood, by being himself abroad, he broke down obstacles and prejudices, inspired confidence . . . In all political and social matters his life was almost faultless.'[7]

The Times printed messages of sympathy and appreciation from every quarter of the globe, although the poet and explorer Wilfred Scawen Blunt noted in his diary that many eulogies made the late King sound like a combination of Solon the lawgiver and St Francis of Assisi. All the traditional ceremonies took place, beginning with the King's lying in state in St George's Hall, and the funeral at Windsor on 20 May was conducted with fitting pageantry. Some of the usual events in the summer social season were cancelled, and ladies dressed in black for Ascot.

Daisy Warwick had more reason than most to reflect on the life that had been so closely entwined with her own; although those glorious years now seemed remote, she remembered his love with pride and affection. But there was a strong sense that King Edward's death signified – in a way that was no less potent for being difficult to articulate – the end of an era.

ᘒ 14 ᘒ

Christians and Socialists

CONRAD LE DESPENSER RODEN NOEL was born into an aristocratic family in 1869, his father being a younger son of the
Earl of Gainsborough. Like several other well-connected men of
his day who experienced a degree of guilt about their own privi-
lege, he had felt called to the priesthood. While a student at
theological college, he had spent some time living in a doss house
in order to experience what real poverty was like. Pinned to the
walls of his student rooms had been the slogans 'Property is
robbery' and 'All things should be held in common'. Noel's passionate concern for social justice was to be the mainspring of his
ministry, and after his ordination in 1894, he joined Father
Stewart Headlam's Guild of St Matthew, a group of like-minded
clergy. Given the prevailing mood of the Anglican Church at that
time, his clearly stated and uncompromising political views had
made him unacceptable in many an average parish. Not only were
politics a stumbling block, so too was the Anglo-Catholic ritual he
favoured.

Conrad Noel's interpretation of the Christian faith came first
and foremost from his reading of the Gospels. He called his belief
'Sacramental Socialism', a creed by which he believed the early

185

first-century Christians had lived. F.D. Maurice, one of the most rigorous theologians among Christian Socialists, had been a strong influence on the movement as it had developed in the generation to which Noel belonged. If the Kingdom of God meant anything, it was to be established here on earth, in the material as well as the spiritual sense. Christianity was not to be seen as a consoling idea, promising a better life hereafter to those crushed by a wicked social system. It must be the inspiration for equality of opportunity and a sharing of wealth. Noel believed this new dispensation was clearly described in the New Testament, but that throughout its two-thousand-year history the Church had moved further and further away from the ideal.

Despite his good character, Noel had spent fourteen years as a curate, facing one refusal after another in searching for a parish of his own. It was this man of deep faith and prophetic voice that Daisy Warwick chose in 1910 as Rector of St Lawrence's, a large fourteenth-century church at Thaxted, close to the Suffolk border. Conrad's ideals were entirely in tune with hers, and she was delighted to bestow the living on him. Not only did she look forward to his fiery sermons at St Lawrence's, she hoped that he would travel further afield to spread the Socialist gospel.

Daisy had already installed another Socialist parson in the parish of Tilty, next to Easton. Edward Maxted harangued his parishioners about the evils of their existence in a capitalist society, wrongly assuming that they felt themselves oppressed and full of revolutionary fervour. Nothing could have been further from the truth. He had come to an overwhelmingly Tory neighbourhood, as he found when touring the quiet villages in his horse and cart. On one occasion he was ducked in the village pond.

Not long before Father Noel's arrival, Maxted had almost caused a riot by a speech he made outside Thaxted Guildhall, from which he had been escorted under police protection. As a result of this performance, some of the more bullish elements in the crowd had threatened that the new vicar, the Bishop and Lady Warwick would be stoned at the induction ceremony. The atmosphere was edgy. Among the party which drove over to Thaxted for Noel's induction was another Christian Socialist, Father James Adderley, son of the first Lord Norton, who was doing dedicated work in the slums of Birmingham, to the great admiration of Lady Warwick. The bells rang in celebration of the new Rector at Thaxted, but not everyone believed that Father Noel would last very long. Those who felt dubious were proved wrong: he stayed till the end of his life, over thirty years later.

During Noel's long tenure, St Lawrence's came to exemplify the High Church tradition at its best. Emphasis was laid on the beauty of liturgy and music, which for some years was directed by Gustav Holst. Candles and incense were much in evidence. In the pulpit, Noel challenged conventional piety, preached Socialism, and exhorted his congregation to change the world. Students from Cambridge came to heckle, but Father Noel was a match for any of them. The charming, rather sleepy village of Thaxted experienced a new vitality; encouraged by the Rector, there was a revival of craft skills in the William Morris tradition, and the village became a kind of pilgrimage centre for Christian Socialists, some of them rambling or cycling across the countryside.

One notorious episode was remembered for many years. Casting convention aside, Father Noel decided that instead of flying a St George's flag from the church tower, he would hoist a red one. This symbol of the International Socialist movement was most displeasing to the Bishop, who ordered the Rector to haul it down immediately. He refused to do so. This struggle with authority became known as 'the battle of the flags', its outcome being more of a tactical withdrawal than an outright defeat. True, the red flag was not kept flying, but it was placed, clearly visible, inside the church.

If politics were central in Conrad Noel's sermons, there was also an emphasis on festive celebrations to mark days commemorating the saints. Processions wound their way round the church and out into the village, accompanied by a full choir and dancing children. At some point, the revived troupe of Morris men would perform. Daisy watched such happenings with interest and satisfaction. At least Conrad Noel avoided a ducking in the village pond.

~

In the autumn of 1910, there was no tranquillity on the wider Socialist scene. The Labour Party and the Social Democratic Federation were at loggerheads over the Liberal budget and the House of Lords. To militant SDF members those concerns were mere bourgeois irrelevance, distracting the electorate from the real issues, such as the fight against poverty. In January of that year, Lady Warwick had said at a meeting that she 'did not know what could have entered the heads of the Labour Party to have sent them headlong into the Liberal camp'.[1] Her statement accurately represented SDF policy.

The bitterness between the Labour Party and the Social Democrats concerned her. She herself looked at the big picture in political objectives, and was exasperated that parties of the Left seemed bogged down in disputes, giving undue importance to minor matters. It was the great ideals that had drawn her and others into the movement, and she was appalled by the lack of perspective and solidarity among many Socialists, a point she made in the *Church Socialist Quarterly*:

The 'reasonable' Socialist will always remember that his and her economic and political faith is only a mere fragment of the great whole of life, the mere fragment of the structure. Do not let the philosophers, the artists, the poets, the theologians, have good reason to turn on us with the accusation that we are harsh Materialists who measure civilisation in the terms of a superficial financial equality. Let us see that we have grasped the bigger truth that our political economy is only a concrete foundation for a superstructure of the life of the mind, which alone matters.[2]

Daisy had persuaded H.G. Wells to rent Easton Glebe, an attractive Georgian rectory on her estate, and into the quiet Tory countryside of north-west Essex he came, a star with the same panache that had made him one of the most successful novelists of the day. Prophet, Socialist, enemy of the conventional world, he attracted a great deal of attention. As an outspoken advocate of free love, he had mockingly revealed the hypocrisy of Victorian values.

His frank writing about sex had caused his novel *Ann Veronica* to be denounced from several pulpits, and *In the Days of the Comet* had portrayed an imagined future of complete sexual freedom, causing Wells to be regarded in some quarters as dangerous. Inspired by his progressive thinking, Daisy was delighted to have secured this literary lion as a neighbour. His wife Jane became one of her closest friends, and their two young sons made friends with her daughter Mercy.

Wells had parted company with the Fabians after a great deal of internal warfare. The Webbs and Shaw had finally prevented Wells and his supporters from carrying a resolution restating the society's aims, an essential change if the group was ever to have parliamentary influence. His ideas on the question of women's rights ran far ahead of many in the cautious Fabian clique, and his theories were not best served by his affair with Amber Reeves, the brilliant and beautiful daughter of two Fabian stalwarts, Pember and Maud Reeves. When Amber became pregnant by Wells, the scandal resounded far beyond the progressive circles in which her parents moved.

At Easton Glebe, 'H.G.' often entertained his many friends for convivial weekends, with no ambience of austere Socialism. Having known hardship in his youth, he now enjoyed offering the kind of hospitality made possible by the huge sales his books enjoyed. As a young man he had wrapped his feet in newspaper to keep warm in freezing digs, while studying under Huxley at the Kensington Science Schools. Now he was very much an insider, at the height of his success, one of the most influential figures in Edwardian literary life. With both Wells and Blumenfeld as neighbours, sitting round Daisy's dinner table, there must have been many stimulating and sometimes explosive arguments.

∼

After the King's death, the peaceful years of Edwardian England gave way to industrial unrest, which broke out significantly in 1911. In the middle of Royal Ascot, on 14 June, a shipping strike started when the crew of the liner *Olympic*, moored at Southampton, left the vessel. They were followed by the men of five shipping lines and the National Sailors' and Firemen's Union. By the end of the week dockers in Glasgow, Newcastle, Hull and Goole had come out in sympathy. There was just over a week before the Coronation, and the strike was a blot on the social landscape. It proved to be the herald of much more disruption.

Wages and conditions were the contentious matters. A basic eightpence an hour was being asked by the dockers, but as yet nothing was on the table, and union leaders, with Ben Tillett to the fore, had waited a long time. They thought that Sir Albert Rollitt, the government-appointed arbitrator, was dragging his heels.

Six weeks later, at the beginning of August, between four and five thousand men at the Victoria and Albert docks stopped work. The National Transport Workers' Federation had come into being the previous year. Tillett, a man small in stature but dynamic in heart, was one of its co-founders, and he now came centre stage.

Tillett's life story was an extraordinary one. Born in 1860, he had received no formal education, began work at the age of eight, and spent some time with a travelling circus. After several years at sea, he eventually gravitated to the London docks and soon established himself as a militant union leader. He had led the men during the previous dock strike of 1889, when Father James Adderley, then at Toynbee Hall, had helped to organise the relief fund. Out of that struggle had come a modest improvement in wages, but conditions had not been greatly ameliorated.

The Thames docklands, usually pulsing with activity, was now a shut and silent area. Without even their usual meagre wages, the strikers were starving. In some cases, their wives earned a little in the East End factories, but there was intense hardship for the families all the same. Tillett led his men, marching through the city, to demonstrate in Trafalgar Square and on Tower Hill. At least being in the open air was an escape from the foetid tenements which were often what they called home.

The strike came to a climax on the August Bank Holiday weekend. On Sunday 6 August, Tillett authorised his dockers to break picket lines and unload ice from container ships, in response to an appeal from the city's hospitals. On the afternoon of that same Sunday, an enormous rally took place in Trafalgar Square, at which the principal speaker was Harry Gosling, co-founder of the National Transport Workers' Federation. With him on the platform was Sir Albert Rollitt. Gosling announced that the dockers had won their eightpence an hour and one shilling overtime. His message was greeted by the assembled men with rousing cheers. The atmosphere had changed from militant determination to euphoria, but the excitement proved premature and, as Tillett warned, the struggle was not yet over. The union leaders were not ready to end negotiations while the claims of casual labourers in the dockyards remained unsettled.

The strike continued, and the situation was grim. Unloaded ships waited, full of imports; worse, some were refrigerated container ships containing perishable foodstuffs. Huge financial losses were being sustained, and severe shortages of meat, fruit and vegetables were becoming apparent. Essential commodities such as water, coal, gas, electricity and petrol were rapidly diminishing. Markets were idle, goods were not moving, and all London seemed to have come to a halt. There was a further exacerbation of the crisis: four thousand railwaymen in Liverpool walked out on Bank Holiday Monday. A few days later, troops in HMS *Antrim* arrived on Merseyside, and it was widely thought that troops would similarly be mobilised to deal with other hot spots of industrial action. Ten million men of the Thames valley were still on strike.

George Askwith, who had succeeded Churchill at the Board of Trade, was not a man in whom Tillett had confidence, and the atmosphere deteriorated when Askwith did indeed threaten the use of troops to break the dockers. The threat was not carried out. Instead, after the brinkmanship, Askwith revealed a settlement package which was acceptable to the dockers' union: raised wages and some employment guarantees were conceded by the dock owners, although the strikers' stated aims were not fully achieved.

Taken in conjunction with provisions in the new National Insurance Bill, the total package was enough to resolve the dispute. Disaster seemed to have been narrowly avoided, but hard on the heels of the dockers' union settlement came a countrywide rail strike. Tom Mann, the railwaymen's union leader, was just as determined as Ben Tillett, and the dispute threatened no less chaos than the crisis in the docks. If the government sent in troops against the strikers, as some of the Cabinet were suggesting, such was the mood that a violent confrontation might be the result. Chancellor Lloyd George stated that he did not believe a settlement could be achieved by force, and was prepared to do whatever was necessary to bring about a resolution of the dispute. He was conciliatory, but he also appealed to the railmen's patriotism, making pointed reference to the threat posed by Germany. Lloyd George's temperate approach brought the railway strike to an end, He was the hero of the hour, and the negotiated settlement a huge relief to Asquith's government.

∼

One result of the 1911 strikes was an appreciable increase in the size and power of the unions which had fought so tenaciously for their members. Women working in East End factories also took a stand that summer against appalling conditions in their factories, which made jam, cigars and matches. Observing the growing movement for workers' rights, Daisy, Wells and other Socialist intellectuals might well have thought the country on the verge of revolution, with which – despite the inconvenience – they would not have been displeased. The power of organised labour to bring the country to the verge of collapse had been clearly demonstrated. That there were powerful forces coming into play was not in dispute, the old order was starting to break up, but what kind of world would replace it?

Daisy and her Socialist friends discussed the future a great deal. One outcome of their discussions was the decision to produce a book, on which Wells, Daisy herself and a number of others would collaborate. It was to be a volume of essays, in which various aspects of a future ideal society would be set out and discussed in some depth. Each essay would focus on one important topic.

G.R. Stirling Taylor and Lady Warwick were to co-ordinate the work, and Wells would act as a kind of executive editor, with the necessary professional acumen. *Socialism and the Great State* was the title chosen, and, as with many joint projects, there were difficulties and disagreements. Although each contributor took sole responsibility for his or her views, Wells was argumentative about anything with which he disagreed.

In 'The Future of Work', it was envisaged that boring repetitive labour would diminish, with machines increasingly replacing manpower. A 'society of leisure' would be ushered in, in which workers would earn a decent living wage without putting in long hours. Emphasis on mass production with all its inhuman characteristics would be a thing of the past, as would all exploitation of workers. The time freed within this new pattern could be spent enjoying many other aspects of life, as the individual desired. At a time when sweatshops and 'dark satanic mills' still existed, this was a revolutionary, even somewhat Utopian concept.

Conrad Noel's essay described the Anglican Church as it might be in the year 2000, and was written as if he had been transported to that date to see how it had evolved. He found that many congregations of Nonconformists had been absorbed 'and now exist within the Church as a guild, with particular methods and standpoint of their own'.[3] To the majority, the idea of competing churches had become meaningless. Within the Church itself, however, there would exist a great variety of ideas and a greater variety of worship.

Father Noel's vision of the future Church was of unity but not uniformity, with members belonging to a fellowship of friends: 'goodness is that which helps, evil is that which injures the community'. Religion was deeply rooted in the eternal realities of human nature: 'People worship no barren and abstract deity called morality . . .'[4] However, the rich Anglican liturgy had survived, in tribute to 'the Supreme Ritualist' who had created the world's pageant of changing seasons. In the wider context, Britain as a Socialist state would exist not in isolation, but within a confederacy of several nations, and all national churches would be members of an Ecumenical Council of Catholic Democracy, which had its headquarters in Rome.

The future of agriculture, land ownership and rural life was Lady Warwick's sphere. In her Socialist blueprint, land would be nationalised and divided into state farms, run by highly trained agricultural experts, with no unskilled labourers. Large areas of moor, mountain and forest would be preserved as national parks. Dirty, oversized industrial cities would disappear, as would remote villages. The new pattern of settlement would be something more like the balance of communities as it was seen in the medieval world. The average town would have fifty to sixty thousand inhabitants, and the countryside would be within easy reach on free public transport. Most of the population would choose to live in co-operative households, rather than in single family units. By sharing mundane household tasks, women would be set free to spend more of their time doing interesting things.

As an atheist, Wells objected to the inclusion of Noel's essay; he thought it badly written, and actually rejected it. Admittedly, Father Noel's undoubtedly brilliant mind was not seen at its very best in his contribution, but the main objection Wells made was really his antipathy to the entire subject. In a disgruntled mood, Wells could only be managed with a great deal of diplomacy.

Nevertheless, despite various disagreements, the book was completed. Published in 1912, it set out a vision of a future polity under Socialism which had plenty of Utopian vision. What it lacked was any description or plan as to how it was to be achieved. Surprisingly, for a book of high seriousness, it sold well, particularly in America.

~

Early in 1912 Daisy renewed her acquaintance with W.T. Stead. For a number of years she had been out of touch with him, but in February she wrote asking for guidance. She was about to embark on a lecture tour in America, and wanted help in planning her talks. Everything had been arranged very quickly, and she needed to shape her ideas in a way that would go down well with enthusiastic but not undemanding audiences. Who was better than Stead as a mentor? He was au fait with current issues and knew the international scene better than most. She particularly wanted his advice about a lecture which would be about the birth of the new era: the rise of democracies, the role of women, and world peace. Undaunted by the prospect of taking on such a big subject in a single talk, Daisy asked Stead if he would be kind enough to set down a general outline. She could do the rest. Another subject was to be 'Warwick Castle and English Life', which would be easy, considering her experience at the centre of Society. The Americans would be sure to gulp down anecdotes about 'all the fabulous people'[5] she had known.

The prospect of actually doing the tour was not pleasurable, but a total of thirty lectures at £300 each was going to make her a lot of money. Daisy Warwick was a desirable acquisition for any American agent, and she was to be paid their estimate of her value. The inside story of her life was exactly what the Americans wanted, particularly because the Countess of Warwick's reputation was already well known across the Atlantic.

She sailed on 2 March aboard the Cunard liner *Mauretania*, holder of the Blue Riband and offering unequalled luxury. In New York she would be staying at the Ritz Carlton. Hordes of hustling reporters were waiting for the *Mauretania*'s most famous passenger to disembark, and when she did so they yelled questions at her: 'Are you an anarchist?' (to which Daisy replied 'Not yet'), 'Why are you a Socialist?' 'When did you become a Socialist?' 'Does smashing windows help the cause of suffrage in England?'[6] It was pandemonium. She informed the reporters that, having lived a simple and secluded life at Warwick Castle, it had been a great shock to see 'the horrible life of a great city'.[7] There were several press conferences, in which Daisy faced the same barrage of questions in uninhibited American style: they wanted to hear her opinions about sex, love, marriage, youth. Traffic was halted on Seventh Avenue, and on a wet, cold night Carnegie Hall was crowded for her first lecture. There was a buzz of anticipation, and then suddenly, there was the Countess centre stage, her appearance greeted with huge applause.

Daisy graciously began: 'I became by marriage the chatelaine of Warwick Castle', and from then on she easily held her audience with all she had to say about her privileged and adventurous life. She sensed very quickly that they did not want any more serious topic such as women's suffrage.

At the house of Mrs Benjamin Guinness in Washington Square, Daisy met some of the artists and literati who were accepted in New York Society. The writer Julian Hawthorne, son of Nathaniel, invited her to his apartment on Riverside Drive, which had spectacular views across the Hudson. It was novel to see that in wealthy American households a lot of work was done by machines, rather than by servants as in England. From New York, Daisy went to Washington, where she met President Taft. Then it was back to New York and on to Baltimore and Philadelphia, giving both afternoon and evening lectures in each city.

The demanding schedule was manageable when she was in front of large, appreciative audiences; however, when subsequently the audiences in some cities were not as large as they had been in New York, she began to feel the strain. The tour was supposed to continue for six weeks and would include Montreal and Toronto, across the border, and then on to Buffalo and the wild west. But the prospect of travelling those vast distances began to seem daunting, and she decided not to proceed. She was breaking her contract, destroying the trust placed in her by American agents, and disappointing her public. Furthermore, instead of being honest about her decision, she made the situation worse by excusing her sudden departure on the grounds of family illness. There was no such thing. Her daughter, Lady Helmsley, had been seen in London, looking perfectly well.

On 24 March, she left her New York hotel, heavily veiled, refused to speak to reporters, and embarked on the White Star liner *Olympic*. So ended a lecture tour which had started so well, and which, had she completed it, would have earned her £10,000.

Once back in England, she wrote to Stead on 1 April, telling him: 'The lectures were a great success, but I could not stick it out! The travelling was killing and the people awful! I mean they only care for dollars and are such snobs!'[8] She invited him to Warwick for part of the Easter holidays, but hoped to see him in London before then, when she would tell him more about her experiences in America.

However, Stead had booked a passage on the *Titanic*, and he was not among the survivors. As he had been a member of the Society for Psychical Research, it seems fitting that Stead's daughter Estelle gave an account of his after-death appearance among a group of his friends; he said 'Everything is just as we imagined.'[9]

✒ 15 ✑

Come the Revolution

FOR EIGHT YEARS, DAISY had been loyal to the Social
Democratic Federation, but in 1912 she left it and joined a
new grouping established by H.M Hyndman, the British Socialist
Party. Her gatherings of trade unionists and Socialist intellectuals
at Easton often featured a rousing version of the *Internationale*, in
which the assembled company would join.

While in America she had received important news from
England about a coal strike. It would be of significance to her personally as an owner of coalfields; moreover, it seemed to herald
further strike activity, which would be of interest to her politically.
The chief protagonists in the looming industrial unrest were
miners and dockers, but other unions – transport workers, gas
workers and general labourers – were all to become involved. In a
letter to Ralph Blumenfeld three years earlier, Daisy had written
that the atmosphere seemed charged with electricity. It was even
more so now, in the spring of 1912.

As leader of the dockers' union, the charismatic Ben Tillett was
gaining a good deal of publicity. Such was the solidarity and determination among the unions that the dispute might well be both
bitter and prolonged. Car men, stevedores, sailors and firemen

were all in support. Demonstrations, rallies and skirmishes with
the police took place frequently. Lady Warwick became quite a
familiar sight in the East End as one of Tillett's strongest supporters, regarding herself as one of his colleagues.

The momentum was building towards another all-out confrontation. On 29 February 1912, 700 miners went on strike at
the largest Lancashire colliery, near Manchester. When the colliery
manager was asked to account for it, he put it down to 'the spread
of Socialist notions'. There was also a dispute in South Wales,
where the *Times* reporter saw 2,500 men come pouring out of the
gates at Tonypandy, the Glamorgan pit which had seen, according
to the newspaper, 'some of the most exciting incidents in the riots
of 1910'.[1]

By 1 March the dispute was official, and within a few days the
Daily Express reported that a million men had joined the first
national miners' strike, asking for a minimum wage of five
shillings an hour for men. Every pit stood idle in Derbyshire, with
56,000 men out. All production in the main Yorkshire coalfields
stopped, 50,000 strikers coming out in Barnsley. In the Durham
coalfields 180,000 men were on strike, and there was widespread
support for the action in Scotland. The *Express* headlines pro-
claimed: 'Paralysis of Industry. Strike Complete. Vast Losses.'[2]

Before long the miners' strike began to have a wider effect on
the railway network and among workers in the Bradford woollen
industry. Owing to the reduced numbers of goods trains and
trawlers, rises in food prices and diminishing supplies of some
foodstuffs had been anticipated in the first week of March: 'Many
householders are placing considerable orders with their trades-
men, who during the weekend found it difficult, and in a few cases
impossible to execute the orders placed.'[3]

A week later *The Times* devoted a leader to the industrial situation. Prime Minister Asquith had made a speech expressing
approval in principle of a minimum wage, and making a pledge to
secure it: 'A case had been made out for ensuring to the underground

workers in the coal industry, in this country, with adequate safe-guards, a *reasonable* minimum wage.'[4] Asquith had asserted that his government would not permit resistance from employers to delay the attainment of this goal indefinitely. Moreover, if the coal owners of Scotland and South Wales persisted in their opposition, the government would introduce legislation.

The miners' delegation were surprised by this offer when they attended a meeting held at the Foreign Office. Prior to the speech, negotiations had been deadlocked, but Asquith had been perceived as putting new life into them. Miners' delegates were satisfied that government sympathy for their cause would give them immense tactical advantage over the employers. *The Times'* Parliamentary Correspondent reported:

> The Labour Party have decided that if the Government do not legislate on the coal dispute, they will themselves bring in a bill to make statutory a minimum wage in the coalfields, and in this bill they will embody the *minimum* scale in the various districts agreed by the Miners' Federation on February 2nd.[5]

By the beginning of April a further 850,000 miners came out on strike, and they were followed on 23 May by transport workers and the London dockers. As Tillett wrote in his account: 'Coal porters', lightermen's, and other men's difficulties were cropping up. The number of meetings was increasing, the enthusiasm was spreading ... The transport workers' fingers were for the time being on the throat of trade.'[6]

The Port of London Authority and the shipowners predictably held their united front. The dockers were again demanding the minimum daily rate of eightpence per hour that they had failed to achieve the previous year. There was to be a minimum wage equal to four hours' pay and bank holidays were to be paid double. They also wanted an agreement on conditions: both day and night shifts were to last nine hours, with paid meal breaks of an hour on all shifts, and with double time to be paid on any meal hours worked. All work was to finish by noon on Saturday. There were to be three set times daily for hiring dockers, at recognised collecting points.

On 12 April the transport workers met in Canning Town, near the docks. Their demands on pay and conditions were confirmed, and the dockers' leaders urged all who had not already done so to join their respective unions. The Shipping Federation and other employers then met the dockers' representatives at the Port of London Authority, but no agreement was reached.

≈

In February, Daisy Warwick and several other prominent members of the Church Socialist League had taken action by drawing up a petition to be presented to the Church of England Convocation at Canterbury. The petition urged the Church to declare itself on the side of workers in their struggle, and to cease defending the existing system of property, private ownership of land and capital. Dr Robert Wakefield, Bishop of Birmingham, had presented the petition, but when the strike began the Anglican leaders remained silent.

Now, two months later, the London branch of the Church Socialist League decided to stage a demonstration against the refusal of the Church hierarchy to support the miners. Over a thousand people arrived at Church House, Westminster on Friday 12 April to take part, young artisans, clerical workers and shop assistants being well represented among them. The hall was packed to capacity, leaving several hundred people outside. It turned out to be a powerful expression of all that the League stood for. To organ accompaniment, the congregation sang 'England Arise' and 'Once to Every Man and Nation'. Then came the procession of speakers, led by George Lansbury, who carried a crimson cross, the League's emblem. Priests in cassocks were much in evidence, as were many church banners.

Conrad Noel took the chair, and started the evening's proceedings with a prayer. He then read a Remonstrance, which was addressed to the archbishops and bishops of the Church. The Church had never questioned the right of men to secure such terms for their work as should give themselves and their families an honourable life, so the petitioners were 'frankly astounded and dismayed' that their lordships did not espouse the workers' cause. Noel, the militant, hoped that please God there would be more strikes, which had an honourable tradition in the Christian Church.

The audience loved that, and cheered loudly. Noel now introduced the Countess of Warwick as 'a member of the Church Socialist League and a coal owner'. Daisy spoke of her feeling of intense gratitude to the miners for the magnificent example they had set, saying that she was glad to be living in an age when at last the workers had been roused to a sense of what they owed to themselves and their families. When she mentioned Tom Mann there were resounding cheers: the railwaymen's leader was awaiting trial for publishing a leaflet urging soldiers not to shoot strikers.

Another platform speaker was G.K. Chesterton, bulky of body but small of voice. If Conrad Noel was a revolutionary socialist, then Chesterton went a step further, calling himself a revolutionist: England had not had a civil war for centuries, that was the trouble, and he thought the sooner there was another one the better. George Lansbury made an impassioned speech, declaring himself sick of the terms palliation, conciliation and arbitration. From now on he would be doing his best to stir up a holy revolt.

Carrying the crimson cross, Lansbury finally led the procession out. Following directly behind was Lady Warwick, wearing a large hat with ostrich feathers and a long black silk cloak. Conrad Noel in flowing black cassock walked with Father Adderley, and other clergy followed behind the League's 'John Ball' banner, which commemorated the medieval priest-agitator from Essex. It was nearly midnight when the procession made its way to Lambeth Palace. Father Noel's thunderous knocking on the door was answered by the Archbishop's secretary, and the Remonstrance was handed over. A benediction was said and the Socialist Leaguers began to disperse. Spurred on by the support evident from the large attendance at their Westminster meeting, further gatherings were organised to carry on the struggle for their own brand of Socialism.

Great meetings were also being held in the docks and on Tower Hill. Provincial ports, including Liverpool and Glasgow, had contributed to the solid support behind the London men. By now several unions were out, which maximised the strike's effect. Every service was being held up by the transport workers: coal, water, gas, electricity and foodstuffs. As Tillett put it: 'Materials for commerce, products of the workshop, the factory and the mill, the meadow and the field, the railway service, transport by road, water and river all ceased their hum.'[7]

Disillusioned by what government had achieved, the unions were not just demanding higher wages, but aiming to change the entire economic system by direct action. If the general population suffered, the militants were unrepentant. Workers had experienced deprivation for generations. Now they could use their power to bring down the activities of civilisation, as Tillett stated.

However, the difficulties of sustaining this militancy with no pay were very much to the fore. Daisy was a staunch supporter, and often travelled up from Essex to speak for the strikers' cause. The newly relaunched *Daily Herald*, under Lansbury's editorship, reported on 8 June that Lady Warwick had made an offer to the Transport Workers' Union to defray the cost of housing one thousand strikers' children as long as the strike lasted.[8] A few days later she appealed in a letter for help in furthering this scheme to none other than readers of the *Daily Express*:

Will everyone with large grounds or open spaces form committees and organise camps for the strikers' children to be cared for in the country districts? A band of helpers is formed here in Essex, and we shall start with a thousand children on this park

ground, and organise committees for the boarding out in villages for many more, as Essex touches the dock district on the
metropolitan side. We shall want money to feed our family, but
it has begun to reach us, and the commissariat is organised in
the most frugal way, to go as far as possible.[9]

Unsurprisingly, the Liberal and Tory newspapers were generally in
agreement that once the miners had secured their demands,
workers in other trades would insist on the same. It was widely
thought that the government would use the army to man ships and
clear docks. Twenty-five thousand soldiers were believed to be on
standby.

If that were so, they were not deployed because wiser counsels
prevailed; Winston Churchill, now Liberal Home Secretary, and
Labour MP John Burns acted as conciliators. Hitherto, Churchill
had been anything but a hero to workers, being held responsible
for the shooting of insurgent Welsh miners at Tonypandy.
Furthermore, he had ordered the violent suppression of demonstrations at ports all over Britain and southern Ireland. When the
situation reached crisis point, Tillett and his committee went to
beard the lion in his den at the House of Commons, just before the
summer recess.

Yet Churchill made a good impression on them. Instead of 'a
man of blood and iron', they saw someone much more amenable.
Tillett compared him to a gentle shepherd, describing Churchill at
this time as 'slightly bent, hesitant of speech, almost an apologetic
manner, youth left in mobile features, ready for boyish fun, the
cares of office sitting lightly on a good sized brow, eyes that
sparkle with a wistfulness almost sweet'.[10]

Even so, there was a lot of straight talking by members of the
deputation. But when they made the point that using brute force
against strikers was reprehensible, the Home Secretary agreed.
There was even a touch of humour in the conversation, much to
the surprise of the dockers.

After a good deal of brinkmanship, the strikers claimed victory. Their demands on pay and conditions having been met, the Port Authority's general manager gave his undertaking that men presenting themselves for work would be reinstated. Nor would proceedings be taken against them for breach of contract. The struggle was not quite over, because subsequently some men were in fact refused work, and further negotiations were needed before a final settlement of the dispute could be reached. This happened on 21 August. The behaviour of the vast body of the comrades had throughout been 'splendid in restraint and firmness', according to Tillett, who also also unreservedly praised the role Churchill had played:

> We found an urbane young Cabinet Minister, apparently fully alive to the duties and responsibilities of his office. We knew that he had exercised great courage in refusing to murder and butcher the men we were fighting for. A clamant press wanted blood; the blood lust had gone from the clubs of the idlers to the seats of the editors; the rich and the powerful saw blood, and gambled on the chances of riots. To the credit of the Home Secretary, so far as our fight was concerned, and we were in daily discourse with him, he turned a deaf ear to these clamours of the cowardly crew who would, under the name of law and order, have gloated over the killing of their fellow creatures . . .[11]

~

Having made some contribution to the strikers' morale, Daisy spent a good deal of the summer at Easton, where Maynard was convalescing from an illness brought on by a heart irregularity. He had collapsed while playing tennis and had to rest for several weeks. His mother rigged up an awning in the garden, so that he could enjoy the glorious weather, but she was hurt that Joe never enquired about his progress. In the autumn, to speed his recovery, Maynard and eight-year-old Mercy were both sent to St Leonards on the Sussex coast, where her friend Arthur du Cros, Conservative MP for Hastings and millionaire managing director of the Dunlop Rubber Company, lent them his house. Maynard, aged fourteen, had already taken to driving, and had a car with him. Mercy had her pony.

In October Daisy rented a house in Ebury Street, full of beautiful French furniture. She thought it a 'slummy' area but a lovely house, and hoped that Joe would visit her there.

Brookie was increasingly suffering with his health, particularly bronchitis, an ailment he had been prone to all his life. Sometimes Daisy was up with him all night. They had been forced to cancel a trip to Canada, where they had intended to travel across British Columbia with Millie and her husband; the Sutherlands had to go alone. Brookie had a particularly bad chest in the winter of 1912, and early in December he left England to spend two months in the West Indies. After his return in February he was stable for a while, but his health was not robust. Over the following months, it was increasingly to be a cause for concern.

∽ 16 ∾

A Brush with the Law

THERE WAS ENORMOUS DIFFICULTY on several fronts throughout 1913. Having been in deepening financial trouble for some time, Daisy was being determinedly pursued by numerous creditors. At the end of February she had to submit to an oral examination of her means, which meant she was forced to disclose details of such valuables as remained at Easton. A few items were put on a bill of sale in favour of the London and Westminster Discount Company, a money-lending organisation to which Lady Warwick apparently owed the sum of £2,420. One of the creditors had an injunction served on her, meaning that removal or sale of those effects was barred pending a hearing.

The following week Brookie suffered a relapse, becoming dangerously ill with lung congestion. Perhaps he had returned too early from the West Indies, and now his condition was grave enough for bulletins to be issued from Warwick Castle. The family kept a bedside vigil and an eminent specialist from London was called in. Many anxious hours passed before an announcement at midnight that the Earl had rallied. It was not till the end of the month that he was able to get up for the first time, although he was still very weak. In a letter to Ralph Blumenfeld Daisy described his appearance as 'very bad'.[1]

Now that she was in her middle years, she genuinely cared about Brookie, and her financial crisis almost seemed less threatening than the worry about her husband. Her main creditor was unsuccessful when attempting to recover the debt owed him by claiming some of Lady Warwick's property. However, her most saleable items were removed, including a portrait by Sargent done in 1902, which was bought by Wertheimer's. The sale meant that the London and Westminster Company could be paid, with money to spare.

But another creditor, a solicitor named William Sturges, was not paid, although by withholding payment from him Daisy risked contempt of court. Sturges, whose several legal actions had been going on for three years, adamantly refused to give up, and his appeal on 24 April was upheld. A receiver was appointed to take over the property assumed to be still at Easton, and Lady Warwick's counter-appeal was dismissed on 24 June. Two weeks later the Official Receiver checked the inventory and found that several valuable items were now missing. When the Sheriff of Essex arrived before the end of July, he ordered seizure of horses, harness and pigs, fodder, and a car. Four hundred head of deer were also rounded up and taken away. Furniture was removed from Stone Hall, even though Brookie's agent was living there. Only ten years before, Daisy had been entertaining splendidly. Now Lord and Lady Warwick were on the edge of bankruptcy.

~

In the spring of 1913 Maynard started his first term at Oundle, where the science facilities and technical training were particularly suitable for him. He thoroughly enjoyed his life there, and wrote the usual schoolboyish letters asking for such things as 'more of those tinned sardines'. Joe Laycock, now with a large family of his own, continued to ignore their son, something Daisy thought less than chivalrous of him. An exchange of letters, with news of life's joys and sorrows, would have been so much more civilised.

Brookie remained an invalid, and everything was very quiet at Easton. Down from Yorkshire, Queenie and Charlie had rented a house nearby, so that they could often visit. Despite her money troubles, Daisy was still living in a tranquil private world. Amateur theatricals took place at the Barn Theatre, a converted medieval tithe barn on the Easton estate. Productions varied in scope from Shakespeare to revivals of obscure dialect plays – when Mercy became a teenager she was to have her first taste of acting at the Barn. Ellen Terry gave professional tips and occasionally played a part herself, on one occasion playing Juliet while Daisy read the Nurse. H.G., with sons Frank and Gip, the Blumenfelds, and other neighbours often joined in; Wells was a squeaky-voiced Duke Theseus in a performance of *A Midsummer Night's Dream*, while Gip, his elder son, played Bottom. It was all great fun, and there were faithful local audiences.

In the autumn Daisy, Brookie, Mercy and the Helmsleys were all staying in Roquebrune, a village in the hills above Monaco. While on the Riviera it was easier to forget those debts: in a letter to Wells, Daisy mentioned the beautiful scents wafting in from the villa's garden, and hoped that he and Jane would visit in the spring. Brookie was in total sympathy with his wife about her financial troubles, which he kindly attributed to bad advice from her lawyers. As he told Moreton Frewen, 'The rascals of men who cheated her ought to have been shown up.'[2]

In the middle of January, Daisy returned to England briefly to deal with some legal matters and to see Samuel Bensusan, who was churning out her articles for the *Daily Express*. Through an action brought by her trustees, she managed to get the deer returned to Easton, but in every other respect her situation was about as perilous as it could be. The Warwick and Easton estates were both heavily mortgaged, the castle had been let to an American, and Daisy's own valuables had mostly been either sold or impounded. By the middle of 1914, she owed approximately £90,000, some £48,000 of that to money lenders.

Her financial situation tempted her to look again at a possible way out which she had previously turned down, namely writing her unexpurgated memoirs. In the spring, while still enjoying halcyon days at Cap Martin, Daisy was reacquainted with Frank Harris, whom she had first met in the 1890s at one of Lady Dorothy Neville's luncheon parties. Harris' glory days had been during the closing years of the previous century. As a rank outsider, without a university education, he had somehow managed to become editor of the *Evening News* at the age of twenty-eight, and later of the influential *Fortnightly Review*. Mercurial by temperament, with a good deal of self-confidence, in his youth Harris had been a member of the Social Democratic Federation. During that time H.M. Hyndman had considered him to be one of the organisation's most effective open-air speakers. Later, swinging to Randolph Churchill's Tory Democracy, he had attempted to become an MP, but had failed in this aspiration. Most memorably, in the 1890s he had spent many evenings at the Café Royal with Oscar Wilde and his circle.

When marriage to a very wealthy widow had provided him with a house in Park Lane, he took centre stage, entertaining many of the people best worth knowing. Peers, politicians and poets all came to luncheons and dinners there. Seated around the table one might have seen guests such as the old Duke of Cambridge, Russell Lowell (the American ambassador), Beerbohm Tree, athlete Willie Grenfell (later Lord Desborough), John Burns, George Wyndham and explorer Alfred Russel Wallace. As the journalist Sir Sidney Low recalled, 'Wilde would toss up scintillating epigrams, countered by the host with fiery thrusts of savage criticism and biting satire.'[3]

In his later life he had descended from those giddy heights. No longer a player in the literary world, as an undischarged bankrupt he had fled to the Riviera. Harris would have been aware that Lady Warwick possessed letters from her royal lover which could potentially make her fortune. Probably also knowing about her money troubles, he saw no reason why her unique letters should not effect her escape from that burden. Harris offered himself as agent in this enterprise, and Daisy took him at face value. After all, he *was* a Socialist and a man of letters. If she had any knowledge of his doubtful reputation, she chose to ignore it. Harris assured Lady Warwick that a likely offer for her memoirs in the United States would be $100,000; his fee for help in the writing and for acting as agent would be £5,000 plus a percentage of the royalties. If for some reason the royal letters were not included, he was to receive £10,000 and his percentage. It seemed like a good plan, and when Daisy left the Riviera she had an agreement to meet Harris again in Paris later in the year, when they would begin work.

In writing a volume of sensational memoirs, she would be entering uncharted territory. Contemporary autobiographies left out what readers most wanted to know, and deliberate silence was kept about sexual matters. In June she had a meeting with Arthur du Cros, friend, creditor and sometime financial adviser. Du Cros had been generous in helping Daisy with her cash flow problems over many years, but he now wanted payment of long-overdue interest.

They met at the house of another Tory MP, Captain George Sandys, in Eaton Square, where Daisy told him about the plan for her autobiography. It is very possible that she did not feel completely comfortable about making her royal love letters public, an action which she probably knew would leave her reputation in tatters. It was simply not done to betray a former lover. It may well be that Daisy was not averse to finding out if the royal family could be induced to pay for the suppression of the letters, and if so, how much they would be willing to give. She knew du Cros to be socially ambitious, and thought that he might see her proposition as an opportunity of serving the Crown. Several ideas were probably going through her mind: one was the possibility that he might buy the royal letters himself for a handsome price, or make known their availability so that someone else might do so. Though startled no doubt by this conversation, he fell in with Daisy's scheme, and asked for an appointment with King George V's private secretary, Lord Stamfordham.

One can only imagine what passed through Stamfordham's mind when confronted with this delicate situation. He knew that the King would wish to spare his mother, Queen Alexandra, who had suffered enough from her husband's indiscretions in his lifetime. Of course, the loyal and wily courtier also knew that he would strongly advise against any payment whatsoever being made. George V, who lived by an inflexible moral code, would not need much persuasion that another way must be found to prevent the damage of disclosure. His consort Queen Mary had moved swiftly to seal the will of her brother, Prince Francis of Teck, thus ensuring that the Prince's bequeathal of most of his estate to his mistress had remained a secret; these love letters written by the old King, so different in temperament from his son, must remain secret too. Daisy suspected nothing, and lived in blissful ignorance of the coming storm.

Du Cros was equally unsuspecting as Stamfordham drew him into negotiations, to preserve the appearance of normality. Meeting at the Ritz in Paris, Daisy, du Cros and Harris considered their position, and felt that everything was going their way. An offer was sure to be made by the royal family. At a meeting in Paris, Harris cockily suggested a revised asking price of £125,000, instead of the original £85,000, which suggests that confidence was high. On the Channel crossing to England, Daisy wrote an ultimatum, stating that unless the money was forthcoming her manuscript memoirs including the letters would be delivered to the publishers, and the original letters would be sold in America within a week for an expected £200,000. Daisy's friend, the businessman and former army captain Bruce Logan, was acting as an extra adviser, and it seems that a deal in America was in progress.

However, Stamfordham and Charles Russell, the King's solicitor, had been planning to take action for some time, and on 29

June it came. Russell served Lady Warwick with an interim injunction, preventing her from putting her royal letters into the public domain.

Thereafter, it was not long before an assassination at Sarajevo shook Europe to its foundations. Once Germany had invaded Belgium on 3 August and war had been declared, everything became secondary to the momentous events that were now unfolding. A mood of patriotic jubilation gripped the country. Rupert Brooke summed it up when he wrote 'Now God be thanked Who has matched us with His hour.' Royal advisers, otherwise engaged, were not immediately concerned with bundles of letters.

Meanwhile, Frank Harris was in difficulty, and needed help from Lady Warwick. His pro-German sympathies had not endeared him to the French authorities, and his life on the Côte d'Azur had become uncomfortable. Where could he go while he made plans? Acting like a good Samaritan, Daisy offered him the use of Brook End, a house on her estate, and provided not only a servant or two but food and cash. While enjoying this refuge, Harris was able to look to the future and book his passage to America.

During the autumn Daisy was busy with the numerous duties which fell to a lady of the manor, such as attending Red Cross meetings and arranging housing for Belgian refugees. Moreover, the Territorial Army wanted to send a contingent for training in her park. Harris therefore had permission to go to the Lodge by himself, and in the time he spent alone was able to have a good look at the private letters and other papers. There was a great deal of interesting material, and Harris could not have failed to see the enormous potential. Before embarking for the United States he wrote a few sample chapters, covering the subject's life up to 1895. However, he longed to be on the other side of the Atlantic, and efforts to get his passage booked, difficult in wartime, superseded any further work on the book.

Prior to his stay in Essex, Harris' relationship with H.G. Wells had become less than cordial – they had met originally years before, when the impecunious young Wells had been trying to get work. Now that Harris had turned up in the vicinity, Wells invited him over to Easton Glebe. When Harris eventually departed for America, Daisy found to her dismay that certain items were missing from her archive, and it was to Wells that she confided her doubts and fears about what might have happened. Wells reacted with worldly-wise amusement as he commiserated with her: naturally, the bounder had been unable to resist taking some of Daisy's royal letters. He would cling to them even if his boat was torpedoed!

In November Daisy called to see Arthur du Cros at his Regent Street office. He was once again pressing for payment, but she parried with subtle hints that there were things in both his private and public life that he would not want disclosed. The message was clear enough for him to give up trying to get the money she owed him.

Then in January 1915 Daisy had to tell du Cros that her £6,000 yearly income from Congo shares had been interrupted by the war. Prompted by this news, he made a very generous offer to pay some of her creditors out of dividends owing to him. Furthermore, he agreed to release £100 a week in dividends for her needs, an act of great practical kindness which saved her from bankruptcy.

But by now there was a full-scale legal action pending. Despite the war, the injunction against Daisy was still in force. Stamfordham and Charles Russell went down to Easton Lodge, where they interrogated Lady Warwick, asking her about Harris and what he had taken to America. After the interview a watch was put on her movements, and arrangements were made for both incoming and outgoing mail to be intercepted.

Early in July 1915, using the Defence of the Realm Act – which enabled the arrest of anyone engaged in activities likely to be detrimental to the nation's war effort – an action was brought in the

King's Bench Division against Lord and Lady Warwick, Bruce Logan and Frank Harris. On 5 July the action was stayed on condition that the letters were handed over by Lady Warwick to be destroyed. She decided on the personal touch, and had an audience with George V. But she was offended by his censorious attitude; after all, she had known him since his childhood. In her eyes a great wrong had been done in bringing the case, and she defended herself:

> I am handing back with splendid generosity the letters King Edward wrote me of his great love, and which belong absolutely to me. I have done nothing with these letters, and have never dreamed of publishing such things . . . every incident of those ten years of close friendship with King Edward are in my brain and memory . . . In fact I am absolutely innocent of any of the charges brought against me which I resent deeply, and shall never forget or forgive.[4]

The matter has been shrouded in mystery ever since. Some indication of Edward's charm and devotion when writing to the woman he adored can be seen in the very few surviving letters. But Daisy's own letters to Edward have not been kept in the Royal Archives, nor has any record of the legal action against the Countess and her co-defendants. The claim that she had never intended publishing them was somewhat disingenuous. In fact her attitude had been quite ruthless, amounting to blackmail, but she had been outwitted. In this episode Daisy was seen in her most unflattering light, but the King and his entourage were both narrow-minded and vindictive. Lord Stamfordham had played his hand consummately.

After the failure of her plans, du Cros enabled Lady Warwick to put her finances on a sounder footing than they had been for years. Chivalrously coming to the rescue, he paid a tranche of her debts in bills of exchange amounting to £48,000. In addition he arranged that dividends due to him were to revert to her as part of her income, and most generous of all he forfeited repayment of the principal during her lifetime.

The following year, 1916, du Cros mysteriously received a knighthood, ostensibly for services to the war effort. As for Daisy, she had lived close to bankruptcy for years, but thanks to du Cros her position was now infinitely improved.

~ 17 ~

The Great War

MANY ARISTOCRATIC WOMEN PROVED their mettle during the Great War, and prominent among them were the Duchess of Sutherland and her younger sister Lady Angela Forbes. Millie's husband, 'Strath', had died in 1913, and Angela's incompatible marriage to Jim Forbes had ended in a divorce for which she had petitioned, a bold move for a woman of her time. Angela had since attached herself to Hugo, the Earl of Wemyss.

Millie had not long been a widow when she unwisely remarried, but we hear little more about her second husband, Percy Desmond Fitzgerald, except for the fact that he served in Palestine from 1915. The war presented her with a great challenge, and she was particularly well equipped for it through her experience of administering great estates in Scotland and Staffordshire. Overseeing households at Dunrobin and Trentham must have taught her a great deal, and big projects did not frighten her: she had exceptional personal drive, patience, persistence and charm, all qualities that enabled her to find ways round seemingly insuperable obstacles. She knew how to make use of her social position and political contacts when necessary, especially with pompous brass hats. In fact she was thoroughly prepared to pursue ambitious wartime goals.

On 8 August 1914 she crossed to France, and made contact in Paris with the Comtesse d'Haussonville, president of the Société Française de Secours aux Blessés Militaires. She briefly joined this branch of the French Red Cross, and was sent to Brussels. Her services having been requested by Dr Depage, head of Belgian medical services, she began organising her own unit to serve the Belgians. By rapidly contacting friends at home she raised £800 within a week, while a surgeon and nine nursing sisters arrived from Guy's Hospital to form the nucleus of a unit which was to be known as the Millicent Sutherland Ambulence.

On 17 August the unit arrived in Namur, where it was based in a convent of Les Soeurs de Notre Dame, and it was quickly caught up in the first wave of hostilities. Five days later, on 22 August, the Germans attacked Namur, and within half an hour nearly fifty casualties arrived. By evening there were many more. Millie and her staff not only had to attend to the patients but had to cope when electricity and gas supplies were cut off. After three days' fighting Namur fell, by which time the unit was caring for a hundred wounded men, including a few Germans. Through this precarious time Millie kept cool and focused on the work in hand, as she later recalled: 'What I thought would be for me an impossible task became absolutely natural. To wash wounds, to drag off rags and clothing soaked in blood, to hold basins, to soothe a soldier's groans – these actions seemed suddenly an insistent duty.'[1]

The situation grew worse when on 24 August the German troops entered the town, and the unit seemed cut off, with enemy troops in overwhelming numbers. Millie's aristocratic disdain for difficulty was useful in her new role and she kept calm under pressure. She also spoke fluent German; because there was no language barrier, she was able to sweep aside objections from junior officers and obtain an interview with General von Bulow, who had set up his headquarters in the Hotel de Hollande.

Obviously impressed by an English duchess who knew both the Kaiser and the Crown Prince, Von Bulow behaved with the

courtesy befitting an officer of his rank, and gave her permission
to move the unit out of occupied territory within a few days. The
wounded were to be transferred to hospitals in Germany. Having
left Namur, the unit reached Mabeuge by 10 September. By way
of Brussels, Maastricht, the Hague and Rotterdam, Millie eventually reached Flushing, where on 18 September she embarked for
England. She had learnt a great deal during the hectic activity
packed into little more than a month, but it was just the beginning.

Once back in England, Millie almost immediately began organising another kind of unit, which would provide a means of
transport for the wounded who were left behind during a retreat.
The urgent need for such an organisation had been highlighted by
the early British reverses. Once again money was raised from the
usual generous friends, but the new venture surprisingly ran into
an obstacle when the Royal Army Medical Corps was not supportive. Millie remained convinced of its importance, and as usual
went straight to the top.

Winston Churchill, now First Lord of the Admiralty, swung his
influence behind the project, and largely thanks to him official
approval was granted. Millie's account of her first experience of
nursing, entitled 'Six Weeks at the War', was published in *The
Times*, and the fee swelled the funds for her new venture. Now that
her scheme had been approved at the highest level, nothing stood
in her way. The new unit was bigger, more ambitious, comprising
surgeons, nurses and eight cars with drivers. They landed at
Dunkirk on 23 October 1914.

Meanwhile, Angela had also crossed to France, and had found
herself nursing wounded soldiers in Paris. She stuck it out for a
few weeks, but nursing was not her forte. At the end of October,
after spending a day in Le Touquet, where the Duchess of
Westminster was running No. 1 Red Cross Hospital, she went on
to Boulogne. It was there that Angela's attention was caught by the
sight of wounded soldiers lying on the quayside. It was impossible

to say how many lay there on the ground, 'but the place looked absolutely packed'.[2]

The port had suddenly been made into a base, which meant that arrangements for the wounded were somewhat chaotic. Red Cross volunteers were in attendance, but each train which steamed in brought a great many more wounded to swell the existing numbers. As many as possible were transferred to hospital ships, but there was always another crowd of men waiting on the quay. Some were put into the Douane, which had been converted into a temporary hospital without beds.

Angela could see that while hundreds of men waited uncomfortably, sometimes for days, they needed to be cheered with tea, buns and cigarettes. She later described how her enterprise had begun:

> I think it was seeing the crowd of unattached wounded on the quay and in the Douane that gave me the idea for a 'canteen' on the lines of the one at Aubervilliers. I was informed it was necessary to get permission from the officer in charge of the station, and accordingly I put the suggestion before him. He welcomed it enthusiastically.[3]

Once back in England, Angela acted with her usual gusto, and having £8 to spend on basic commodities, she swept into Fortnum and Mason to buy them. Within twenty-four hours, having said goodbye to her daughters Marigold and Flavia, she returned to France. The station waiting room was assigned to her, and quickly unpacking her £8 worth of stores, she was able to feed the men who came in on the very next train. With hot water supplied by Monsieur Gerard, manager of the station restaurant, Angela's 'British Soldiers' Buffet' was just about up and running.

The *batterie de cuisine* was extremely basic: 'an iron boiler, two or three old jugs and a pail for washing up in'.[4] Somehow they managed, and the 'Angelina' was a welcome sight for battle-weary troops. Gradually the Red Cross became involved, helping with the supplies, and soon gigantic cargoes of tea, coffee and other groceries began arriving weekly, driving the military transport officer to distraction. With a newspaper appeal bringing a generous response, Angela was able to start equipping her canteen properly.

There was an early setback when she suspected that Blanchie Gordon-Lennox had tried to undermine the enterprise out of jealousy. So when the adjutant, Sir Arthur Sloggett, tried to close down the buffet, Angela's response was typically robust. On her behalf Lord Esher contacted Sir Alfred Keogh at the War Office, and the matter proceeded up the chain of command to Lord Kitchener. He gave permission for the Soldiers' Buffet to continue its excellent work, and Hugo Wemyss had a straight talk with Blanchie, who was persuaded not to interfere again.

Once given official approval in the highest quarters, Angela's organisation went from strength to strength, but as the service had to operate night and day there was not much sleep, only with luck about four hours in twenty-four:

> The time of the arrival of the trains was more or less a matter of conjecture, and as I had only one assistant during the first strenuous days it meant spending the greater part of the night as well as the day on the station, and also being there at about 5 a.m. to supply the queue of orderlies from the trains who were waiting for hot drinks.[5]

In those early days of war, hospitals were being set up everywhere near the Channel ports. Mrs Keppel and Lady Sarah Wilson had installed their unit at Boulogne in the Hotel Christal, and Lady Dudley was organising the Australian hospital nearby. In England Violet Granby, now Duchess of Rutland, made part of her house in Arlington Street into a hospital. For a time her youngest daughter Lady Diana became a nurse at Guy's Hospital, a sudden awakening to very hard work and the strict discipline imposed by senior staff. Subsequently she applied her experience at Guy's to Arlington Street. Having spent much of their lives adorning King Edward's court, these women were now revealing unexpected talents. One of the very few of that coterie not involved in nursing was Daisy Warwick.

~

Millie Sutherland had lost no time in getting her convoy fully functioning, and it was first used by the French in retreat from the Marne between October and December 1914. Night and day the ambulances shuttled between the front and hospitals at Zydecote and Dunkirk, or to the waiting hospital ships which were filled with wounded and dying men. While her ambulances continued to serve behind the lines, notably at Boesinghe, and a month later at the battle of Neuve Chapelle, Millie established a temporary hospital at Malo-les-Bains on the outskirts of Dunkirk.

However, once the German bombardment of Dunkirk began, the French authorities decided that the severely wounded should be moved. Millie's unit retreated some miles to Bourbourg, where her tent hospital had an exceptionally peaceful atmosphere. As the war of movement gave way to a war of attrition in the trenches, the unit returned to Malo-les-Bains.

On 5 April 1915 Julian Grenfell, son of Lord Desborough, visited the hospital with Millie's son, Alistair. Grenfell was returning from what proved to be his final leave. Summing up his impression in a letter to his sister, he wrote: 'It was great fun. All the picture postcard celebrities were there . . . Millie looking too lovely, lovelier than anything I have ever seen. How much prettier she is than any of the younger generation, and how fascinating. I simply loved seeing her. She looks radiantly happy.'[6]

Before rejoining his regiment, the First Royal Dragoons, he also enjoyed a festive high tea with Angela. She remembered how they had played chemin de fer on the marble tables in the restaurant near her Soldiers' Buffet, in 'hilariously good spirits'.[7]

'Into Battle', Grenfell's memorable poem with the opening line 'The naked earth is warm with spring', evoked the mood of those final few weeks of his life. On 26 May 1915, he died of his wounds at Boulogne. Millie's friendship with his mother, Lady Desborough, would have made his loss very personal. A month earlier, Rupert Brooke had died in the Dardanelles. On hearing the news, Millie had written to Edward Marsh: 'The wind is in the northeast and the guns go on and on. I shall be very old soon, like a grey moth that has lived in dust and darkness too long to remember that its underwings were orange.'[8]

By October 1915, her unit had moved to Calais in order to serve the British forces, which were filling that area in increasing numbers. The French had not recognised the port as a British military base, so it was impossible to site any official British army hospitals there. The unit's Red Cross status and Millie's diplomatic skill with the French meant that her hospital could fill the need. Situated near the Gravelines Road, once again it comprised tents and huts on the sand dunes, giving it a temporary appearance. For all that, it was an oasis of safety for men who had been through hell.

Nearby was a small copse and a marsh, where in the spring nurses picked yellow iris to put in the wards. Not far away were the town's ramparts, where the Last Post was sounded every night. When fully established, No. 9 Red Cross Hospital had a staff of four doctors, a matron, a theatre sister, eighteen trained nursing sisters, twenty-one Voluntary Aid Detachment nurses, six mechanics and chauffeurs, seventeen British orderlies and twelve French women workers. Among those new to nursing who worked with Millie were her daughter Rosemary, her daughter-in-law Eileen Sutherland, Diana Wyndham, Katherine Asquith and 'Tommy' Rosslyn, Harry's wife. By January 1916 there were eight wards, equipped to deal with a hundred patients. Six months later, during the Somme offensive, scores of wounded were brought either by ambulance or hospital barge down La Bassée Canal. Enemy air raids were frequent, especially at full moon, when Calais was bombed by zeppelins making their way to England. For patients whose nerves and bodies had been shattered in combat, those raids were a fearful reminder. Sister Millicent would appear in pyjamas and tin hat moving round the wards at night, and seemed able to bring reassurance. Knowing that she had this ability to comfort the patients gave her a sense of fulfilment.

The staff needed respite from the physical and emotional strain of their work, and guests were invited for convivial evenings, with gramophone music. Millie liked to roll up her sleeves and help with the nursing, but some time had to be spent in administration, to keep the hospital financially viable. The Red Cross gave a grant of £50 a month, but apart from that it was entirely dependent on voluntary donations. In New York Mrs Benjamin Guinness started a fund into which dollars poured generously. In addition Millie found time to visit the Carrell Dakin Hospital in Compiègne to learn a new technique: a more rapid and less painful method of sterilising wounds using sodium hypochlorite. Not only was the method a remarkably good antiseptic, but it caused less pain and healing was more rapid. Soft tissue wounds averaged a healing time of six to twelve days. The method, first introduced to Millie's unit in January 1917, was to be of great value in the terrible months of the Somme offensive.

The King and Queen, along with the Prince of Wales, visited No. 9 Hospital in June 1917, when they were accompanied by Earl Haig. Another visitor was the Prime Minister's wife, Margot Asquith. The third battle of Ypres took place at the end of July. With extra funds from the army medical authorities, the Red Cross was able to add another hut, so that by August 1917 the hospital had 160 beds. During the terrible days of Passchendaele in October and November, when those beds were filled with wounded and dying – many gassed and covered with the mud that seemed to permeate everything – Millie's presence was again of comfort.

In March 1918 the hospital moved yet again – this time to a park outside the town of St Omer. Millie rented a chateau in the grounds, and invited her nurses to lunch there every Sunday. In the hospital mess hut was pinned up Haig's message: 'No Retreat'.

~

The war seemed interminable, and as the numbers of fighting men multiplied with each offensive, so did the need for Angela's Soldiers' Buffets. In one centre, Etaples, the number of 'Angelinas' rose to fourteen. An average of five thousand men daily were supplied with meals or snacks. Before the Somme offensive of July 1916 Angela and her assistants had fried eight hundred eggs between four and seven in the morning. During another period they produced tea and sandwiches for ten thousand men. Expeditionary Force canteens had been gradually set up, but faced with this competition Angela decided to make her own buffets distinctive by selling a different, wider range of food: everything from porridge and rice pudding to sausages, mince and green vegetables. She also thought of offering small but essential items such as combs, handkerchiefs and socks.

Lady Angela was a strong character, and there were times when certain people made things difficult for her. Vague accusations about Angela's morality – inspired by the fact that she had been sighted smoking a cigarette – reached Field Marshall Haig, the British Commander-in-Chief, and were regarded as serious enough for him to order her deportation. But other circumstances were also responsible for this overbearing decision. On the eve of Haig's offensive at Passchendaele, there had been a mutiny of British troops at Etaples. The town had become a training and transit camp, a place of notorious brutality, dealing with the raw recruits from England and also battle-weary troops from the front. Angela had set up one of her *estaminets* in the middle of the parade ground, known as the bull ring. She was very popular with the men, and Haig tried to pin blame for the mutiny on her influence.

Lady Angela was definitely not the kind of woman to take such unfairness, and she fought back, using her contacts in England to take up her cause. Hugo Wemyss even spoke about the matter in the House of Lords, but the dispute was still reverberating when the war ended. Some of the men who had been involved in the Etaples mutiny were shot at dawn, and many more were killed at Passchendaele.

'Angelinas' had made a special contribution to soldiers' welfare, dispensing welcome hospitality on those bleak quaysides, and in fact an estimated four and a half million men had been fed. With her flair for organisation, Angela had made the buffets a resounding success, and she ended the war £3,000 in credit. When offered this sum, the Army Council refused it, on the grounds that they did not have the proper administration for such gifts.

~

Daisy Warwick neither went to France nor did she engage in unquestioning patriotism. Her attitude was more complex. As a Socialist she regarded the war as a capitalist venture, with strong overtones of imperialism; as an internationalist, she had not attributed the war simply to Teutonic aggression. Although both her sons were serving in the forces, she was a pacifist at heart.

Moreover, although Daisy had not been sent to complete her education in Germany, like so many girls of her class she spoke the language fluently and admired German culture – another factor which made her equivocal about the conflict. When German prisoners were held in a camp at Dunmow, she went alongside them in the fields as they worked, and was able to talk with them. She criticised the enrolment of elementary schoolchildren to do land-work at the age of twelve, because in her view it was inexcusable that the education of a new generation should be curtailed in such a way. Besides, why should not agricultural labour be done by public schoolboys, gillies, gamekeepers or footmen? It would make more sense than depriving disadvantaged working-class children of their already meagre education. If she was deliberately courting controversy, it would not be for the first time.

Guy had been appointed aide-de-camp to the General Officer Commanding the British Expeditionary Force, his mother's friend General French. He attained the rank of Brigadier-General in 1915 at the age of thirty-two, and commanded first the Fourth and then the Twelfth Canadian Infantry brigades. He was to emerge with both the French and Belgian Croix de Guerre.

In 1915 Maynard had joined the Royal Flying Corps, but was grounded because he had not reached the minimum age for pilots. However, he was filling in the time with a practical job as a mechanic, for which he had shown a natural aptitude from childhood. According to his mother, he was crazy to be airborne, but happy working in an aircraft factory at Farnborough in the meantime. Daisy rented a cottage nearby, so that she could see as much of him as possible. She was glad that he was on the ground, fearful that eventually he might lose his life in a flying machine, or at any rate get badly shot up. Had it not been for the outbreak of war he would have been going up to Cambridge, reading for a science degree at Trinity Hall.

In H.G. Wells' *Mr Britling Sees it Through*, a novel which sought to convey the atmosphere of an English village during the war, the character of Lady Homartyn was based on Daisy, whose wartime life was centred upon her duties in Essex. These included the Red Cross, and contact with no less than thirty-two hospitals. Easton had been taken over by the Third Army, under Sir Alfred Coddrington, and there were several 'sleepy old generals'[9] in attendance. Occasionally younger officers were attached to the staff, and they told her the latest war news. She enjoyed their company, and liked being in the know about developments.

In October 1915 Daisy wrote to Joe Laycock as armoured biplanes were buzzing over Easton; the letter was addressed to Lieutenant-Colonel J.J. Laycock, Notts RHA, II Mounted Division of the Mediterranean Expeditionary Force. The self-portrait given in this letter is vivid: Daisy, now a woman in her fifties, is still full of vitality, driving herself all over England from Easton to Warwick, Farnborough and Yorkshire.

She knew how to do running repairs (no longer did she have her chauffeur, Rabett), and her luggage consisted of a single dressing case. Apart from all her other activities, she was writing articles for the American press and getting around £3,000 a year out of it. Giving an account of Maynard, Daisy described him as 'a real good high principled boy, full of fun, but absolutely simple and loving home life'.[10] He was very musical, but like his father he could be obstinate. Joe's daughter Mercy had also turned out well, and was about to start at Roedean, where her course would prove somewhat tempestuous. She was tall for an eleven-year-old and could be taken for sixteen; she had a strong will, but her mother seemed pleased with her all the same: 'she is so like you, Joe, with your wonderful eyes, and my figure and legs! . . . The most delightful companion'.[11] Mercy displayed a talent for writing and acting, and a lightning imagination. She was a great animal lover, and with her boundless vitality was always either riding her horses, playing tennis or cycling. According to her mother Mercy adored men, and seemed 'to know all about everything!' She wanted the moon, 'and when she succeeds in getting it, tires, and wants a new moon!!'[12]

In this very long letter, it is clear that even after a decade Daisy still has some feeling for the man who had given her two children. She tells him how on one occasion, when on the way south from Yorkshire, she had motored to Wiseton and looked intently at the once so familiar house. Sitting outside the gates Maynard had remembered being taken to see 'Soldier Joe' as a little boy. When his mother had seemed surprised, he had affirmed the strongest memories of those visits. This poignant experience had caused Daisy to reflect that 'all playing at love is a sham, and that the reality was the *big* love of all my life'.[13]

~

The British Socialist movement was divided during the war, just when it ought to have been speaking in unity. In one camp were Blatchford, Hyndman and Wells, who regarded defeat of Germany as the priority. In the other were people within the Independent Labour Party, who regarded the conflict as a capitalist war, of which the working class on both sides were the victims.

Passionate as she was about Socialism, 'the one cause I hold worth living for'[14] and in her opinion the only long-term hope for humanity, Daisy tried to be a conciliator. But it was a hard task. In April 1916, the British Socialist Party was approaching its conference in Manchester, and it was widely believed that the differences simmering in the party would boil over. To someone who saw the big picture this strife was frustrating. After all, surely what united the feuding groups was greater than anything that divided them? What mattered was faithfulness to the ideal; the superstructure of internationalism could only rise on that basis. The world would then awake at last to the truth that it was rulers who make wars and their subjects who perish by them. But Comrade Warwick's clear-sighted view did not prevail, and as predicted at the April conference profound disagreements caused the Socialist Party to split. Hyndman and most of his former SDF associates broke away and formed the National Socialist Party, which strongly supported the allied war effort. Compared with the ebullient optimism of the pre-war years, the movement was no longer inspiring to the many loyal Socialists like Lady Warwick who knew that unity was strength.

That year, 1916, an eloquent description of the devastation in Europe was written by Walter H. Page, the American ambassador in London, addressing a friend back home in Virginia:

> You will recall more clearly than I certain horrible catastrophic, universal ruin passages in Revelation – monsters swallowing the Universe, blood and fire and clouds and an eternal crash, rotting ruin enveloping all things ... There are perhaps ten

million dead of this war, and perhaps a hundred million persons
to whom death would be a blessing. Add to these as many millions more whose views of life are so distorted that blank idiocy
would be a better mental outlook, and you'll get a hint . . . of
what this continent has already become – a bankrupt slaughterhouse inhabited by unmated women . . . The hills about
Verdun are not blown to pieces worse than the whole social
structure and intellectual and spiritual life of Europe. I wonder
that anybody is sane.[15]

In March 1917 had come news that reverberated all over the
world. Revolutionary forces had stormed the Tsar's Winter Palace,
seized the imperial family, and set up a provisional government
which was pledged to guarantee democracy. It soon became clear
that Russia was in turmoil, with the Bolsheviks fighting opposing
forces, which were fiercely resisting. European Socialists welcomed the new dispensation, while European governments
watched and waited for clarification of a volatile situation.

Daisy Warwick hoped that the end of imperial rule in Russia
might signal an end to monarchies right across Europe. Writing in
the *Daily Chronicle* the following month, she was exuberant:

I hail the Russian Revolution as the one great good that has
come to the world so far from nearly three years of heartbreaking war . . . My hope is that the people of Russia will by
their mandate abolish monarchy for good and all, and give the
tragedy of war the happy ending that freedom alone can confer.
They can by their vote shatter into ruins every throne that holds
an absolute monarch, they can give Social Democracy its voice
and then, and then only, man will be free and war impossible.
Vive l'Internationale![16]

During the first three years of the war, Daisy had been a good deal
occupied with journalism: with the faithful co-operation of

Bensusan, her ghost-writer, articles in her name proliferated in English, American and colonial magazines. Some of the topics on which Lady Warwick expressed her views were women's work in wartime, wartime divorce, illegitimacy and the effect of war on moral standards generally. With so many features appearing under her controversial name, unsuspecting people would have thought her to be a one-woman hive of industry. A New York literary magazine, *The Bookman*, regarded her as the most brilliant writer on social and 'Socialistic' subjects in the English-speaking world. In fact she and Bensusan met frequently to discuss ideas, sometimes at lunch or tea; he would take a few notes, and when a basis for a feature had been agreed he would start writing.

One of their more sensational features was Daisy's version of the Beresford affair, published by *Pearson's Magazine* in New York (1915), of which the editor was none other than Frank Harris. Accompanying the article was a drawing of a rumpled bare-legged lady on a couch. In 1916 a collection of Lady Warwick's articles was published under the title *A Woman and the War*. Ralph Blumenfeld, editor of the *Daily Express*, saw to it that the book received a kind review in his paper; despite that, sales in Britain were slow, though they were better in America. Indeed, the USA was the pair's most favourable foreign market. In Britain, Europe and the Empire, they were represented by the London Literary Agency, and later by the Authors' Syndicate. Neither dealings with agents nor the Warwick–Bensusan collaboration were always smooth, and Bensusan did not always receive the payment due to him without a struggle.

If she was disappointed by the wrangles among Socialists during the war, the Anglican Church establishment also alienated Daisy. Naturally Conrad Noel and other Christian Socialists were people whose commitment she much admired, and whose ideals she shared. But too many clergymen seemingly preached as if God in heaven was waving the Union Jack and could be asked to give victory to 'our' side.

The brutality of war had also turned Daisy against fox hunting, as if the association with killing was now unbearable. Therefore the local pack of hounds no longer ran over the Easton estate, which had become a dedicated animal habitat instead, in memory of author and naturalist W.H. Hudson. A modest book, *Nature's Quest*, which came out a few years later, was her personal celebration of the countryside, which she had loved from childhood.

~

On 19 February 1918 Maynard was married in a quiet ceremony held at Little Easton church. He was not quite twenty, but his bride, Dora Pape, was thirty-five. Whether by choice or because the war was still on, the wedding seems to have been in such a low key that Mercy was the only bridesmaid. It is more than likely that Maynard had met Dora through her eldest brother, Lt. E.L. Pape, RFC, on whose arm she walked up the aisle of the beautiful twelfth-century church. Another RFC officer, Lt. R. Joynson Hicks, was best man, and celebrations went on sporadically for two days.

Then, in the early hours of 22 February, a maid at Easton Lodge was woken by a crackling sound next to her bedroom. Looking out, she saw flames filling the Tudor section of the house and raised the alarm. The fire was spreading rapidly, but, quickly alerted by the maid, Daisy escaped down an emergency staircase, carrying her favourite parrot. Brookie was also led out safely from his room at the opposite end of the wing.

Most unfortunately, the Easton telephone was out of order, so a messenger had to be sent to Dunmow in a motor to call out the fire brigade. As reported in a local paper, Police Inspector Flack, along with some firemen, at once proceeded to the mansion with hydrants and hose to start getting the fire under control. The rest of the brigade from Dunmow followed, and were joined by other contingents from the county. Special constables as well as regular police turned up in force to assist the firemen, but flames were spreading so quickly that it was some time before they began to gain control.

The blaze had apparently been started by a monkey which had been sitting on top of a stove, clinging to an old blanket. The culprit caused a great deal of damage. Spreading along the west wing, fire engulfed one bedroom after another, and in the rooms underneath ceilings came thudding down. Windows and doors burst with loud reports. Having made his way out through clouds of smoke, Brookie was wrapped in blankets, and sitting on the lawn in a chair tried to direct the firemen to help rescue some of the art collection. Luckily some old masters were saved. The moon was hazy that night, but flames lit up the sky for miles around, clearly showing the people gathered in Easton Park.[17] The chatelaine with her parrot looked on. She had been about to open Easton as an officers' convalescent home, and some eighty beds had been prepared.

By the time the fire was put out, the entire west wing had been gutted. Daisy's bedroom was burnt out and all her clothes destroyed, as well as books, personal papers and other valuables. Some twenty-eight bedrooms and the kitchens had also been destroyed. Of the Tudor building (which had survived a fire seventy years previously), nothing remained except some huge charred oak beams, while stags' heads lay around bizarrely in the old hall. By the afternoon, firemen were directing a flood of water on to those smouldering heaps.

Although thousands of pounds' worth of damage had been done, it could have been worse had it not been for an internal concrete wall which stopped the fire spreading throughout the mansion. All the staff emerged safely from that terrible night. Wearing a skirt borrowed from Jane Wells, Daisy soon departed for London to equip herself with some new clothes. It would cost nearly £30,000 to repair the fire damage.

❦ 18 ❧

The Aftermath of War

ALL THAT WALTER PAGE, the American ambassador, had written in his letter of 1916 was accentuated by the war's end, some of the fiercest battles having been fought in the two final years. C.F.G. Masterman wrote of the colossal change in society: in the vast raw cemeteries of Europe and the Middle East lay 'seven hundred thousand of the beauty and pride of Britain . . . silent and cold among the unanswering generations of the dead'.[1] He singled out the retreat from Mons and the first battle of Ypres as the fields where 'the flower of British aristocracy' had perished, but there were other territories where they had fallen. When the guns had stopped and the great armies had melted away, humanity was still stunned – no longer by the noise but by the silence, a great silence in which those four years of uncertainty and madness seemed like a nightmare.

The men who had come through returned to a precarious world, and found whatever employment they could. Work was scarce even for the able-bodied, but for the disabled it was almost non-existent. It was not the reward they might have expected. As Masterman put it: 'those now engaged in the selling of ribbons or the speeding of the plough . . . are men who once held the Ypres salient, or stormed through the Hindenberg line, or marched into Bulgaria or Baghdad, or bivouacked outside Jerusalem.'[2]

Many families felt their bereavement reinforced, realising finally that their loved ones would not be returning. It was most unusual for a mother to welcome home two sons. Queenie's husband Charlie Helmsley had been killed on the Western Front in September 1916, three weeks after succeeding his grandfather as Earl of Faversham. The following year Queenie would marry Sir Gervase Beckett, the veteran Conservative MP, a widower who belonged more to her parents' generation than her own.

The economic cost of the war was felt throughout the country. There was no greater sign that the old world had ended than the huge sale of land: a million acres came on to the market during the immediate post-war years, the largest transfer since the Norman Conquest. The loss of so many sons who would have inherited significant estates was a factor in the great land sale. A general feeling of instability was another. Many people would have agreed with the critic and Liberal MP Augustine Birrell when he said: 'I am far too much in doubt about the present, far too perturbed about the future, to be otherwise than profoundly reverential about the past.'[3]

Daisy Warwick began selling land in September 1918. Forty-six acres at Passenham were sold to tenants at a price of £17,000; 659 acres at Ingarsby, Leicestershire were also sold to tenants for £18,000. The following year she put land up for sale on a much bigger scale, nearly a third of her total inheritance around Easton: 5,133 acres were sold, realising £97,017.

Once again many of the buyers were tenant farmers; in fact well over half the sitting tenants bought their farms. At the end of the sale, one spoke for them all when he thanked Lady Warwick for treating them so well. She had been anxious to avoid encouraging speculators to move in, and in that she had succeeded. Sales of the colliery villages of Bagworth and Thornton in Leicestershire followed, and brought her £90,017. The money raised by the multiple sales was certainly needed. Despite the generosity of Arthur du Cros, Daisy's position was nothing like as secure as it had been in the old days. During the war she had lived on capital, selling off blocks of Katanga shares to the Franco-Belgian company which controlled the business. The war had undermined the position of great landowners, with higher taxation, particularly of unearned income. There had been a revival of agriculture, but by 1917 wages were rising faster than agricultural prices.

The fact that she had been forced to sell land which had been held in her family for generations did not dismay Daisy at all. Her conversion to Socialism had led her to believe that the landowning classes were doomed anyway. Democracy would one day carry them away completely. The old order had been based on feudalism, and the sooner the last vestiges of it were swept away, the better it would be for Britain. Brook House in Park Lane was sold, an address full of memories of grand pre-war entertaining. Daisy's household at Easton had been considerably diminished, with far fewer servants.

Even so, her life was hardly threadbare. At the end of the war Philip Tilden, now established as an architect, carried out some restoration work at Easton. With the very limited amount of money available to spend, it was his aim to gather the raw ends of the house together, 'so that posterity would not miss the vast chasm that separated the old Dutch-looking house from its bastard child and single isolated block that trespassed upon the edge of the lawns'.[4]

Whereas Tilden favoured symmetry his client believed that asymmetry equalled originality. Some accommodation was finally reached, though Tilden was not completely happy with the results. Frustrating as the project may have been at times, the architect saw it all with humour: 'Daisy Warwick cared so much more for people, animals and the beauties of nature that, as she said a hundred times "A shack will do for me, dear thing."' He discovered very soon, however, that the shack would have to contain 'a

Ritz-like bathroom, a most sunny, large and beautiful bedroom with a sitting room alongside, and the service round the corner so that there should be comfort in velvet slippers'.[5]

~

After the war, Daisy had set about buying the reversion of Easton from Guy in order to settle it on Maynard, who was living with his wife Dora in a house on the Easton estate. Their only child, born in 1919, was a daughter named Felice, whom her grandmother Warwick called 'the adorable Bunty'.

Guy had emerged from the Great War at the age of thirty-six as Brigadier-General Lord Brooke, and should have been set on a course to fulfil his earlier promise. That he failed to live up to expectations had a lot to do with his increasing alcohol addiction. Early in youth he had set his sights high, but after the war all his burning ambition seemed to evaporate, and the man of action he had been became a man who did nothing.

The acrimonious break-up of his marriage was one milestone, after which he only met his ex-wife occasionally to discuss business matters. Guy's erratic and unstable behaviour was disruptive within his family, as his mother wrote to Ralph Blumenfeld two years after the war's end. She described how he had turned up suddenly with some Americans, expecting her to put them up: 'He was very bad indeed! In fact a scandal, but after two days here on water he became normal and innocently asked me what the fuss was about! What *is* one to do? But I fancy now he is quite quite hopeless and I don't know what my Xmas will be like!'[6] She had been intending to give a small New Year dance, but could not face it with Guy in the house: 'Mercy and I and Maynard find our Xmas dislocated!'[7]

Guy formed some shadowy attachments with women, enjoyed a little fishing and shooting and club life in London, but this seemed to be the limit of his aspirations. After his alcoholic excesses he spent time drying out at The White Cliff, his mother's house in Devon, set in the loveliest bay. Daisy referred to a female companion who went with him as 'the barmaid'.

In the same letter she also wrote to Blumenfeld about the post-war situation, and predicted the collapse of world financial markets which would happen before the end of the decade:

> Every day brings us nearer to a terrific smash, financial of course, but especially industrial! The unemployed will get out of hand ere long – Heavens what a life for the soldiers who fought for England! Sometimes I wish the Germans had come! By this time we should have been 'organised' and at work!'[8]

She was receiving charming letters from the prisoners of war who had been incarcerated at Dunmow: 'They never forget us and write so cheerfully and bravely of their work and country. I feel the French are more and more despicable – what *do* they want! . . . They can not even be grateful to England and America . . .'[9]

~

Daisy had been out of touch with Lord Rosebery for many years, but in the spring of 1922 she was moved to write to him from The White Cliff: 'Long ago we laughed and joked and "Catherine" confided troubles that in those days weighed heavily, but were really light compared to the world's agony since. Perhaps you have forgotten me? But I hear of you now and then from "Sister Millie" . . .'[10]

Rosebery's elder son had been killed during the war. Daisy had seen pictures of her old friend in the newspapers, showing him looking sad. They had brought tears to her eyes, and given her the courage to write: 'I know all you suffered in the war; it was too deep to write words of sympathy – but please believe that I never forgot you – in our short intimacy your kindness to me – and all the dreams built up around your political career that you were too indifferent to grasp!'[11] Her use of the word 'intimacy' is interesting. Is it a clue that they had enjoyed a relationship as more than friends?

In November 1922 Daisy was in Paris to give Rodin the sittings he needed to complete the marble 'Greek Goddess' on which he had been working for a long time. She stayed at the Mercedes Hotel in the Place de l'Etoile rather than the Ritz, her favourite in those now remote pre-war days. And it was from Paris that she wrote a ten-page letter to Rosebery in which, obviously feeling that he had misunderstood the concept, she tried to set him right about the meaning of Socialism.

She had been so glad, she said, to get such a kindly letter from him, and to know that he had not forgotten her. Twenty years before, Daisy had wanted him to take on the mantle of leadership in progressive politics, but he had declined. Having desired to see him in the forefront of the great reform movement she reminded him of 'the frank genuine *longing* I had to see your great talents used for the People . . . whom you might have led with your gifts of intellect and eloquence . . . you *wilfully* dropped behind, and I had to go on.'[12]

Now she felt glad to have even a humble place in the great movement that would free the world: 'And a wide river rolls between us now and neither of us can bridge it. It is unlikely that I shall ever see you again – but when you lay down your mantle at the end, perhaps you will think after all that I have chosen the better part.'[13]

Like all thoughtful men, she suggested, he was too intelligent to underrate the forces which were going to submerge the present political parties. If only he could have been part of it. She herself had been amazed by the progress of radical thinking the world over, and she had the temerity to explain: 'Nine tenths of the argument against Socialism dissolves into mist the moment one states the single fact that Socialism is a science of *economics* . . . and as such the only thing to which it can be logically and intelligently opposed is Capital.'[14]

In her view, Socialism was not about controlling people and taking away individual freedom. Neither did it aim to systematise thought; the only systematising would be industrial. People would be set free from the competitive struggle in which they had to engage so as 'to deprive other men of the necessities of life in order to prevent *them* from depriving *you*',[15] and the development of real individuality would become possible for the first time.

Reflecting on her own life, Daisy told her old friend that whereas in the past she had given her all in loving an individual, with the passing of years the same impulse had merged into the love of Humanity, 'and under that banner I have found the courage to lose all that once seemed essential to life and happiness'.[16]

❧ 19 ❧

The Labour Candidate

MERCY, NOW EIGHTEEN YEARS OLD, had very striking looks and great intelligence. She was keen on having a profession and refused to be presented at court. Daisy was slightly shocked that her daughter wanted to work, but Mercy responded: 'But Mother, you're always saying people should *do* something!' There was still enough of the old aristocrat in her Ladyship for her to greet Mercy's ambition with caution, but she also recognised that they were living in a new world. Women were becoming emancipated and wanted to experience everything.

Ellen Terry encouraged Mercy's ambition to be an actress, having seen her performances at the Barn, where at the age of fifteen she had played Prince Arthur in Shakespeare's *King John* (with Terry as Hubert), and Katherina in *The Taming of the Shrew*. The veteran Kate Phillips offered to coach her. Luckily, Miss Phillips knew Basil Dean, a distinguished producer-director, and wrote to him about her protégée. With some reluctance he agreed to see her, but during the interview Mercy's charm and intelligence made a good impression, and Dean invited her to join his theatre company. On 1 March 1923 a contract arrived, offering her the same terms as other beginners. In a tribute to her wanton ancestor she chose the stage name Nancy Parsons, and within three months the fledgling actress was playing a parlour-maid in *Lilies of the Field*, a comedy starring Meggi Albanesi and Edna Best. Several members of Mercy's family were among the first night audience at the Ambassadors Theatre early in June.

Basil Dean's career had begun in the last years of the nineteenth century, when he had been an actor with a ramshackle company, mostly touring the north of England. Eventually realising that he wanted his future to be not in acting but in directing, he had worked with Miss Horniman's Company in Manchester. On coming to London, Beerbohm Tree had taken him on as assistant producer at the Haymarket Theatre. By the early 1920s Dean was among the best-known names in the theatrical world, working both with veteran actors of the Edwardian period and new young talent such as Noël Coward. Besides the Ambassadors, Dean also ran the St Martin's Theatre nearby, and putting on plays in both houses kept him extremely busy. He had a reputation for being a perfectionist, and indeed his productions usually attained an overall quality that justified his approach.

There had been some stirring of attraction to Mercy from the beginning, although Dean was still married to his first wife, by whom he had three sons. However, after the curtain had come down, company members would often go to one of many supper clubs to dance, and Mercy and Basil would join them. Dancing had become a craze after the war, probably stemming from an instinct to affirm life and vitality. The Embassy in Bond Street, where the impeccable Luigi showed regular patrons to their favourite tables, was one of the best known of these clubs. It was to the Embassy that Basil and Mercy most often went after the theatre, to join the jostling throng on the dance floor. It was the beginning of a love affair, and before long news reached Lady Warwick that her daughter's name was being linked with Dean.

Not only was he a married father of three, he was also a great deal older than Mercy; but the couple ignored the gossip and continued dancing. Then came the summons to meet her Ladyship, by way of an invitation to spend an August bank holiday weekend at Easton. The couple were met at the private station once used by the Prince of Wales, and entered Easton Park via the Blue Gates on the far side of the Stortford Road. As they drove through, they passed an occasional retainer who bobbed a curtsey or doffed a cap. Though much changed since the days of great splendour, there was still an element of the feudal way of life on the estate. If the butler and footmen were no longer in evidence, there was a cohort of maids in starched white caps and aprons who attended to everything, and bedrooms were still comfortable in the Edwardian fashion.

Dean was not at all daunted by the prospect of meeting Lady Warwick. As he was to say later: 'Ours was a fairytale and I was completely lost in it.'[1] 'Nancy' was eager for her mother to meet the man with whom she had fallen in love. They whiled away some time in the saloon 'crowded with Edwardian gilt mirrors, enormous Chinese vases with sheaves of pampas grass protruding, Dresden figurines, priceless bibelots competing with the nouveau art of the nineteenth century'.[2] There were signed photographs everywhere, ranging from royalty to trade union leaders. Lady Warwick now made her entrance: she had chosen to receive Dean in the Garden Room (built after the 1918 fire) in which there were frescoes by 'Teddy', son of theatre director Edward Gordon Craig. Dean retained a clear memory of that first meeting with his future mother-in-law:

> Instead of condescension there was interest; instead of criticism there was tactful enquiry about my work and interests . . . soon we were deep in talk about the theatre . . . our talk was punctuated by the screeching of parrots, the chatter of monkeys and the yapping of dachshunds. None were house-trained, but Lady Warwick did not seem to mind . . .[3]

The entire weekend was idyllic. The countryside was never seen to better advantage: sometimes it seemed to be swathed in a pale blue gauze of mist, behind which the distant fir plantation stood up, 'dark sentinels against the high bright sky, where larks were singing . . . in and out of the rose garden we went, carrying the scent of its blooms into the dairy, where thick yellow cream from the Jersey herd was standing in earthenware jars, waiting to be turned into delicious butter'.[4]

The famous gardens were maintained to a standard which seemed as high as in the great days, even though only eight gardeners were employed. Bank Holiday Monday began with a cloudless blue sky, hot and sunny, and it was a big day in the calendar: the annual Easton flower show, with a fairground thrown in. For form's sake they were present for the judging, but Nancy quickly grew bored and skipped away to the fairground, with Basil in pursuit. They stayed until the last rays of the setting sun were glistening behind the old oak trees and blue mist was once again shrouding the landscape: 'the coloured globes looping the fairground had already been switched on, and the younger children taken home, loudly complaining, but the older ones and their boy friends were still swinging excitedly or aiming at the last of the coconuts . . .'[5]

They went back to a riotous supper at the Lodge, which to Basil already felt like home: all the house party was euphoric, their mood induced not by alcohol but simply by the joy of living. After supper, the lovers left the others playing card games and went for a walk in that most romantic of settings. Crossing the tennis courts, then through the sunken Italian garden, they passed along the avenue of pleached limes till they reached a lake, where they sat gazing at the scene in silence for a long time, as a harvest moon floated over the trees.

∼

At the end of October 1923 *The Times* carried a report that the Countess of Warwick had agreed to fight the constituency of Warwick and Leamington as Labour candidate in the forthcoming by-election. The correspondent wondered if the red flag would be raised from the castle tower, but was assured that was not to be.[6] The secretary of the Warwick and Leamington Labour Party, Mr J.T. Duffield, said that having had the honour of knowing Lady Warwick for several years, he believed her to be the very best of candidates: 'She is a most charming woman, and a most effective platform speaker.'[7] She had proved her earnestness as a Socialist. Labour had a good cause, and it might well be to the party's advantage that for the first time about 18,000 women voters would have the chance to exercise the franchise. Lady Warwick intended to make a special appeal to them, said Mr Duffield.

One of the drawbacks in fighting Warwick and Leamington for Labour was the comparative weakness of the party organisation in the constituency. The local party was nevertheless optimistic, but a more objective assessment would have taken account of the opposition. The Tories were fielding an ideal candidate, the debonair Anthony Eden MC, son of a baronet, who would soon be marrying Beatrice, daughter of Sir Gervase Beckett. With his good war record and undoubted charm, Captain Eden had all the credentials to appeal in a constituency which was natural Conservative territory. The Liberal candidate was George Nicholls, once an agricultural labourer, who had sat in the Commons since the election of 1906.

Early on there was a rumour that Lady Warwick was daunted by the challenging task ahead, and was about to withdraw 'from sheer terror at the largeness of the constituency'.[8] Speaking at Leamington Town Hall, she denied any such thing: 'I am here and I am going to stay until after the polling has taken place.'[9] Conscious of being up against a strong Liberal candidate who was focusing on agriculture, she homed in on the subject: 'a bold national agricultural policy, aiming at stability of prices for the farmer and an adequate living wage for the labourer, was the goal.'[10] Casting herself in the role of the lady who had come out of Warwick Castle to assist the poor and lowly, Daisy made much of her association with Joseph Arch, who had been born at Barford, a few miles from Leamington. Moreover the Arch family had been employed at the castle for generations.

Just when the campaign was beginning to warm up came news that the Prime Minister, Stanley Baldwin, had decided to call a general election. The Dissolution of Parliament took place on 16 November, and polling day was to be on 6 December. The King's Dissolution speech referred to the grave problems and deep anxiety caused by the position of agriculture and the problem of unemployment, the latter being something with which post-war governments had failed to deal in any significant way. The outgoing government held the view that no permanent improvement could be expected without measures for safeguarding and developing the home market, and therefore Baldwin was seeking a mandate for protectionism. According to Sir William Joynson Hicks, Health Minister, the government had been trying to remedy the situation, but the only remedy of a permanent character was 'to increase the possibilities of real commercial work by protecting the home market'.[11] The Prime Minister also intended to give preferential treatment to the colonies; he proposed 'development of the greatest asset in the world, the Empire, by British sinews and by British capital . . . However, it is no use sending either men or money to the Dominions or the colonies . . . unless we are prepared to secure them markets here by means of a preferential tariff.'[12]

The Clarion's editorials, speaking for the Left, tried to point out the fallacies inherent in the current debate:

> . . . nowhere in the world has a policy of Protection, such Protection as Capitalist Governments apply to industry, ever abolished unemployment . . . Surely they would find a remedy for unemployment if they could!
>
> Yes, if they could find a remedy that would at the same time enable the profiteer to profiteer and the landlord to wax fat on

unearned land values, and the financier to take his customary toll ... What has terrified the Government into taking this plunge into the fiscal controversy is not a desire to abolish unemployment. It is merely a desire to lessen the dangers that may arise from unemployment. During the war, the governments in power absolutely abolished unemployment. They could do the same again in peace if they wanted to. They don't want to. Therefore I think the Labour Party is on safe ground in challenging the efficacy of the proposed Tory Protectionist policy . . .[13]

A second editorial came the following week, in the wake of a pronouncement from John Galsworthy – speaking as a company promoter – that 'though science, finance and the Press at the moment seem to doubt it, there is still more money to be made out of the salvation of mankind than out of its destruction.' *The Clarion* thought that if Mr Galsworthy knew how to make money out of mankind's salvation, he had better set about the job at once:

It is rather wonderful that the guardians and owners of the Capital of the country have never thought of this themselves. Merely as a change from their age-long habit of thinking that money-making must necessarily involve the degradation and the depression of the masses, whose only Capital is their Labour-power . . .

During the war we had just a glimpse of the possibilities of money-making that would evolve themselves in a country where all the people were employed, and fed and clothed with decent comfort . . . But our poor Captains of Industry were so sodden and dazzled with their ancient wage-reducing prejudices that they were unable to see the vision. As soon as the war was over they cried aloud with one voice for the old-time 'freedom' to condemn millions of their fellow creatures to the hell of poverty and semi-starvation . . .[14]

The Labour manifesto proposed a capital levy on fortunes over £5,000, for reduction of the war debt; national schemes for productive work; nationalisation of mines and railways; taxation of land values and corporations; and generous provision for the aged, as well as the sick, the disabled, and widowed mothers. Policies to abolish food duties and to reduce income tax were set out. Labour also advocated a revision of the Treaty of Versailles.

Daisy entered the fray with some of her old panache, and as reported in the *Daily Express* drove a phaeton with a team of white ponies, a *coup de théâtre* of the kind for which she had an unerring instinct. Sporting the red and gold Labour colours, weaving in and out of the other traffic, she was unmistakable. Her daughter-in-law, Dora, and Percy Widdrington, the Socialist Rector of Great Easton, were sometimes to be seen with her.

When addressing meetings Lady Warwick concentrated on unemployment, housing, education and agriculture. Speaking at Stoneleigh, she told her audience that on the 500 acres she owned in the constituency, her farm labourers were paid thirty-six shillings a week. She emphasised the importance of a standard wage, which should not mean loss of benefits such as the old age pension.

She was matching the Liberals: Nicholls had emphasised that his party would give farmers the right to purchase land, would make rapid provision of houses, and remove thrift disqualification from the old age pension. In a meeting at Kenilworth, she also called for a national housing scheme to prevent young people from leaving villages. If, she said, the people of that division elected her, she hoped to have opportunities for answering their questions on issues of vital importance to them, but whatever the result, she would continue to work as she had done for the last thirty years, a pledge which received applause.

The election atmosphere was far from cordial. Having countered her claim to a connection with Joseph Arch by pointing out that he had himself been Arch's colleague, and they had worked together to secure farm labourers' rights, George Nicholls was scornful about Lady Warwick being put forward as a Labour candidate. He said that everyone knew her to be an out-and-out Socialist whose wearing of the Labour mantle was just a stunt.

Captain Eden played to his strength, claiming that his party understood farming better than his rivals. With the Conservatives proposing policies that included special assistance to industries suffering from unfair foreign competition, negotiation for a reduction of foreign tariffs, and substantial imperial preference, he insisted that Conservative governments had traditionally been the best friends of all who depended on agriculture for their livelihood, and that they had continued to be so in recent times.

Apart from stalwart supporters Maynard and Dora, Daisy was undermined by her own family, with their strong Conservative connections. Elfrida, Guy's wife since 1909, was the sister of Anthony Eden; Guy thought it fitting to write to his brother-in-law, wishing him every possible success. Queenie was married to Tory MP Sir Gervase Beckett, and Eden's marriage to her step-daughter Beatrice in early November gave another reason, if one was needed, for Queenie to support her mother's Conservative opponent. Daisy must have been only too painfully aware of how much her immediate family loathed her politics.

As if to underline their antipathy, Brookie's brother Louis Greville sent a telegram saying 'My brothers and I send best wishes for your success in coming contest for the Conservative cause.' The implication was that Lord Warwick was included, as if dissociating him from his wife. Eden was on the crest of a wave, and on 9 November had the pleasure of reading out this greeting. It stung his Labour opponent, as it had been intended to do. And it made her very angry, for Brookie had stayed out of the fray, living quietly in Devon. Although the Labour cause could not have been dear to his heart, he was far too kind to say anything publicly against his wife, and had told her that if she felt called to continue her work, then she should do so.

Daisy took the opportunity of replying on that same evening, 9 November: 'how low down a trick this is to play on a man so ill that even I was too proud to ask him for a message to bring to you. He would certainly have given it because what Lady Warwick does Lord Warwick always endorses.'[15] He was a true gentleman, and to imply that he had sided with his brothers was the act of cads.

With her family so antagonistic, strong support was needed from elsewhere, and it came. High-profile Labour figures spoke in the constituency, among them George Lansbury, Beatrice Webb and Arthur Henderson, the first Labour MP to become a Cabinet minister. However, Lord Algernon Percy, Duke of Northumberland, spoke for Eden on the hustings; although she was perfectly direct when talking about the key issues, he accused Lady Warwick of indulging in platitudes and talking about high ideals without defining how they could be made into reality.

Eden held several winning cards. With good looks and a commendable war record, he also stood for the kind of views acceptable to what might nowadays be called 'middle England'. In the heart of hunting country, Daisy had stated her opposition to blood sports, courageously disregarding how that might affect her chances on polling day; Eden made it clear that he believed foxhunting was the right and proper sport for English men and women. Eden was a churchgoer, and said that he would resist any move to disestablish the Church of England; he would also oppose legislation to make divorce easier. He was tailor-made to represent the traditional Conservative supporters who rallied to his cause.

Lady Warwick's outlook was probably more closely reflected by *The Clarion*, still under the editorship of her old mentor, Robert Blatchford. She was in favour of recognising the Soviet government, and revealed her sympathy with conscientious objectors. Eden could not have hoped for a better gift: the war was still very much on people's minds, and heroism was associated with the men who had fought and died, decidedly not with 'conchies'. Besides which, to the people of Warwick and Leamington the Soviet government was seen as highly dangerous. Even the Labour Party liked to put as much distance as possible between itself and any Communist-Marxist connection.

It was a gruelling campaign for Lady Warwick, now in her sixties. On 2 December she addressed five open-air meetings in drizzling rain. Supported by several 'comrades', she was giving it all she could. The day before polling, she addressed no less than nine meetings, ending up in Warwick marketplace. Her car was dragged through the streets by her supporters, and a large crowd escorted her homeward.

On election day *The Times* published a leader, under the heading 'The Voice of Britain', which left no doubt about its allegiance:

> Rarely has there been an election fraught with graver consequences at home and throughout the world. The issues are large and clear. Are we to look on while unexampled unemployment is eating into our national life, or are we to strive resolutely for its cure? Are we to abdicate our rightful influence in Europe or are we to assert it? . . . Today will show whether we are resolute to have a strong government or not . . . [The people of Britain] can secure such a government by giving Mr Baldwin a large majority over Labour and the reunited Liberals combined; they can secure it in no other way . . .[16]

According to 'The Thunderer' a Liberal victory was out of the question; the Liberals had criticised Mr Baldwin's foreign policy, but had nothing to offer in its place. In any coalition Labour would set the pace, and the paper did not welcome such influence: 'The Labour Party put forward a hazy internationalism as a cure for the ills of Europe . . . Their very active left wing is, moreover, connected to some of the most dangerous forces of European unrest . . .'[17]

In Warwick and Leamington at least, Eden's victory with 16,337 votes was hardly a surprise. Nicholls, with 11,134, split the non-Tory vote: Lady Warwick polled just 4,015 votes, a poor third, and a hugely disappointing result. But the odds had been heavily stacked against her: had it not been for a strong Liberal candidate making it a three-cornered fight, she might well have done a good deal better. It would also have helped if her constituency organisation had been stronger. On the whole, however, it would have taken a miracle for Labour to win in such a Tory heartland.

If that miracle had happened and Daisy Warwick had been returned, she would have probably been capable of making an effective contribution in the House of Commons. It would have been interesting to see her take on the Conservative Lady Astor, who was re-elected for Plymouth Sutton, a woman who concerned herself with many of the same issues. The election result, however, gave Labour 191 members, an increase of nearly fifty seats, making it the second largest party in the Commons, with no party holding an overall majority. And there were some interesting results countrywide: Labour improved its overall position in Wales, and Ramsay Macdonald increased his majority in Aberavon. Elsewhere Frederick Pethwick Lawrence defeated Winston Churchill in West Leicester. Margaret Bondfield won Northampton, and was later to be the first female Cabinet minister in a Labour government. Another female Labour luminary, Susan Lawrence, took East Ham. Within a year, in 1924, Ramsey Macdonald was to lead the first Labour government.

~

Daisy hardly had time to recover from the hard campaign before Brookie died in Devon on 15 January 1924. During his last years he had done a little painting, and sometimes enjoyed gentle motoring excursions with Philip Tilden and his wife. Local architecture and antique shops added to the pleasure of those trips. Daisy had increasingly respected him for his gentlemanliness, and during the latter years they had reached an understanding. After forty years of marriage, sometimes far from smooth, Daisy was bound to feel some sense of loss, even if Brookie had always been rather in the background.

Brookie's funeral took place in Warwick four days later. With all due solemnity, the coffin was carried from the castle on a gun carriage through the streets; there were several carriages of flowers, and the Warwickshire Yeomanry provided a guard of honour. The fifth Earl was laid to rest with his ancestors in the family vault beneath St Mary's Collegiate Church.

A memorial to him in the church at Little Easton was inscribed with lines by the American Quaker, John Greenleaf Whittier:

> And now he rests
> His greatness and his sweetness
> No more shall seem at strife
> And death has moulded into calm completeness
> The statue of his life.

❧ 20 ❧

The Play's the Thing

LORD WARWICK HAD DIED a comparatively poor man, leaving only £10,749 gross. In addition he had a life insurance policy of £139,000, which had to be used to redeem debentures on the Warwick estates, benefiting his heir, not his widow. Guy, now the sixth Earl, was in a bad way and, according to Bensusan, two months after inheriting the title was in a nursing home being treated for alcoholism.[1]

In midsummer 1924 Daisy had reason to write to Ralph Blumenfeld to complain about the way his paper had treated one of her political friends:

> I am hurt by the *Daily Express*. I think it is mean . . . You have all the money on your side, but you need not degrade your paper by trying to hurt people like Ben Tillett. He needs food and rest. His great *heart* and *soul* in a body always suffering and in pain, should save him from personal insult – even if you differ from him politically . . .[2]

She would always stand 'in the last ditch with the disinherited', and pleaded with Blumenfeld: 'Don't go on playing up for the capitalists. You are too *good* for such dirty work and too *clever* not to despise it . . . You and I are friends – my friend hurts *me* – so forgive me if you can.'[3]

In September Daisy wrote to Blumenfeld from Yorkshire. She had been staying at Nawton Towers, where Queenie had lived with her first husband, and had been surrounded by Tories such as the Londonderrys, who were all saying that England was finished. 'Such rubbish makes one sick,' she commented, but it was true that the Tory Party was fairly demoralised, 'and the Lord knows when and how it is to be recovered!'[4]

～

But something else had preoccupied Daisy Warwick's mind for a while, a matter she had so far been unable to resolve. Once life settled down after the war, she had turned her attention to retrieving her papers from Frank Harris. While he continued to hold them, there was always the danger that he would make use of them in some way, knowing all too well the rewards he could reap. Daisy needed help in dealing with Harris, and she found a man to fill this role. Grant Richards had once worked with W.T. Stead and had subsequently started a successful publishing company, with a list that included Shaw, John Masefield and A.E. Housman. So when Richards agreed to act as intermediary, advising about the right approach and how to phrase letters, Daisy began a correspondence with Harris, attempting to put just the right amount of pressure on him in order to secure her objective.

Harris was adamant about his rights. Under the terms of their agreement in 1914 he had been promised a certain sum of money for ghosting her memoirs and acting as agent. He claimed to have kept his side of the bargain, having produced a number of chapters for which he had not received a penny. He was not prepared simply to hand over all his work for nothing. While Lady Warwick might complain that he had duped her and taken advantage of her trusting nature, Harris took no notice, and resisted all her entreaties.

Then in 1922 he had named his price: for £1,000 he would return the royal letters as well as the partially completed manuscript. In view of the terms of their original contract it does not seem unfair on his part. At this point, Harris had been in transit. After selling his share in *Pearson's Magazine*, he had left the United States and retired permanently to the South of France. Negotiations got no further, but Richards encouraged Daisy to revive the idea of writing her memoirs, and suggested as amanuensis a certain Charles Kenyon, who had been music and drama critic on the *Manchester Courier* before the war. At the end of 1924 that was where things stood, inconclusively.

Then, in January 1925, came the last episode of the protracted quarrel. Having gone to visit Frank Harris on the Riviera, Richards returned to London with his mission accomplished. He had managed to persuade Harris to hand over Daisy's letters, and must have thought he would be greeted by a grateful recipient. Nothing of the kind: Daisy heard the news of his success without enthusiasm, and refused to reimburse him for his expenses. She pronounced Harris' incomplete manuscript to be a tissue of lies, and burnt it. Any idea of writing her memoirs appeared now to be finally dead. Daisy told the persistent Richards that she had no interest in gossip, nor in her frivolous youth; neither did she want to lose her friends. He told her sternly that it was no use talking about 'blackmail' in regard to Harris, who deserved his payment, but as Lady Warwick was crying her 'poverty' he would not insist on his own expenses being repaid. In the end, after threatening to sue, Harris received just £750. It was the end of a bitter story.

~

Meanwhile, there were more interesting happenings in the theatre. The relationship between Mercy and Basil had been developing, although the amount of time they were able to spend together was severely limited by his professional life. In the autumn of 1924 the pressure was exacerbated by the knowledge that his wife intended to seek a divorce. Fortuitously, Basil had agreed to produce *Peter Pan* in America, and in fulfilment of his contract sailed for New York on the SS *Majestic* in mid-September. One of his fellow passengers was Somerset Maugham, whose edgy plays he would soon be producing.

There were some difficulties with casting the American version of *Peter Pan*, but it eventually opened in Buffalo and after two weeks transferred to New York's Knickerbocker Theater. By November Dean was homeward bound, planning a Christmas production of *A Midsummer Nght's Dream* at Drury Lanc, with choreography by Mikhail Fokine. It would be a spectacular, in the finest tradition.

In January 1925 Mercy had a part in Frederick Lonsdale's *Spring Cleaning* at the St Martin's, one of a clutch of plays that – like Maugham's *Our Betters* and Noël Coward's *The Vortex* – were breaking new ground. Their common denominator was frankness, particularly about sex, reflecting changing attitudes in the post-war world.

Whenever possible, through those months of non-stop activity, Basil and Mercy would drive down to Easton after the curtain came down on a Saturday night. Their fifteenth-century manor house needed a lot of work. Daisy stated to Joe Laycock that it was a gift; in contrast, Dean states that he had purchased it from the Maynard estate on condition that his payment would be placed in trust for Mercy and her children, augmenting the money to which she was entitled on marriage.

Daisy introduced them to an eccentric local character known only as 'the Marquis', a keen antiquarian who was to supervise the manor's restoration. It began with very basic items. The leaded casements and chimney were smothered with ivy, there was a lot of dilapidated Victorian wallpaper, rusty iron fire grates hid the original open hearths, and fungi were growing out of some walls. With architectural drawings supplied by 'the Marquis', a local builder began work. When rotting plaster was knocked down, original oak beams were revealed, and under deal boards were original oak floors. Glancing at the plans now and again, scratching his head with his bowler hat, the head builder got on with the job, using common sense and his knowledge of traditional crafts.

Mercy and Basil were more or less engaged, and with Lady Warwick's blessing they began thinking of marriage. Once solicitors had resolved the money matters, everything went smoothly. Mercy celebrated her twenty-first birthday over Easter with just a few distinguished guests at Easton: Basil brought Fay Compton, one of his leading ladies. Eugene Goossens and Gustav Holst with his wife were also of the party. A week later, in the spring of 1925, Daisy wrote to Joe Laycock to tell him about Mercy's forthcoming marriage. She was sad about it, she said, 'as he isn't half good enough for her, but they are devoted to each other'.[5] The Socialist countess did not neglect to mention that Mercy had her own money.

She conceded that Dean was clever, and with typical exaggeration said that the couple had wonderful plans for theatres all over the world. Daisy was keen for Joe to see his daughter, and suggested that they arrange lunch or dinner. Moreover, she wanted Mercy's father to get to know her – hitherto he had never maintained contact – and the proud mother told him about her brilliant conversational gifts. She had done a three-week cultural tour of Italy with one of her girlfriends, and returned full of vivid experiences.

Whether or not Joe ever agreed to meet his old lover and her daughter is not known. They were now distant, as Daisy wrote: 'the worlds we live in now seem so far apart that it is difficult – isn't it? To find mutual understanding?'[6] The emotional subtext, here as elsewhere, is clear: she had never quite got over losing Joe.

'Madre', as Daisy liked to be called, generously left the way clear for the couple's engagement party by taking herself off to Scotland. 'Nancy' said that she wanted the event to be a feast of wit and wisdom, and as Noël Coward was one of the guests there was probably an abundance of wit. The violinist Jascha Heifetz was present, as were several musicians who had clustered round Diaghilev's ballet and Sir Thomas Beecham's National Opera. The party lasted over three days of a Whitsun weekend, and there was plenty to do: tennis, visiting Wells at the Glebe, motoring round some of the ancient Essex villages, and entertainment by Coward and Eugene Goossens who improvised at the piano. Mindful that alcohol was always in short supply at Easton, Basil laid in a generous stock.

~

In May, John French, the 'little General', died. The man in whom Daisy had confided her grief about Joe Laycock all those years ago, soon after giving birth to Mercy, had been one of her closest friends. Another of those friends, George Curzon Marquess of Kedleston, had died during the winter, and Daisy missed him. When such people left the scene, it emphasised how much the world was changing.

Daisy had found a large part of her happiness in the children Joe had given her. Having worked since 1922 as motoring correspondent on the *Morning Post* – the editor, H.A. Gwynne, was a friend of his mother's and a neighbour in Essex, where Ellen Terry sometimes stayed with him – Maynard had become a successful journalist: he had recently driven a thousand miles in his Bentley to write a series of articles for the paper entitled 'Ways Out of London'. He had also put his mechanical skills to good use: according to his mother he had revolutionised the sign shows outside the *Post* building, making it 'the best show in London signs',[7] and he was experimenting with wireless communication to America. In his own way, Maynard was a genius, thought his mother, and she still very much wanted Joe to meet his son as well as his daughter. She would have liked Joe to share her pride.

Mercy and Basil's wedding took place early in the morning of 1 July 1925 at a register office in Covent Garden. The bride wore a crêpe de chine ensemble and a fashionable tricorn hat. A register office would not have been the location of choice for the bride's mother, but she tried to make the best of it by filling the room with masses of flowers. If she thought of the contrast with Queenie's wedding, it might have brought to mind the vast social change that had come about in the intervening years; things which would have been unthinkable a generation before were now accepted as a matter of course.

The wedding night was also the opening of a new Galsworthy play at the St Martin's. It was given a mixed reception: at the end of the performance there was hardly any sound from the stalls, but the gallery regulars produced so much applause that Basil mistook it for approval of the play, when in fact it was his marriage which was being cheered. After the final curtain call the entire company came on stage to present a silver salver engraved with all their names. The couple drove down to Beer for a few days' honeymoon, but the holiday in Devon was slightly marred: not only had notices for the Galsworthy been poor, but Somerset Maugham's *Rain* was not doing great box-office business, and much of the responsibility for the company's financial success fell on Dean.

By mid-August the couple were on board the SS *Majestic* bound for New York, where Basil was to be responsible for a total of four productions on Broadway. Among them was *The Vortex*, which had been launched modestly the previous year at the Everyman Theatre, Hampstead. Mercy's mother had armed her with several letters of introduction to members of old New York Society, although the social register no longer had the influence it had once enjoyed. On the strength of a recommendation from Mrs Merryweather Post, the Deans were invited to visit the legendary Mrs K. Vanderbilt in her brownstone mansion on Fifth Avenue. Basil did not particularly relish meetings with Society ladies who belonged to the past. Far more to his taste were Fred and Adele Astaire. Most of Mercy's age group seemed to be heirs or heiresses to fortunes in tobacco or sugar, who drank a great deal despite Prohibition, which was being increasingly flouted.

The Vortex had a memorably successful first night at New York's Henry Miller Theatre – 'stupendous' was the word Dean used in his autobiography. At Coward's request, 'Nancy' was hostess at a celebration party given at the Embassy Club, which she carried off with great aplomb; it was an art she had probably inherited from her mother. Dean always found New York exhilarating, and at that time the city's vitality was stronger than ever, its pace of life ever faster. A typical rehearsal day would end in a quick dash by taxi to the hotel, a change into white or black tie, a hurriedly eaten dinner, and then another taxi ride to catch curtain up at one of the theatres. Basil's theatre obligations meant four months of hard work, and Mercy had no choice but to accept the demands being made on her husband, although she was yet to have a proper honeymoon. Just before Christmas the pair embarked on the *Mauretania*, glad to be on the way home.

The following year was taken up mainly by *The Constant Nymph*. Adapted by Dean from Margaret Kennedy's popular novel, the play opened at the New Theatre on 14 September 1926, starring Edna Best and Noël Coward. The actress Mrs Patrick Campbell bumped into the producer at the final dress rehearsal. 'Beautiful play, Mr Dean,' she murmured in her most seductive tones, 'beautiful play, and how bad Noël is! I *must* go and tell him!'[8]

The Constant Nymph was received very favourably, and was instantly snapped up by an American impresario who persuaded Dean to direct the play quickly in New York. The play opened at the Selwyn Theater early on 9 December, but its London success was not repeated. However, its failure made less impact on the director than it might have done; he scarcely remembered it, for a very good reason. On 11 December Mercy gave birth to their daughter, Tessa, at Swan House, Chelsea, Daisy's current London home, and Dean was very much the proud father. The couple did not care a great deal about the formalities, but Grandmother Warwick did, and she arranged for Tessa's christening by Conrad

Noel at St Lawrence's, on a bright spring day. Two of the god-mothers were Margaret Kennedy and Edna Best. After the ceremony the party drove back from Thaxted to Easton for a celebration lunch. For Daisy's daughter and son-in-law, all seemed set fair.

ꞓ 21 ꞓ

Struggles and Disappointment

EASTON PLAYED A CONSIDERABLE part in Labour life during the 1920s. As a young man, Fenner Brockway experienced the heady atmosphere. Brockway, a leading pacifist, had been secretary of the No Conscription Fellowship in 1917, and in 1922 became organising secretary of the Independent Labour Party. When reflecting on that period much later in his life, he paid Lady Warwick a generous tribute, saying: 'She really did stir the consciences of large numbers of people.'[1] According to Brockway, the Countess could be mischievous. When delegates were intrigued by the many photographs of King Edward on display, she needed little prompting to tell some very risqué anecdotes. Arthur Henderson, a Methodist and total abstainer, would have been profoundly shocked, had he been present.

A very important matter had been concerning Lady Warwick for quite a while, one which had national, potentially international importance. In the post-war world, it was no longer an asset to own a vast house of the kind which had been run in the old days by armies of servants. Domestic help was much less readily available, and a building such as Easton Lodge which had once been a centre of luxury in Edwardian England was now more of a white elephant.

She had been ruminating about what she could do with the house. Although it had served them well for three summers, the ILP had decided not to continue meeting at Easton, mainly for financial reasons. But might there be another use for the house as a meeting place for Socialists? She was prepared to present it for use by the Labour Party as a centre for conferences, consultations and residential study groups. Ramsay Macdonald, together with Beatrice and Sidney Webb, visited the mansion to get the measure of what was being offered.

Some of the Left had reservations: they wondered whether 'the Party could touch the pitch of luxurious living without being defiled',[2] as Beatrice Webb noted in her diary. But Mrs Webb did not appear to share this hesitancy, believing Lady Warwick to be a generous well-wisher, a committed Socialist, and not to be despised: 'a benign and hard-working old woman who has gained the respect of her neighbours by a sterling public spirit . . . and by opening her park to all sorts of festivals and jaunts for the common people.'[3] In 1924, just before the first Labour government came to power, there was a move in what seemed to be the right direction, when the party's executive decided to provisionally accept the offer. During the short period before the election which brought Labour to power, Easton was in constant use by the hierarchy.

The agreement was initially to be for a trial period of one year, during which time the Labour Party would have full and free use of the house and grounds. The fee for these amenities was £300, with an additional sum to cover payment of the rates. With a low tariff for food to be supplied, the total package was one which gave the party great benefits for modest expenditure. The arrangement seemed to be satisfactory all round.

However, after the year's trial period, some began to question the suitability of the premises on practical grounds. Beatrice Webb, who had previously not raised objections, now thought differently: 'The house is far too gorgeous in its grandiose reception rooms and large extravagantly furnished bedrooms. Owing to the devastation (by fire) of 28 bedrooms during the war, there is an absurd disproportion between the *number* of the bedrooms . . . and the plenitude and magnificence of the reception rooms . . .'[4] Furthermore, some members of the puritan tendency may have felt the luxurious surroundings to be out of keeping with the Socialist ethos, probably believing that the prerequisite of high thinking was a measure of austerity.

The fact that the Countess was constantly on the premises also seemed to be a problem. Labour people did not always feel comfortable in her presence. She could be autocratic, and apparently sometimes made individuals feel that they were there 'on suffrance' rather than by right. This lack of harmony might have been due to feelings of inferiority on the part of Labour people who had never encountered Lady Warwick's world before; Socialist she was, but never proletarian. Probably feeling out of their depth, some of the groups may have become prickly, not an uncommon reaction when people feel overawed.

For whatever reason, by Christmas 1924 the arrangement had come to an end, and Daisy spent the following two years trying other approaches. The ILP had already held a national summer school at Easton in 1924, and in March 1925 decided to do so again. At a time when the vigorous ILP was influential in Labour politics, its summer schools took place under the charismatic chairmanship of the pacifist radical Clifford Allen. Here Daisy was in her element. As a member of the British Socialist Party, with revolutionary sympathies, she had much more in common with the ILP than with the first Labour government. With uninhibited debates and jolly social evenings these were outstanding events. Several young people who attended would make their names as politicians in the future, Clement Attlee and Jennie Lee among them; Jomo Kenyatta, future president of Kenya, wore his leopardskin and carried a spear.

Daisy still harboured the hope that her house might play a part in the politics of the Left, and went to considerable trouble to free the entail so that she might be able to dispose of it as she wished. She favoured the idea of an educational centre, on the lines of Ruskin College, Oxford. She approached the Trades Union Congress, not only offering Easton during her lifetime but also proposing to bequeath it to them, and at first they seemed interested.

The TUC general secretary, Walter Citrine, handled the negotiations, but although the initial offer was welcomed no definite answer was forthcoming. Almost inevitably when dealing with a body weighed down with bureaucracy, progress was slow and tedious. Daisy wished for a more dynamic response, in keeping with her vision of Easton as the nucleus of a future Socialist university. Frustrated by the delay, at the end of December she wrote to Citrine, saying that with increasing taxation and responsibilities to her employees it was imperative for her to know where she stood.[5]

In response to this appeal, members of the TUC General Council visited Easton for the weekend of 16–17 January 1926. They were able to make a full inspection of the property, besides which there were consultations with Lady Warwick, her solicitor, and the TUC's own architects and solicitors. Everything seemed satisfactory, and an agreement was reached. At last, the outcome was positive, and on 24 February members of the TUC Council arrived to take formal possession of Easton Lodge. There were specially invited guests present, as well as members of the press. After lunch, the handing-over ceremony took place in the library, as described by a reporter from the *Manchester Guardian*:

At the head of the table is the Countess of Warwick, beautiful and charming, who is giving away her house and nine hundred acres out of pure idealism and enthusiasm for the education of her 'comrades' in the movement . . . This day was for her the climax of a generation of wholehearted devotion to a class not her own.[6]

In her speech Lady Warwick expressed her hopes that the college would bring international solidarity and friendship among the world's workers. She was not being turned out of her home, she said, but would have her small domain in the stable yard.

After the ceremony, the assembled company wandered round the gardens, followed by a film crew. Lady Warwick leant on the arm of Margaret Bondfield, who had risen from assistant in a draper's shop to leading light in the Labour Party.

The scheme had now been publicly confirmed, but the legal transfer was still pending. During the interval Daisy immersed herself in planning: she wanted to increase chicken and egg production and restore the grounds to their pre-war standard. In pursuance of the latter aim she hired a groundsman to restore the cricket pitch and tennis court. The TUC chairman, Arthur Pugh, suggested that a schedule of Socialist summer schools and conferences should be organised, and speeches would be made to publicise the venture. G.D.H. Cole was proposed as principal of the college and was asked to prepare a memorandum on the academic curriculum.

Then came the first snag to mar the plans: the TUC suggested that the park could be turned into a source of income. Lady Warwick became apprehensive about possible speculative building, and she inserted extra clauses in the contract to forestall such an eventuality. Solicitors for the TUC responded that their clients would thereby be deprived of all the usual rights of ownership.

Lady Warwick had to explain her point of view, and did so in an open letter to the TUC Education Committee:

In my lifetime I have promised to keep intact the legacy of my ancestors, the love and care of the animal and bird life established on the ground for generations. It is because I wished that those brought up in less fortunate conditions should find here the joys of quiet, of solitary places, when our students could dream dreams of a happier world for the masses, and because the big things in life have always come from meditation, that I have wanted the workers to share in all that has been denied them.[7]

A meeting was held at the TUC headquarters in London, and the union leaders assured Lady Warwick that none of the parkland would be sold or mortgaged during her lifetime without her permission. Safety clauses would be inserted to this effect. Once again the scheme seemed to be on track. However, there was still peripheral criticism. Students of the London Labour College disliked the idea of Easton Lodge on principle. Ruskin College had been unenthusiastic from the beginning, the main objection being that the house was isolated, not sufficiently accessible, whereas in fact it had been well served by the railway for years. For good measure, the National Union of Railwaymen, King's Cross Branch, passed a critical resolution. The wording mentioned lavish ornate furnishings and decorations, which it was felt were out of keeping with the simplicity desirable in a Socialist institution. People with vested interests seemed to be doing all they could to get the scheme abandoned. And apart from those public bodies which were against it, there was also opposition from the family.

In April everything was thrown into confusion by the General Strike, and although the main activity collapsed in nine days, the miners continued on strike till summer. Socialists believed that the Conservative government now in power was determined to break the unions, and in fighting back they faced serious financial outlay. This stroke of bad luck further hampered the progress of the proposed Easton College.

By June there was still no firm undertaking. Lady Warwick was feeling increasingly anxious and tired. She had been working to make this interim period successful by welcoming large parties of Labour supporters and others, who enjoyed lunches, teas and speeches in aid of the cause. Although willing to do anything which would help, she could not go on indefinitely. For one thing, the fees being paid were insufficient to cover the cost. In July there was no let up: a teachers' fellowship arrived and put on a Shakespeare performance. The educationalist Margaret McMillan, founder of the Nursery Schools Association, brought a party of nursery school children from Deptford, the last group to come to Easton that summer. It was non-stop activity.

Lady Warwick told Citrine that if he would be honest with her, she would make every possible adjustment to bring their plan to fruition. She declared herself willing to run the house as a college for two or three years, until the TUC was ready to build the extensions required. On top, she offered to teach foreign languages and horticulture. She was still thinking about how the scheme could be made to work when she went to Paris late in the summer, and made the suggestion that an architect could draw up plans for the extensions at her expense. Without immediate alterations to the house, they could open the college the following Easter. She even offered, as a goodwill gesture, to tour Europe with some trades union delegates, in order to drum up sympathy for the miners' cause. All these suggestions were declined.

In August, at the annual TUC Congress, a vote was to be taken on the proposed capital levy for necessary building at Easton Lodge; the estimate was an initial £50,000, some of which would be raised, if agreed, by small contributions from all union members. Both Lady Warwick and Citrine were pessimistic as the Congress opened in Bournemouth, where the Council put forward the proposal.

The resolution ran into difficulties immediately, with several speakers from the floor raising objections. There seemed to be a general antipathy to spending money on residential education for the few instead of providing industrial areas with workers' evening classes. A union MP named Jack Jones poked fun at men who had gone to Ruskin College dressed as workmen and returned wearing plus fours.[8] He seemed to catch the mood of Congress when he said that such colleges created a snobbish elite, and many delegates were swayed by the speech. A motion was proposed to refer the whole matter back to the General Council. It was carried by a million votes, clearly signalling an end to the scheme.

Daisy felt the rebuff keenly. She had imagined a future for Easton, which meant a great deal to her, and the plans had been ambitious, as always. Now the dream of an international college was over. Prejudice had played a part in ending it. There were people in the Labour movement who had always resented her, never considered her to be 'one of us'. Class war is not always one-sided. Lady Warwick had done everything possible to be accepted in the Socialist world, displaying courage, commitment and tenacity. H.M. Hyndman had recognised her qualities right at the beginning, but others saw her as an aristocrat who could never be completely within the fold.

~

Two years after her disappointment over the TUC rejection, Daisy faced a more personal sorrow when, on 31 January 1928, Guy died at Hill Street, Mayfair. He was laid to rest in the family vault at Warwick only four years after his father. For the last few years of his life, he had lived with Olive Baldwin, a woman of uncertain background who seems to have been touchingly devoted to him. Three years earlier they had sailed for Majorca to enjoy a winter holiday, seeing Lisbon and Tangiers en route. Olive was sadly conscious of her awkward position – their relationship had never been openly acknowledged. Consequently, she felt compelled to leave the house immediately, and did not attend the funeral.

A sad figure, Olive slipped back into the obscure background from which she had come, with only the settlement of £200 a year made by Guy for her lifetime. Daisy wrote to her kindly, and a few surviving letters of Olive's reveal her as self-effacing and loyal. All the same, she had been rather a strange choice on Guy's part: his mother had once said how much she wished he had married Lady Marjorie Manners, the Duchess of Rutland's eldest daughter, and had he done so how different the course of his life might have been.[9]

∾

More unhappiness was to come. The following year, Basil Dean was in New York when he received an unexpected letter from Paris. Although he recognised Mercy's writing on the envelope, he was totally unprepared for the shock contained within. Mercy was announcing that she had eloped. The impact of this news, Dean later wrote, was as if someone had kicked him in the stomach. He felt 'an agonising sense of loss'.[10]

There had been no sign that anything was wrong only a couple of weeks earlier, when Basil had said goodbye to his wife and daughter at Easton. It transpired that Mercy and her lover, Ian McGilchrist, had been holed up in a small hotel near the Rue de la Paix in Paris, before departing for the Riviera on Le Train Bleu. 'Madre' took charge of the situation, no doubt furious with Mercy and deeply shocked. She appointed herself Tessa's de facto guardian, and the three-year-old, along with her nanny, moved in with Grandma.

The lothario, McGilchrist, who had been running an air taxi service between London and Paris, was killed in the summer of 1930 flying one of his own planes, and Mercy found refuge in the famous Cavendish Hotel, Rosa Lewis' old establishment. Over the following two years, 'Madre' would try to effect a reconciliation between her and Dean, believing that the marriage which had begun so well could not be finally doomed. In his autobiography, Dean wrote very warmly about his mother-in-law:

> Through all the pain and stress that followed upon our separa-
> tion, Lady Warwick remained steadfastly my friend, continuing
> her 'guardianship' of Tessa, keeping an eye on Nanny and our
> domestic arrangements . . . From time to time she would try and
> convince us both of the folly of our ways, me for my obvious
> neglect . . . and Nancy for her refusal of responsibility . . .[11]

A family dinner was held at the Savoy, when the couple were urged to rekindle their marriage. But it was all to no avail, and in 1932 Mercy and Basil were divorced. Thereafter Mercy showed no interest in Tessa, and for many years there was no contact between mother and daughter. But Basil was a reliable father, notwithstanding his busy professional life, and in his absence Grandma Warwick provided the security of her home.

~ 22 ~

Last Years

ALTHOUGH SHE HAD SAID she would never write her autobiography, in 1929 Lady Warwick's partial life story, *Life's
Ebb and Flow*, was finally published. But it was nothing like the
strong, honest book she could have written. Unsurprisingly, it was
not all her own work, but had been taken in hand by Elspeth
Keith, wife of the journalist John Robertson Scott. What emerged
was a hotch-potch of memories which lacked coherence.

Despite this, the book quickly went into three impressions and,
two years later, Hutchinson published her second volume of
memoirs, with the title *Afterthoughts*. Written by the indefatiga-
ble S.L. Bensusan, it was an improvement on the first volume. In
1930 Lady Warwick's translations of two German books
appeared, the more interesting being *My Experience as a Miner*,
written by a young German nobleman who had been employed in
the Ruhr coalmines during the previous decade.

In the same year, a kind of ginger group, calling themselves 'the
loyal grousers', was set up within the Fabian Society. Under this
umbrella, a wide cross-section of intellectuals and left-wing politicians met at Easton. Margaret Cole was often there with her
husband George, and she described the impression the house made
on her:

It was a great lump of a building . . . set in large and ill-kept gardens in the midst of a huge and very untidy park . . . It had enormous rooms, several painted in colour throughout; one, the Peacock Room, contained the vast fourposter in which Edward VII used to sleep, another, the library, had shelves full of books bound in scarlet morocco to match the room – which books on examination, were not great classics but complete sets of minor thriller-writers of late Victorian times; its roof and plumbing were continually coming to pieces. Outside there was a terrace along which raucous peacocks in rather shabby trim marched up and down and interrupted discourses on economics with squawks of 'Pigou! Pigou!'[1]

There was simply not enough money for the refurbishment which was so badly needed.

Daisy had grown fat, but even in her last years still had her famous pink and white complexion and the 'electric light' smile, both of which seemed to belong to a different era. Her mind had embraced the modern world, but there was something distinctly Edwardian about her appearance. She was sometimes given to sudden gusts of temper, and it was known that H.G. Wells experienced occasional violent explosions.

Beatrice Webb wrote to her early in 1931 mentioning the enthusiastic accounts she had been receiving about those meetings of 'the young people' at Easton Lodge. She felt that all three main parties seemed to be very confused by the world slump which had spread from the United States to Britain, Europe and beyond since the Wall Street Crash of 1929, and the situation called for study: 'For that reason I rather hope the government will go out in the near future, so that the Labour Party can get to work and make up its mind what it ought to be proposing. I am sure that the meetings at Easton Lodge are a very great help in this direction . . .'[2]

Desperate economic conditions were to prevail during Daisy's last decade, yet there was never a definite swing to Socialism, which she found baffling. Although disillusioned, like many, by the lack of Socialist progress in the early 1930s, she was always willing to try and help those struggling for a more equitable society, and she gave generous assistance to the hunger marchers. Moreover, she admitted to being receptive to Communism, and as early as the mid-1920s had jointly stood bail with George Bernard Shaw for twelve Communists accused of seditious consipiracy.

~

Away from the political world, one of the special friendships which Daisy developed in the last part of her life was with the eminent physicist Sir Oliver Lodge, whose son Raymond had been killed in the war. Lodge had written an account of alleged communications with his son through the medium Mrs Osborne Leonard, and the book was a runaway best-seller. Lodge had been forthright in expressing his belief in personal survival of death, and as a world-class scientist his dedication to the cause of Spiritualism had given the movement a considerable boost. Whether or not Daisy was ever entirely converted is open to speculation, but she was certainly very interested, and claimed to have had various experiences of her own psychic power.

Nearer to hand were other good friends, the historian Philip Guedella and his wife Nelly, who lived on the estate in a house called the Old Laundry, which was exactly what it had been. Dear older friends remained in touch. Ben Tillett wrote her very florid letters, full of warmth, even a kind of love. By the early 1930s Daisy's sight was impaired, and there is reference to her problem in one of his letters, addressed to 'My dear Comrade and friend':

I am still hoping for the best that your sight may be saved. You know how I feel when such pain and distress comes to you. You have always been very courageous and brave-hearted in your life, giving to our Labour movement gracious and splendid service at all times. Our women folk miss you badly! . . . and are very anxious as to your sight. If the prayers and good wishes which they offer can create miracles I feel you will be spared the agony and pain which is now your grave burden.[3]

In answer to her offer to provide furnishings for the new rooms occupied by the National Trade Union Club, of which Tillett was now chairman, he responded that tables and chairs would be welcome, as well as screens. Such items would be a reminder of her presence, her beautiful personality, which had helped the Labour movement so much. He ended the letter 'God love you'.

In another letter he wrote that 'nothing in the heavens would be a sweeter vision than your beautiful self . . . If there is a possibility of you being able to come to our Carnival, you would be received by all the loving loyalty and devotion of a vast crowd who adore you . . .'[4] Six months later he wrote to his 'dear old Sweetheart: How beautiful you are to me, and the years but make you more beautiful still . . .'[5]

~

As old age approached, Daisy took pride in making the adjustment. A champion of youth, believing that young people in the 1920s and 1930s had a freedom, frankness and individuality about them which was to be admired, she encapsulated her philosophy in an article published in the *Daily Express*:

The way not to admit age, not to brand oneself as a back number, is to keep heart and faith and enthusiasms . . . Let all your thoughts be hopeful. Study always. Keep as active mentally as you were physically active . . .

Old age may be the happiest of all those periods which Shakespeare catalogues. I mean to make mine the happiest period in my life.[6]

Daisy took her own advice during her last years, which were hard-working. One very successful venture was her pedigree Jersey herd, which was housed in the stables at Brook End Farm, originally built for Lord Rosslyn's racing stud. She started managing the herd herself in 1932, when she had ten heifers and one bull, and she would travel to Jersey to choose stock. Three years later, the herd amounted to twenty-six cows and heifers and two bulls. Her stock won prizes not only at the local Essex Show but also at the London Dairy Show, a success topped by breeding the Dairy Champion at the Royal Agricultural Show.

One by-product of the Jersey herd was development of a more humane method of slaughter on farms and in abattoirs. Lady Warwick had been campaigning for this cause for many years, and it was at Easton that the first demonstration of the bolt gun was given, a great advance on the previous 'pole-axe'. In 1936 the Slaughterhouse Act – which made the old method unlawful, and allowed the slaughter of animals for human consumption only under licence – was put on the statute book

As chairman of the Essex branch of the RSPCA, Daisy was certainly not a mere figurehead. She cared deeply about animal welfare, and Basil Dean noticed her natural affinity with the animals she kept as pets. During her last years she kept a group of retired circus ponies at Easton, free to roam the park, but coming to the door every morning to be fed.

In the 1930s the Easton estate took on a new role as a film location. Basil Dean's involvement with Ealing Studios prompted him to make use of the pastoral setting which looked so well on camera. *Mr Midshipman Easy*, from a story by Captain Marryat, was one of the early productions, directed by Carol (later Sir Carol) Reed. Another, based on an Edgar Wallace story, was shot almost entirely on the estate. The final scene showed the stars, Evelyn Laye and Frank Lawton, enjoying a screen kiss in one of the summerhouses. Then there was *The Perfect Alibi*, directed by Dean himself under contract to the American company RKO. A principal part was played by C. Aubrey Smith, who would stand in the courtyard at the Lodge exchanging reminiscences with the chatelaine while waiting for the next shot to be set up.

Always a person to move with the times, Daisy must have thoroughly enjoyed the atmosphere. These film and theatre people brought a certain glamour to the old place. At the conclusion of filming she put on a fête, on which more money was spent than the company had paid for using the location. It was an elaborate affair, with a military band, balloon flights, catering by Rumpelmeyer's, and a dance by floodlight to conclude. There was also to be a performance of some one-act plays, given by Sir Gerald du Maurier and 'Full West End Company'. The wooden stage had been built out over a lake, where the vista of a Chinese pagoda provided an ideal backcloth. Unfortunately, the day of the party turned out to be very windy, and besides, the floating stage had not been anchored sufficiently well. Consequently, the moment Sir Gerald stepped on to it, the scenery began to bob up and down ominously. Sadly, the performance had to be abandoned, but dancing took place as planned, and the evening was a great success.

Sometimes, at weekends, guests staying with Wells at the Glebe would call on Daisy, or vice versa, and there might be a ramble over the park on Sunday morning, as Basil Dean recalled. On one occasion Charlie Chaplin was of the party, when they came across a Jersey cow barring the footpath: 'Wonderfully comic, a cow, don't you think?' said Chaplin, with his famously bemused expression.

∽

In the winter of 1933, aged ninety, Daisy's mother Blanche Rosslyn died at her home near Regent's Park, where she had lived for many years. She had lived to be a great-great-grandmother. Blanche had always been a woman of strong character and deep faith, and in her latter days had been received into the Roman

Catholic Church. Nevertheless, a memorial service was held for her at Little Easton church, marking the end of her exceptionally long and fulfilled life.

Daisy's attention in these last years was focused very much on her granddaughter Tessa, with whom she had formed a strong bond. Accompanied by the faithful Nanny Tresham, they went on summer holidays in Scotland. Basil's three sons were often invited to Easton during their school and later their university vacations, so that Tessa could get to know her half-brothers. They grew very fond of her. The Barn Theatre now had heating and electric light, and the boys once performed a play there to an audience of four: Tessa, Grandma Warwick, Nanny Tresham and their father.

~

Daisy was now in her mid-seventies, and for more than fifty years had been a presence on her estate and in the local area. She had been known all her life for having abundant energy, but now people close to her became concerned that her strength seemed considerably diminished. She was no longer seen driving errati- cally round the familiar country lanes. Gone was her hearty appetite, and she was losing weight.

A consultant physician made a diagnosis of colonic cancer. As the disease took its toll, she was to be found lying on a sofa, beau- tifully dressed, with a careful maquillage to hide the ravages of illness. She received friends individually, sometimes for Sunday luncheon. Right to the end she was concerned with the well-being of all, but thought particularly about Tessa's future, her dear granddaughter. She wished Basil well when he told her of his plans to remarry. Finally, individual members of her family were invited, so that she could say goodbye. All farewells said, Daisy passed away peacefully on 26 July 1938, aged seventy-six.

Her coffin was taken to Little Easton church, where a simple service was held, ending with the Nunc Dimittis: 'Lord now lettest thou thy servant depart in peace: according to thy word. For mine eyes have seen thy salvation.' Then to Warwick, where she was placed in the family vault, an idea she had never liked: 'all that marble on top of me', she used to say.

Obituaries in both the London and New York *Times* recalled her as a great figure in Edwardian Society. Both discreetly mentioned her friendship with Edward, as Prince of Wales and King, but stopped short of naming her as the mistress who had been his great love. A friend, 'P.G.', contributed a personal reflection, remembering 'a great lady who employed a notable position for those who were not great: a friend of many causes, of which each involved befriending somebody or something weaker than herself . . . Having an assured position, she seemed determined to secure one, if she could, for every other creature . . .'

Daisy Warwick's life spanned a period of enormous change. Born into the old aristocratic world, she had known many of the great, the good, and the not so good. She saw the more egalitarian, less formal world after 1918 as a sign of progress, and wholeheartedly embraced the new era. If she remained in part forever Edwardian, with gracious old world manners, her mind was thoroughly modern. She enjoyed contact with leading thinkers and politicians during the 1920s and 1930s. As people of a later generation would have said, she was 'with it'. There was something about her that appealed to people as diverse as Ben Tillett, the trade unionist, and the architect Philip Tilden, who wrote: 'All people forgave her everything, for they loved her so very much. Her human instincts and interests were many and marvellous, her sense of humour and infectious laugh tied one to her for life . . .'[7]

But words do not completely capture her essence. Personality is elusive, indefinable, and Daisy's charisma will always remain.

SUSHILA ANAND

1942–2007

From an address at her funeral by her cousin, Ann Jasper

∞

I was not quite eight when my cousin Sushila was born, in wartime London in August 1942. I was taken by my mother and father to 8 St George's Mews off Regent's Park Road, the flat where Sushila's parents Kath and Mulk lived, to see the new baby. Kath was my father's sister. I was thrilled to be allowed to hold the baby, who had a quiff of dark hair and was wearing a woollen knitted dress. The baby was named Rajani Kumari. She herself changed it to 'Sushila' later in life. Rajani grew into an exceptionally beautiful child and remained a beautiful woman until the end. Sadly, Sushila never really forgave her father, the celebrated Indian writer and activist, Mulk Raj Anand, for leaving when she was a small girl. I know this was a grief to him. I wish she could have remembered, as I did, how thrilled he was when she was born.

Sushila's mother Kath, when a young girl, had had great success at RADA – according to family legend beating Celia Johnson to a gold medal. But she had to withdraw after one year because of lack of funds. She decided to send her daughter to the Cone Ripman Arts Educational School, where Sushila excelled in everything from tap dancing to acting to ballet. Her love of ballet was life-long. I remember her as an extremely conscientious, hard-working child, always aiming for excellence, quite hard on herself. We all dreamed of her becoming a prima ballerina. But after one Christmas pantomime season in the corps de ballet, Sushila decided the theatre was not for her after all; she felt her academic education had been neglected at theatre school. In 1974/75 while travelling in India, the BBC accepted an interview she had recorded there, and this led to a new career as a freelance broadcaster and writer.

Sushila was unworldly inasmuch as she never aspired to own a home or a car or to acquire status symbols. Her ambitions were literary and she set herself very high standards. Her research was thorough and painstaking. Her books, *Queen Victoria's Maharaja*, co-authored with Michael Alexander, and *Indian Sahib*, about Queen Victoria's Munshie, are a great credit to her. And we were all so pleased, as was she, that before she succumbed to illness she managed, by what must have been a supreme effort of will, to finish the book she'd been working on for a few years about Daisy, Countess of Warwick. It is very sad she won't be here for that.

Sushila was a lover of beauty, in art and in nature. She loved to get out of London into the countryside, and I won't forget one mild and sunny Christmas Day a few years ago. We drove to West Wittering for a walk along the beach. Sushila took off her coat and joyfully ran and skipped along the shore, bare-armed. My husband Peter and I felt like the parents of an exuberant child. She was thrilled when she moved from St George's Mews to Oppidans Road, where for the first time in her life she had a garden. Like Kath, she had a good sense of humour and I think I'll always remember the lovely way she laughed.

Perhaps partly because she was an only child brought up by a single parent, Sushila was something of a loner, though she didn't really want to be. I think in the last months of her life, because of all the people who supported and visited her, she came to realise that she was much loved.

Notes

~

Abbreviations:

CSA = Caroline Spurrier archive
ETA = Emma Temple archive
RP = Rosebery Papers, National Library of Scotland
SP = Salisbury Papers, Hatfield
StP = Stead Papers, Churchill College, Cambridge

Chapter 1 The Heiress

1 Countess of Warwick, *Life's Ebb and Flow*, Hutchinson, 1929
2 Ibid.
3 Ibid.
4 Ibid.
5 *The World*, March 1880
6 *Vanity Fair*, December 1879
7 *The World*, January 1880
8 Daisy Maynard to Lord Brooke, March 1880 CSA
9 *The World*, March 1880
10 Horatia Stopford to Lord Rowton, 5 May 1880
11 Lord Rowton to Lord Beaconsfield, 11 May 1880
12 Lord Beaconsfield to Lord Rowton, 12 May 1880
13 Ibid.
14 Daisy Maynard to Lord Brooke, early summer 1880 CSA

Chapter 2 Marriage

1 Lord Brooke to Daisy Maynard, 27 March 1880 CSA
2 Ibid.
3 Daisy Maynard to Lord Brooke, March 1880 CSA

4 Countess of Warwick, *Life's Ebb and Flow*
5 Ibid.
6 Daisy Maynard to Lord Brooke, undated CSA
7 Lord Brooke to Daisy Maynard, undated CSA
8 Daisy Maynard to Lord Brooke, undated CSA
9 Daisy Maynard to Lord Brooke, 20 May 1880
10 Ibid.
11 Lord Rosslyn to Lord Beaconsfield, 19 June 1880
12 Lord Beaconsfield to Lord Rosslyn, 20 June 1880
13 *The World*, 23 June 1880
14 Daisy Maynard to Lord Brooke, summer 1880 CSA
15 Daisy Maynard to Lord Brooke, summer 1880 CSA
16 Lord Brooke to Daisy Maynard, 20 December 1880 CSA
17 Daisy Maynard to Lord Brooke, 9 September 1880 CSA
18 Daisy Maynard to Lord Brooke, 27 September 1880 CSA
19 Daisy Maynard to Lord Brooke, October 1880 CSA
20 Daisy Maynard to Lord Brooke, 14 October 1880 CSA
21 Daisy Maynard to Lord Brooke, 19 October 1880 CSA
22 Lord Brooke to Daisy Maynard, October/November 1880 CSA
23 Daisy Maynard to Lord Brooke, November 1880 CSA
24 Lord Brooke to Daisy Maynard, 7 February 1881 CSA
25 Lord Brooke to Daisy Maynard, 22 February 1881 CSA
26 Lord Brooke to Daisy Maynard, 26 February 1881 CSA
27 Lord Brooke to Daisy Maynard, 28 February 1881 CSA
28 Daisy Maynard to Lord Brooke, 22 March 1881 CSA
29 Elinor Glyn, *The Reflections of Ambrosine*, Duckworth, 1904
30 *The World*, 7 May 1881
31 Poem celebrating the wedding of Daisy Maynard to Lord Brooke CSA

Chapter 3 Grand Passion

1 Lord Rosslyn to Lord Brooke, May 1881
2 Ibid.
3 Lord Brooke to Lady Rosslyn, May 1881
4 Daisy Brooke to Lady Rosslyn, May 1881
5 Lady Angela Forbes, *Memories and Base Details*, Hutchinson, 1921
6 Elinor Glyn, *Romantic Adventure*, Duckworth, 1936
7 Ibid.
8 Lord Rosslyn to Lady Brooke, 31 December 1882; quoted in Margaret Blunden, *The Countess of Warwick*, Cassell, 1967
9 Ibid.
10 Ibid.
11 Conversation with Basil Dean, Daisy's son-in-law, related in a letter to the author by Winton Dean, one of his sons

12 Lady Beresford to Lord Salisbury, 22 July 1891 SP
13 Ibid.
14 Ibid.
15 Countess of Warwick, *Life's Ebb and Flow*
16 Lord Charles Beresford to the Prince of Wales, summer 1891 SP
17 Ibid.
18 Lady Beresford to Lord Salisbury, 22 July 1891 SP
19 Ibid.
20 Ibid.
21 Lord Charles Beresford to the Prince of Wales SP
22 Ibid.
23 Ibid.
24 Ibid.
25 Ibid.
26 Sir Henry Ponsonby to Sir Francis Knollys, 20 December 1891 SP
27 Lord Marcus Beresford to Lord Charles Beresford, 30 November 1889 SP
28 Ibid.
29 Ibid.
30 J.K. McDonnell, memo to Lord Salisbury, 17 December 1891 SP
31 Lord Salisbury to Lord Charles Beresford, 10 August 1891 SP
32 J.K. McDonnell to Lord Salisbury, 17 December 1891 SP
33 Lord Charles Beresford to the Prince of Wales, 18 December 1891 SP
34 Prince of Wales to Lord Charles Beresford, 19 December 1891 SP
35 Lord Charles Beresford to Lord Salisbury, 23 December 1891 SP
36 Prince of Wales to Lord Charles Beresford, 24 December 1891 SP
37 Marquess of Waterford to Lady Brooke, 24 March 1892 SP
38 Prince of Wales to Marquess of Waterford, 6 April 1892 SP

Chapter 4 **Queen of Society**

1   Glyn, *Romantic Adventure*
2   Ibid.
3   Ibid.
4   Ibid.
5   Glyn, *Reflections of Ambrosine*
6   Ibid.
7   Ibid.
8   Lady Warwick to W.T. Stead, 10 September 1893 StP
9   *The World*, 21 September 1892
10 *The World*, September 1892
11 Lady Brooke to Lord Rosebery, 29 September 1892 R.P 10090, fol 174
12 *Warwick Times*, 15 December 1894
13 *The World*, 5 February 1895
14 *Queen Magazine*, 9 February 1895

15 Ibid.
16 Lady Warwick to W.T. Stead, February 1895 CSA
17 Ibid.
18 *The Clarion*, 16 February 1895
19 Ibid.
20 Ibid.
21 Countess of Warwick, *Life's Ebb and Flow*
22 Ibid.
23 Robert Blatchford, *My Eighty Years*, Cassell, 1931
24 Ibid.
25 Blunden, *The Countess of Warwick*
26 *Pall Mall Gazette*, January 1895
27 Ibid.
28 Ibid.
29 Lady Warwick to Lord Rosebery, 18 February 1895 RP 10102, fol. 140
30 *The Times*, 7 January 1896
31 Ibid.
32 Lady Warwick to W.T. Stead, 5 January 1896 StP
33 Lady Warwick, letter to *The Times*, 7 January 1896
34 Ibid.
35 Lady Warwick to W.T. Stead, 24 March 1896 StP
36 Duchess of Sutherland to Lord Rosebery, July 1896 RP 10107, fol. 197
37 Forbes, *Memories and Base Details*
38 Duchess of Sutherland to Lord Rosebery, 14 August 1896 RP 10107, fol. 207
39 Ibid.
40 Lady Warwick to Lord Rosebery, 14 September 1896 RP 10108, fol. 23
41 Ibid.
42 Lord Rosebery to Lady Warwick, 16 September 1896 RP 10108, fol. 38
43 Ibid.
44 Lady Warwick to Lord Rosebery, 6 October 1896 RP 10108, fol. 86

Chapter 5 **New Love**

1 Sir Francis Knollys to W.T. Stead, 28 June 1891 StP
2 Lady Warwick to Lord Rosebery, 21 December 1896 RP 10109, fol. 290
3 Ibid.
4 Lady Warwick to W.T. Stead, 2 May 1897 SP
5 Ibid.
6 Ibid.
7 Lady Warwick to W.T. Stead, undated StP
8 Preface to *Autobiography of Joseph Arch*, 1897
9 Ibid.
10 Prince of Wales to Lady Warwick, 17 June 1897 CSA

11 Prince of Wales to Lady Warwick, 4 June 1898 CSA
12 Ibid.
13 Prince of Wales to Lady Warwick, 7 June 1898
14 Ibid.
15 Ibid.
16 Lady Warwick to W.T. Stead, April 1898 StP
17 Prince of Wales, quoted in letter from Lady Warwick to W.T. Stead, summer 1898 StP
18 Ibid.
19 Lady Warwick to W.T. Stead, late summer 1898
20 Prince of Wales to Lady Warwick, undated (c. 1898) CSA

Chapter 6 Turbulent Times

1 *Review of Reviews*, 1 November 1899
2 W.T. Stead to Arthur Balfour, 26 September 1896 StP
3 Arthur Balfour to W.T. Stead, 30 October 1899
4 Lady Warwick to W.T. Stead, quoted in Countess of Warwick, *Life's Ebb and Flow*
5 Joe Laycock to his mother, 25 October 1899
6 Ibid.
7 Ibid.
8 Prince of Wales to Lady Warwick, 10 December 1899 CSA
9 Prince of Wales to Lady Warwick, undated (spring 1900) CSA
10 Prince of Wales to Lady Warwick, undated (spring 1900) CSA
11 Prince of Wales to Lady Warwick, undated (spring 1900) CSA
12 Ibid.
13 Ibid.
14 Prince of Wales to Lady Warwick, late spring 1900 CSA
15 Lady Warwick to W.T. Stead, summer 1900 StP
16 Prince of Wales to Lady Warwick, undated (c. August 1900) CSA
17 Ibid.
18 Prince of Wales to Lady Warwick, undated (autumn 1900) CSA

Chapter 7 The Hero's Return

1 Lady Warwick to Joe Laycock, undated (autumn 1900) ETA
2 Joe Laycock to Lady Warwick, undated (spring 1901) ETA
3 Lady Warwick to Joe Laycock, spring 1901 ETA
4 Ibid.
5 *New York World*, 8 February 1901
6 *The Nineteenth Century*, July 1901
7 Ibid.
8 Countess of Warwick, *Life's Ebb and Flow*

9 Lady Warwick to Joe Laycock, summer 1901 ETA
10 King Edward VII to Lady Warwick, 22 August 1901 CSA
11 Ibid.
12 Countess of Warwick, *Afterthoughts*, Hutchinson 1931
13 Lady Warwick to Lord Rosebery, 18 December 1901 RP 10115, fol. 232
14 Lady Warwick to Joe Laycock, 18 December 1901 ETA

Chapter 8 Coronation Year 1902

1 Countess of Warwick, *Life's Ebb and Flow*
2 Lady Warwick to Joe Laycock, 1 January 1902 ETA
3 Marquess of Downshire to Marchioness of Downshire, January 1902 ETA
4 Ibid.
5 Lady Warwick to Joe Laycock, undated (January 1902) ETA
6 Lady Warwick to Joe Laycock, undated (February 1902) ETA
7 Ibid.
8 *The Candid Friend*, March 1902 ETA
9 Professor Meldola to Lady Warwick, March 1902 CSA
10 Private detective's report, 21 March 1902 ETA
11 Lady Warwick to Joe Laycock, spring 1902 ETA
12 Lord Charles Beresford to Lady Warwick, spring 1902 ETA
13 *The Times*, 1902
14 Lord Brooke to Lady Warwick, 29 March 1902 ETA
15 Telegram, Lady Warwick to Joe Laycock, late April 1902 ETA
16 Lady Warwick to Joe Laycock, 1 May 1902 ETA
17 Ibid.
18 Telegram, Helena Clarke to Joe Laycock, 21 May 1902
19 Telegram, Willie Low to Joe Laycock, 24 May 1902
20 Lady Warwick to Joe Laycock, undated (prob. late June 1902) ETA
21 Ibid.
22 Telegram, Helena Clarke to Joe Laycock, 25 May 1902 ETA
23 Lady Warwick to Joe Laycock, June 1902 ETA
24 Mary Hunter to Joe Laycock, early June 1902 ETA
25 Mary Hunter to Joe Laycock, 6 June 1902 ETA
26 Ibid.
27 Lady Warwick to Lord Rosebery, 9 May 1902 RP 10129, fol. 245
28 Ibid.
29 Ibid.
30 Marchioness of Granby to Lady Warwick, June 1902 ETA
31 Lady Warwick to Joe Laycock, summer 1902 ETA
32 Ibid.
33 Kitty Downshire to Joe Laycock, July 1902 ETA
34 Ibid.
35 Kitty Downshire to Joe Laycock, early August 1902 ETA

36 Lady Warwick to Joe Laycock, July 1902 ETA
37 Lady Warwick to Joe Laycock, August 1902 ETA

Chapter 9 **Late Summer 1902**

1 *The World*, July 1902
2 Kitty Downshire to Joe Laycock, undated (August 1902) ETA
3 Ibid.
4 Kitty Downshire to Joe Laycock, 31 August 1902 ETA
5 Ibid.
6 Kitty Downshire to Joe Laycock, undated (September 1902) ETA
7 Ibid.
8 Kitty Downshire to Joe Laycock, September 1902 ETA
9 Ibid.
10 Lady Warwick, recounting her conversation to Joe Laycock, autumn 1902
11 Lady Warwick to Joe Laycock, undated (September 1902)
12 Kitty Downshire to Joe Laycock, 26 September 1902

Chapter 10 **A Journey South**

1 *The Onlooker*, 20 December 1902
2 Lady Warwick to Joe Laycock, early January 1903 ETA
3 Ibid.
4 Lady Warwick to Joe Laycock, 23 February 1903 ETA
5 Ibid.
6 Ibid.
7 Ibid.
8 Lady Warwick to Joe Laycock, 6 March 1903 ETA
9 Telegram, Lady Warwick to Joe Laycock, 23 March 1903 ETA
10 Telegram, Joe Laycock to Lady Warwick, March 1903 ETA
11 Lady Warwick to Joe Laycock, 30 March 1903 ETA
12 Ibid.
13 Lady Warwick to Joe Laycock, 30 March 1903, 2nd letter ETA
14 Lady Warwick to Joe Laycock, 31 March 1903 ETA
15 Lady Warwick to Joe Laycock, 2 April 1903 ETA
16 Ibid.
17 Lady Warwick to Joe Laycock, 4 April 1903 ETA
18 Lady Warwick to Joe Laycock, April 1903 ETA
19 Lady Warwick to Joe Laycock, April 1903 ETA
20 Lady Warwick to Joe Laycock, 5 April 1903 ETA
21 Ibid.
22 Lady Warwick to Joe Laycock, 12 April 1903 ETA
23 Ibid.
24 Lady Warwick to Joe Laycock, 13 April 1903 ETA

25 Lady Warwick to Joe Laycock, May 1903 ETA
26 *The World*, summer 1903
27 Lady Cynthia Asquith, *Haply I May Remember and Haply May Forget*, 1950
28 Lady Warwick to Joe Laycock, June 1903 ETA
29 Lady Warwick to Joe Laycock, summer 1903 ETA
30 Lady Warwick to Joe Laycock, 5 April 1903 ETA
31 Lady Warwick to Joe Laycock, summer 1903 ETA

Chapter 11 Reunion

1 Lady Warwick to Joe Laycock, September 1903 ETA
2 Lady Warwick to Joe Laycock, September 1903 ETA
3 Fitzroy St Clair Erskine to Lady Warwick, January 1904 ETA
4 Dowager Lady Helmsley to Lady Warwick, January 1904 ETA
5 Lady Warwick to Joe Laycock, 15 February 1904 ETA
6 Marchioness of Granby to Joe Laycock, undated (February 1904) ETA
7 Joe Laycock to Marchioness of Granby, undated (February 1904) ETA
8 Marchioness of Granby to Joe Laycock, undated (February 1904) ETA
9 Joe Laycock to Elinor Glyn, undated (winter 1904) ETA
10 Mary Hunter to Joe Laycock, March 1904 ETA
11 Edward VII to Lady Warwick, March 1904 ETA
12 Marchioness of Granby to Lady Warwick, March/April 1904 ETA
13 Lady Warwick to Marchioness of Granby, April 1904 ETA
14 Lady Warwick to Joe Laycock, April 1904 ETA
15 Lady Helmsley to Lady Warwick, 10 April 1904 ETA
16 Marchioness of Granby to Lady Warwick, undated (mid-April 1904) ETA

Chapter 12 Comrade Warwick

1 Lady Warwick to Joe Laycock, August 1904 ETA
2 H.M. Hyndman, *Reminiscences*, Macmillan, 1912
3 Lady Warwick to Joe Laycock, August 1904 ETA
4 Ibid.
5 Ibid.
6 Ibid.
7 Ibid.
8 Joe Laycock to Lady Warwick, September 1904 ETA
9 Ibid.
10 Lady Warwick to Joe Laycock, autumn 1904 ETA
11 H.M. Hyndman to Lady Warwick, autumn 1904
12 Lady Warwick to Sir John French, 14 October 1904
13 Ibid.
14 H.M. Hyndman to Gaylord Wilshire, 4 January 1905

15 *Labour Leader*, 3 March 1905
16 Ibid.
17 H.M. Hyndman to Gaylord Wilshire, 16 March 1905
18 *Wilshire's Magazine*, 19 August 1901
19 *Fortnightly Review*, March 1906
20 Speech at Passenham, Northamptonshire, 20 April 1905
21 Ibid.
22 H.M. Hyndman to Gaylord Wilshire, 19 May 1905
23 *Daily Express*, 12 January 1906
24 *Daily Chronicle*, 18 April 1906

Chapter 13 **The King is Dead**

1 Lord Warwick, letter to *The Times*, 28 August 1907
2 Countess of Warwick, *Life's Ebb and Flow*
3 Minutes of Studley Castle meeting, 8 April 1907, quoted in Blunden, *The Countess of Warwick*
4 Lady Warwick to Ralph Blumenfeld, 10 November 1907
5 Preface to Countess of Warwick, *William Morris: His Home and Haunts*, T.E. & E.C. Jack, 1910
6 *The Times*, 7 May 1910
7 *The Times*, 10 May 1910

Chapter 14 **Christians and Socialists**

1 *The Times*, 4 January 1910, quoted in Blunden, *The Countess of Warwick*
2 *Church Socialist Quarterly*, October 1910, quoted in Blunden, *The Countess of Warwick*
3 Conrad Noel, 'The Church of the Future', in H.G. Wells et al., *Socialism and the Great State*, Harper & Brothers, 1912
4 Ibid.
5 Lady Warwick to W.T. Stead, winter 1912
6 *New York Daily News*, 11 March 1912, quoted in Blunden, *The Countess of Warwick*
7 *New York Herald*, 10 March 1912, quoted in Blunden, *The Countess of Warwick*
8 Lady Warwick to W.T. Stead, 1 April 1912
9 Estelle Stead, *My Father W.T. Stead*, Heinemann, 1913

Chapter 15 **Come the Revolution**

1 *The Times*, 29 February 1912
2 *Daily Express*, 3 March 1912
3 *The Times*, 4 March 1912

4 *The Times*, 11 March 1912
5 Ibid.
6 Ben Tillett, *History of the 1912 Dock Strike*
7 Ibid.
8 *Daily Herald*, 18 June 1912
9 *Daily Express*, 11 June 1912
10 Tillett, *History of the 1912 Dock Strike*
11 Ibid.

Chapter 16 **A Brush with the Law**

1 Lady Warwick to Ralph Blumenfeld, March 1913
2 Lord Warwick to Moreton Frewen, 21 December 1913 quoted in Blunden, *The Countess of Warwick*
3 Hugh Kingsmill, *Frank Harris*, Biografia, 1985
4 Theo Lang, *My Darling Daisy*, Michael Joseph, 1966

Chapter 17 **The Great War**

1 Denis Stuart, *Dear Duchess*, Gollancz, 1982
2 Forbes, *Memories and Base Details*
3 Ibid.
4 Ibid.
5 Ibid.
6 Julian Grenfell to his sister Monica, quoted in Stuart, *Dear Duchess*
7 Forbes, *Memories and Base Details*
8 Duchess of Sutherland to Edward Marsh
9 Lady Warwick to Joe Laycock, October 1915
10 Ibid.
11 Ibid.
12 Ibid.
13 Ibid.
14 Lady Warwick, article in *Justice*, 13 April 1913
15 Walter H. Page to a friend in Virginia, USA, quoted in C.F.G. Masterman, *England After the War*, Hodder & Stoughton, 1923
16 *Daily Chronicle*, 11 April 1917
17 *Essex Herald*, 26 February 1918

Chapter 18 **The Aftermath of War**

1 Masterman, *England After the War*
2 Ibid.
3 Ibid.
4 Philip Tilden, *True Remembrances*, Country Life, 1954

5 Ibid.
6 Lady Warwick to Ralph Blumenfeld, 17 December 1920 House of Lords Library 3928/14
7 Ibid.
8 Ibid.
9 Ibid.
10 Lady Warwick to Lord Rosebery, 16 May 1922 RP 10127
11 Ibid.
12 Lady Warwick to Lord Rosebery, 23 November 1922 RP 10129, fol. 257
13 Ibid.
14 Ibid.
15 Ibid.
16 Ibid.

Chapter 19 The Labour Candidate

1 Basil Dean, *Seven Ages*, Hutchinson, 1970
2 Ibid.
3 Ibid.
4 Ibid.
5 Ibid.
6 *The Times*, 25 October 1923
7 Ibid.
8 *The Times*, 6 November 1923
9 *The Times*, 9 November 1923
10 Ibid.
11 Ibid.
12 Ibid.
13 *The Clarion*, 2 November 1923
14 *The Clarion*, 9 November 1923
15 *Morning Post*, 12 November 1923, quoted in Blunden, *The Countess of Warwick*
16 *The Times*, 6 December 1923
17 Ibid.

Chapter 20 The Play's the Thing

1 S.L. Bensusan, diary 25 March 1924
2 Lady Warwick to Ralph Blumenfeld, 21 June 1924 House of Lords Library 3928/22
3 Ibid.
4 Lady Warwick to Ralph Blumenfeld, 24 September 1924
5 Lady Warwick to Joe Laycock, 17 April 1925
6 Ibid.

7 Ibid.

8 Basil Dean, *Mind's Eye*, Hutchinson, 1973

Chapter 21 **Struggles and Disappointment**

1 Fenner Brockway quoted in Blunden, *The Countess of Warwick*

2 Beatrice Webb, *Diaries 1912–1924*, quoted in Blunden, *The Countess of Warwick*

3 Ibid.

4 Beatrice Webb, *Diaries 1924–1932*, quoted in Blunden, *The Countess of Warwick*

5 Lady Warwick to Walter Citrine, 29 December 1925, quoted in Blunden, *The Countess of Warwick*

6 *Manchester Guardian*, 26 February 1926, quoted in Blunden, *The Countess of Warwick*

7 Lady Warwick, open letter to the TUC, *The Times*, 22 March 1926, quoted in Blunden, *The Countess of Warwick*

8 TUC Annual Report 1926, quoted in Blunden, *The Countess of Warwick*

9 Lady Warwick to Joe Laycock, undated ETA

10 Dean, *Mind's Eye*

11 Ibid.

Chapter 22 **Last Years**

1 Margaret Cole, *Growing Up Into Revolution*, Longmans, 1949

2 Beatrice Webb to Lady Warwick, 24 February 1931

3 Ben Tillett to Lady Warwick, 29 November 1934

4 Ben Tillett to Lady Warwick, 19 February 1935

5 Ben Tillett to Lady Warwick, 23 August 1935

6 *Daily Express*, 7 September 1928, quoted in Blunden, *The Countess of Warwick*

7 Tilden, *True Remembrances*

Picture Credits

~

The publisher is grateful to Ms Caroline Spurrier, great-granddaughter of Daisy, for kindly allowing access to her family's paintings and photographs, which were photographed by Fisher Hart. Brian Creasey also allowed access to the collection of photographs and paintings held in Easton Lodge Gardens.

P. 2 (*top left*) © Hulton-Deutsch Collection/Corbis; P. 3 (*top left*) Hulton-Deutsch Collection/Corbis; P. 4 (*top left*) © Hulton Archive/Getty Images (*top right*) © Lafayette/V&A Images (*bottom left*) © Walery/National Portrait Gallery; P. 5 © Lafayette/ V&A Images; P. 6 (*bottom*) courtesy of Essex Record Office; P. 8 (*top*) courtesy of Essex Record Office; P. 11 (*top right*) © Martin/ National Portrait Gallery; P. 12 (*top left*) © Bettmann/Corbis; P. 13 (*bottom*) © Bettmann/Corbis; P. 14 (*bottom*) © Hulton Archive/Getty Images.

Every effort has been made to identify and acknowledge the copyright holders. Any errors or omissions will be rectified in future editions provided that written notification is made to the publishers.

Index

~